MW01484430

Post-Manifesto Polygamy
The 1899–1904 Correspondence of
Helen, Owen, and Avery Woodruff

Volume 11
Life Writings of Frontier Women

Courtesy of the Lambert and Woodruff families

Helen Woodruff

Courtesy of the Lambert and Woodruff families

Avery Woodruff

Courtesy of the Lambert and Woodruff families

Owen Woodruff

Post-Manifesto Polygamy

The 1899–1904 Correspondence of
Helen, Owen, and Avery Woodruff

Edited by

Lu Ann Faylor Snyder

and

Phillip A. Snyder

UTAH STATE UNIVERSITY PRESS
LOGAN, UTAH
2009

Utah State University Press
Logan, Utah 84322–7800
www.usu.edu/usupress

Manufactured in the United States of America
Printed on acid-free paper

ISBN: 978–0–87421–739–1 (cloth)
ISBN: 978–0–87421–740–7 (e-book)

Library of Congress Cataloging-in-Publication Data

Post-manifesto polygamy : the 1899-1904 correspondence of Helen, Owen, and
Avery Woodruff / edited by Lu Ann Faylor Snyder and Phillip A. Snyder.
    p. cm. – (Life writings of frontier women ; v. 11)
  Includes bibliographical references and index.
  ISBN 978-0-87421-739-1 (cloth : alk. paper) – ISBN 978-0-87421-740-7 (e-book)
  1. Polygamy–Religious aspects–Church of Jesus Christ of Latter-day Saints. 2.
Polygamy–Religious aspects–Mormon Church. 3. Woodruff, Abraham Owen,
1872-1904–Correspondence. 4. Woodruff, Helen May Winters, b. 1873–Corre-
spondence. 5. Lambert, Eliza Avery Clark Woodruff, b. 1882–Correspondence.
I. Snyder, Lu Ann Faylor. II. Snyder, Phillip A.
  BX8641.S65 2008
  289.3092'2–dc22
  [B]
                                2009007441

For the descendants of Helen and Owen and Avery

And also for the descendants of Lu Ann

Contents

Illustrations

Acknowledgments

First of all, I must thank Maureen Ursenbach Beecher, my former colleague in the English Department at Brigham Young University, without whose influence this project on the Woodruff correspondence would not have been developed and completed. My wife Lu Ann began work on it during a senior seminar she took from Maureen on the personal writings of nineteenth and early twentieth-century Latter-day Saint women. She continued working on it during her PhD studies in history at the University of Utah. My own understanding of the importance of recovering, documenting, and publishing these women's writings deepened one spring when Maureen asked me to substitute for her in teaching this seminar after she had become ill halfway through the term. Lu Ann and I ended up team-teaching the class and had a wonderful experience together with the students. Further, after Lu Ann's death from colon-to-liver cancer on January 15, 2000, Maureen gently but persistently pushed me to finish Lu Ann's work on this project, which I have finally done.

Next, I must thank John Alley, executive editor of Utah State University Press, for his patience and guidance as I completed this project. He and Maureen provided excellent suggestions to both Lu Ann and me for revisions and additions to earlier drafts. In addition, I must thank Lowell "Ben" Bennion, Jr., one of the manuscript's outside reviewers, for his invaluable suggestions for further research and revision, particularly regarding the introduction, for which he provided especially detailed notes. Thanks also to Benjamin Wood, a senior English major at USU, for his help with the final proofing of the letter transcriptions. Many thanks to Mel Thorne, director of BYU's Humanities Publication Center, and to his students for their invaluable work on the index. Lu Ann's and my son Travis drafted the maps. It is gratifying to have him contribute to this project. I appreciate all the historians and archivists who helped me — an English professor — to get the cultural context and the historical details of this project right. Any errors here are mine alone. Thanks as always to

BYU's College of Humanities and English Department for their support of my scholarship.

By the time of her death, Lu Ann had completed the transcriptions of the letters, done most of the documentation, compiled most of the Woodruff Circle entries, and drafted the introduction. I reorganized the letters and sections of Avery's autobiography in chronological order to provide a more coherent narrative, added additional documentation, reorganized and standardized the Woodruff Circle entries, checked the transcription against the original letters, and did several revisions of the introduction. In addition, I presented a paper based on Lu Ann's introduction at a 2000 symposium sponsored by the Joseph Fielding Smith Institute for Latter-day Saint History at BYU, which was published as "The Woodruff Correspondence, 1899–1904, in Polygamy's Last Days," under Lu Ann Snyder's name, in *Times of Transition, 1890–1920,* edited by Thomas G. Alexander.

Lu Ann would want me to thank the Lambert and Woodruff families for their donation of the original letters, journals, autobiographies, and other items to the L. Tom Perry Special Collections at BYU and for their support of this project. Richard Lambert was particularly helpful in securing the photographs for this volume. She would also want me to thank everyone at BYU's Special Collections and the LDS Church Archives who helped her with her research, and particularly her professors and classmates from BYU's American Studies Program and the University of Utah's Department of History. She loved working on her scholarship — especially the Woodruff correspondence — and treasured her professional relationships. Although her cancer prevented Lu Ann from completing her PhD, I trust this publication will stand in its place as public evidence of her scholarly ability. She admired Helen, Owen, and Avery for their commitment to their religion and for their generosity toward one another under very trying circumstances.

Finally, Lu Ann would want me to note, as she often did during her last months and always with a twinkle in her eye, that it is possible for certain extraordinary people to publish *after* they have perished. And so it is with her.

Phillip A. Snyder
Salem, Utah, 2009

Preface

The complete 1899–1904 correspondence among Helen, Owen, and Avery Woodruff are published here for the first time along with excerpts from Avery Clark's autobiography. The documents are taken from the Abraham Owen Woodruff Collection (Vault MSS 777) housed at the L. Tom Perry Special Collections, Brigham Young University, Provo, Utah. According to the register compiled by David J. Whittaker and Erin Parker, the collection

consists of journals, notebooks, letters, and other miscellaneous items arranged into six boxes. The first box contains Woodruff's mission journals (1) from 23 January 1894 to 31 October 1894, and (2) from 1 October 1895 to 26 May 1896, a journal from 1 January 1899 to 31 December 1900, a journal from 1 October 1901 to 24 April 1902, a letter record book beginning in 1894, a notebook of 1898, and a letterbook from 6 March 1900 to 18 April 1900.

The second box contains a scrapbook of various dried plants, a book of music, and a notebook belonging to Helen Winters, Woodruff's first wife. The third box contains letters to and from various family members, including: Wilford Woodruff, Emma L. Woodruff, Helen Winters Woodruff, Avery Clark Woodruff, Asahel Woodruff, and other family members. Box three also contains Woodruff's mission correspondence to his family.

The fourth box begins with miscellaneous mission correspondence, including several letters written in German. It also includes correspondence with members of the Church of Jesus Christ of Latter-day Saints living in Mexico and correspondence with many prominent church figures, including: Heber J. Grant, George Albert Smith, Joseph F. Smith, and Lorenzo Snow, among others, as well as miscellaneous religious correspondence.

Box four also contains correspondence with members of the U.S. Congress. Box five contains correspondence regarding the Big Horn Basin of Wyoming, including numerous letters from DeForrest [sic] Richards, Governor of the State of Wyoming.

Box six continues the correspondence from the Big Horn Basin and also contains receipts, announcements and invitations, and miscellaneous correspondence. Folders nineteen and twenty of box six contain photocopies of letters from the Eliza Avery Clark Woodruff Papers, from Church Archives of the Church of Jesus Christ of Latter-day Saints in Salt Lake City, Utah. Folder nineteen also contains an explanation of codes and references to the letters, prepared for Church Archives by D. Michael Quinn. Folder 21 contains a photocopy of the "Autobiography and Recollections of Eliza Avery Clark (Woodruff) Lambert, 1882–1953."

In accordance with the editorial procedures of Utah State University Press, we have prepared the typescript to reflect the original manuscript as closely as possible. We have retained the original spelling, punctuation, and syntax, only standardizing some marks, such as dashes, and spacing to reflect current practice.

Editorial interpolations within the text of the letters and other supporting documents are noted by roman brackets, as in "Soda [Springs, Idaho]." Framing and internal editorial interpolations describing the letters are noted by roman brackets with italicized comments, as in "[*LDS Church letterhead, handwritten*]" and "[*halfway in left margin*] 1901." When the text to which these interpolations refer is unclear, the referenced text is also placed within the brackets, as in "[Owen and Kate Spilsbury took care of Rhoda *in left margin*]." Corrections and insertions above the line in the original text are noted with carets, as in "such as ^the boys^ milking cows."

To help readers identify key figures, we have included endnotes on first reference as well as on any unclear references. In addition, we have included a register of names under "Woodruff Circle of Family and Friends" at the back of the book, the sources for which are Latter-day Saint family group sheets available through the Family History Library, Salt Lake City, and Andrew Jenson's *Encyclopedic History of the Church of Jesus Christ of Latter-day Saints* (1941) and *Latter-day Biographical Encyclopedia* (1901). Code interpretations in the letters come from Quinn's explanation prepared especially for the Woodruff collection. Other commentary on the contents and source documentation is included in endnotes.

Introduction

*Therefore, prepare thy heart to receive and obey the instructions
which I am about to give unto you; for all those who have this
law revealed unto them must obey the same.*[1]

Reinterment and Restoration

Over two hundred Woodruff family members gathered on July
17, 1993, in the Salt Lake City Cemetery, to witness the reinterment of
Abraham Owen Woodruff and his wife Helen May Winters. This family
celebration ended the eighty-nine-year separation of Helen and Owen
after their unexpected deaths from smallpox in June 1904 in Mexico
City and El Paso, respectively. Grandsons of the Woodruffs, with funding
from Brigham Young University and approval from Mexican authorities,
arranged to exhume the bodies and bring them to Salt Lake City, along
with their original headstones. The reburial served as the culmination of
family efforts to restore them to one another, as reported by grandson
Wilford Bruce Woodruff:

> As plans for this significant event have proceeded, a wonderful
> spirit of unity has grown in the family. We felt that a husband
> and wife separated 89 years and by more than 1,000 miles
> should be brought together and buried side by side. It is the
> result of a series of wonderful experiences.[2]

One of the "wonderful experiences" mentioned by Bruce included
the fortuitous timing of the reinterment. Because no one paid Helen's
grave fees for nearly nine decades, the Mexican authorities had declared
her grave abandoned and scheduled the reburial of her remains in a common grave and the reselling of her plot. Arriving just in time to pay the
fees and exhume the body, the Woodruffs made a posthumous reunion
for Helen and Owen possible. In addition to bringing together husband
and wife, the burial also reunited their family. Helen and Owen were
reinterred alongside their three deceased children — Wilford Owen,

*Abraham Owen
Woodruff*

Courtesy of the Lambert and Woodruff families

Helen Mar, and Rhoda — and Owen was buried near his father and mother, Wilford and Emma Woodruff. At the Woodruffs' original memorial service on June 26, 1904, Seymour B. Young, then president of the First Council of the Seventy of the Church of Jesus Christ of Latter-day Saints (LDS), said he "hoped that at some future time the couple could be brought back home and reunited with loved ones."[3] The Woodruffs' reunion in the Salt Lake City Cemetery in 1993 paralleled a reunion of family artifacts — letters, journals, and autobiographies — now preserved at Brigham Young University's L. Tom Perry Special Collections as the Abraham Owen Woodruff Collection. These artifacts provide firsthand accounts of Owen and his wives, Helen Winters and Avery Clark, as post-Manifesto polygamists and demonstrate some of the personal effects of plural marriage.

This essay focuses mainly on the correspondence between Helen, Owen, and Avery. The eighty-five-letter Woodruff Correspondence includes Helen's thirty-two typed and *handwritten* letters to Owen and his five to her; Owen's thirty-one typed and *handwritten* letters to Avery and her nine to him; Avery's four letters to both Owen and Helen, her two letters to Helen, and Helen's two letters to Avery. This collection spans the period 1899–1904, covering the five years of Helen and Owen's marriage and the three years of Owen and Avery's polygamous marriage. Transcribed and historically documented here, these letters place the Woodruffs' marital experience in Utah's turn-of-the-century context with particular emphasis on religion, culture, and politics. In addition, a few of Owen's journal entries; excerpts from Avery's 1952 autobiography; journal entries by Alonzo Taylor, an LDS missionary who cared for Helen at the time of her death; and recollections of Kate Spilsbury, who cared for Helen and Owen's baby when Helen became ill, supply further perspectives on the day-to-day logistics of the Woodruffs' relationships and the joys and sorrows they produced. The Woodruff Collection also adds a significant personal and familial perspective to Mormon culture and social history. For example, most previous books about late nineteenth-century polygamy, such as Annie Clark Tanner's *A Mormon Mother* and Ida Hunt Udall's *Mormon Odyssey*, are based on journals and other autobiographical writings edited by succeeding generations to display their ancestors as both heroes and victims. Written as public reminiscences, these accounts reflect a certain bias in their retrospective public transmissions.

Antithetically, because the Woodruffs' letters are immediate and relatively unmediated in articulating their struggles with their polygamous marriage, with their absences from each other, and with their sometimes wavering self-confidence, they represent a private account of a public issue, one that developed during the LDS Church's transition from isolation to integration into mainstream American culture, which celebrated monogamy. Perhaps most importantly, while generalizations can be made from this collection as a significant case study of post-Manifesto life in the polygamy "underground" set against the backdrop of such historical events as the Smoot Senate hearings, this analysis focuses most specifically on how the Woodruffs' commitment to plural marriage as a fundamental religious principle complicated and disrupted their personal lives and relationships.

Abraham Owen Woodruff

Abraham Owen Woodruff, born November 23, 1872, in Salt Lake City, was raised in a polygamous family. His mother, Emma Smith, became the third wife of Wilford Woodruff in 1853 and had eight children, Owen being the youngest son. Each of Woodruff's four wives produced a large family, but even with so many siblings, Owen captured much of his aging father's attention and support. Raised in a primitive log house built by his father in 1847, Owen grew to manhood learning and performing the labors of farm life. Like his father, he loved outdoor activities, especially fishing and hunting. A young and enterprising Owen attempted to earn pocket money by gathering watercress from Liberty Park Springs and then selling it at the local market.

The familial circle of Owen's childhood was surrounded by an intense anti-polygamy environment. From 1843 to 1852, a limited number of Latter-day Saints practiced plural marriage as an essential tenet of their faith with only isolated persecution, partly because these plural marriages initially were kept secret from even general church membership, but whenever Utah applied for statehood, polygamy became the central problematic issue. Plural marriage had been practiced by selected Latter-day Saints as early as 1843 when in Nauvoo, Illinois, the Prophet Joseph Smith had William Clayton record a revelation from God, which offered the conditions and sanctions for polygamy under the "new and everlasting covenant."[4] According to Richard L. Bushman in *Joseph Smith: Rough Stone Rolling*, it is possible that Joseph entered into plural marriage with Fanny Alger sometime before 1836, with Louisa Bateman in April 1841, and then with an additional thirty women before his death in 1844.[5] Bushman argues that the primary motivation for these plural marriages was not sexual lust but spiritual necessity and summarizes Joseph's plural marriage practice as follows:

> He did not court his prospective wives by first trying to win their affections. Often he asked a relative — a father or an uncle — to propose the marriage. Sometimes one of the current wives proposed for him. When he made the proposal himself, a friend like Brigham Young was often present. The language was religious and doctrinal, stressing that a new law had been revealed. She was to seek spiritual confirmation. Once consent was given, a formal ceremony was performed before witnesses, with Joseph dictating the words to the person officiating.[6]

In addition, Bushman stresses Joseph's insistence that anyone entering into polygamy have priesthood sanction first and that men were not to proceed independently.[7] Other Latter-day Saint men who were sanctioned to take additional wives were expected to follow Joseph's example in that process, stressing always the spiritual imperative of the practice.[8] Further, Bushman reports that the accounts of plural wives published in the decades after the Mormon migration West also reflect this spiritual focus as well as the importance of divine confirmation.[9] In *Solemn Covenant*, B. Carmon Hardy adds that the LDS Church considered polygamy to be "the family order of heaven" and proclaimed that "it would regenerate mankind, nurture a superior civilization, and eliminate sexual wickedness."[10]

Increasing LDS acknowledgment of polygamy fueled the anti-Mormon criticism and persecution that followed the pioneers as they made their way west after 1846. In the years following Mormon settlement in Utah and the Intermountain West, polygamy's profile was raised even higher both within and without the church. In response to the national anti-polygamy outcry, Congress enacted the 1882 Edmunds Act, which defined "unlawful cohabitation" as supporting and caring for more than one woman, legally disenfranchising polygamists and their supporters. The Edmunds Act forced polygamists, especially those among the church hierarchy, to go underground to avoid arrest, so ten-year-old Owen was left fatherless for extended periods of time as his father, Wilford, attempted to stay a step ahead of law enforcement. Congress passed the Edmunds-Tucker Act in March 1887, which required wives to testify against husbands, abolished woman suffrage in Utah, and dissolved the Nauvoo Legion and the Perpetual Emigrating Fund, which had aided foreign Latter-day Saints in their immigration to Utah. Congress enacted these laws as a way to force the LDS Church to discontinue what outsiders saw as a depraved practice rather than as a doctrinal mandate to which the church subscribed. These two acts created an almost unbearable situation for the polygamists who were separated from their families through incarceration, seclusion, or missionary service to foreign lands, causing them to rethink the practicality of a now-illegal practice. Four months after the passage of the Edmunds-Tucker Act, President John Taylor died, leaving Wilford Woodruff to preside over the church. Owen was then fifteen years old.

President Woodruff issued his anti-polygamy Manifesto in September 1890, announcing that the church would discontinue the practice of plural marriage and conform to the laws of the United States. He declared in the Manifesto that his advice to the Latter-day Saints was to "refrain from contracting any marriage forbidden by the law of the land."[11] He said that he received this proclamation as an answer to his prayers "by vision and revelation" and that the Lord "told me exactly what to do and what the result would be if we did not do it."[12]

A month later, this "Official Declaration" was sustained unanimously by the general church membership during General Conference on October 6, 1890, and later added to the 1908 edition of the *Doctrine and Covenants*, thus making it part of canonized LDS scripture.[13] In this context, George Q. Cannon, counselor to President Woodruff, expressed the political effects of continuing the practice of plural marriage: "I have ever been assured hundreds of times, by men, too, of wisdom and discernment, that our overthrow was inevitable unless we conformed to the demands of public opinion and renounced all peculiarities of faith."[14]

However, appeasing the national public also sowed seeds of confusion among the Latter-day Saints because the Manifesto raised

Owen Woodruff with his father, LDS President Wilford Woodruff, 1897

fundamental questions regarding the implications of polygamy's abolition: How does this change affect the revealed doctrines of the church? What happens to the polygamous families already established? Kenneth Godfrey notes this confusion in *Women's Voices*: "It was not without struggle and sorrow that Latter-day Saint men and women let go of plural marriage and of their hopes for a unique political and economic kingdom."[15] Although many Latter-day Saints reluctantly accepted the loss of polygamy as a requirement necessary for Utah and the church to enter into mainstream American society, many did not, especially some in general church leadership positions. The United States government continually monitored the church's adherence to recently passed anti-polygamy laws and continued to pass additional anti-polygamy legislation. The Enabling Act of July 16, 1894, for example, forever prohibited polygamous marriages, not just cohabitation. Clearly the government felt it could not yet trust the Latter-day Saints to adhere fully to their own Manifesto renouncing polygamy as church doctrine and practice.

This transitional time for the church coincided with Owen's entrance into adulthood. He was eighteen years old and studying at the LDS College in Salt Lake City with noted Professors James E. Talmage and Karl G. Maeser when his father issued the Manifesto. Upon his graduation, Owen worked at Zion's Savings & Trust Co. in Salt Lake City as a collector and as an assistant bookkeeper.[16] In 1893, at age twenty-one, Owen received a call to serve in the Swiss-German mission. In a somewhat unusual beginning, he served without a companion for the first five months and learned the language from a German family where he recited lessons with the children each morning.[17] Owen distributed religious tracts during the day and held meetings in the evening where he preached in broken, stammering German. Once the mission president finally assigned a companion to Owen, a branch of the church was soon organized.[18] Owen labored diligently, even disguising himself as a peasant worker when the German civil officials banished LDS missionaries, so he could continue his work. Owen returned home in 1896 and resumed his work in the bank. He met Helen May Winters that same year.

Helen May Winters Woodruff

Woodruff family tradition holds that when Owen's father, then president of the LDS Church, first saw Helen, he introduced himself to her. He then told her that he would like her to meet his son Owen and that, if they married, they would be happy together and would not be separated, even in death, by more than two weeks.[19] More important than President Woodruff's encouragement to Owen and Helen, however, was

Helen May Winters

their meeting and falling in love; they were married on June 30, 1897, as described in the *Deseret News*: "President Woodruff, though feeling quite feeble today, went to the temple and performed the ordinance of marriage between his son Abraham Owen Woodruff and Miss Helen May Winters."[20] President Woodruff also recorded this event in his journal:

> June 30th I slept fairly well the latter part of the night & this morning. Felt better of myself. Arose shaved & dressed myself and went to the office. Attended a special meeting of the Board of Directors of Z. S. B. & T co at 10.30 am. Declared a dividend for 6% for the past six months. This afternoon at the Temple I performed the marriage ceremony uniting Miss Helen Winter to my son A. O. Woodruff, and then drove home. There was a family gathering at the residence of Br Heber J Grant this evening. I did not attend.[21]

On October 7, 1897, a month before Owen's twenty-fifth birthday, President Woodruff called him to be an apostle. Owen's appointment was sustained by the church membership at that October General Conference, and he was then set apart by his father. This assignment entailed traveling to various LDS congregations to dedicate buildings, call church leaders, and generally oversee the operations of the church. Owen also served on the General Board of the Sunday School as part of his apostleship and on business boards such as the Logan Knitting Factory. Thus, within only three months of their marriage, young Owen and Helen became prominent members of the church's religious and social hierarchy.

Helen May Winters, born September 24, 1873, grew up in Pleasant Grove, Utah, the youngest of eight children. Today the graves of her parents, Oscar Winters and Mary Ann Stearns, retain a prominent place in the city's cemetery, as befitting two of the founders of Pleasant Grove. One of Helen's sisters described her as "always the one who first came out of the gloom if a shadow fell upon the household, and who by her very nature and presence brought the sunshine back again."[22] Helen attended district schools, later took a course at the Brigham Young Academy in Provo, Utah, and taught in the public schools of Sevier and Summit counties. She returned to school as a student at the University of Utah in Salt Lake City, where she became acquainted with Owen.[23]

Like Owen, Helen was no stranger to polygamy. Her grandmother, Mary Ann Frost Stearns Smith Pratt, became a bride in April 1832, a mother in April 1833, and a widow by August 1833. Alone in Nauvoo, Mary Ann married the Prophet Joseph Smith as a polygamous wife. Widowed again at the Prophet's death, she married Parley P. Pratt after the death of his wife, Thankful. Pratt later married ten other wives, without the permission or knowledge of Mary Ann. She raised four children with Parley, in addition to her only child, Mary Ann Stearns, by her first husband. Daughter Mary Ann, Helen's mother, married Oscar Winters at the age of nineteen and, although surrounded by practitioners of plural marriage, chose to remain in a monogamous marriage, even though she believed in plural marriage as a tenet of LDS doctrine. She records her personal coming to terms with polygamy in the following excerpt from her autobiography:

> It was while located on the boat at St. Louis that I saw the little book published by Martha Brotherton on polygamy. She with her family had visited at our house before they left England, and being acquainted with her made me very curious to know what she had to say about it, so I took the book, went into my berth, drew the curtains, and proceeded to investigate. I had always been taught to believe in the Bible, and when I came to the place where it quoted Abraham, Jacob and others as having more than one wife, I decided that the principle must be true, coming from that source and also, though right for others, not for me was my firm conclusion. An[d] though thus steeled against it for myself, I always honored and respected those living in it.[24]

Accordingly, Mary Ann supported her daughter Hulda Augusta when she became the second wife of Heber J. Grant in 1884 at the age of twenty-eight.

Only two of Helen's letters to Owen prior to 1900 remain, but those letters and other remembrances demonstrate the mutual love and devotion we traditionally associate with monogamous marriage. Their correspondence manifests a physical and emotional intimacy unmatched by many nineteenth-century marriages, as evidenced in the following reminiscence in an October 27, 1903, letter from Helen to Owen:

> I have thought and thought of the many sweet experiences of our lives together and have lived again those happy days when first you took me to your heart and then to "our" home. How free from care and sorrow those days. We were children then, boy and girl together. I remember how I used to watch and wa^i^t for your home coming and when you came would always welcome you with a smile and a "bebe kiiss" (I can't

spell German). How we used to sit for hours and never tire of

spell German). How we used to sit for hours and never tire of telling each other of our love for each other. (Letter 59)

During the first few years of their married life, Helen and Owen frequently traveled together in Utah, Wyoming, and Canada on church assignments. Owen ministered as an apostle, and Helen assisted the Young Ladies Mutual Improvement Association (YLMIA), beginning in May of 1898. Because Helen represented the YLMIA General Board, she had her own leadership status, apart from being an apostle's wife.[25] Helen's responsibilities also required her to serve on various committees, such as the Library Committee, where the board members devised plans to help various branches of the church set up "Traveling Libraries" to provide books for study and reference.[26] As May Boothe Talmage wrote in a 1904 memorial to Helen, those who served with the Woodruffs in their church callings could easily observe their loving relationship:

> None who have ever been fortunate enough to be intimately acquainted with Brother and Sister Woodruff could ever doubt that they were given each other of God. No outward demonstration was necessary. There was something so genuine, so frank and sincere, yet, withal, so tender and affectionate in their bearing toward each other that their unostentatious devotion was often commented kindly upon by their friends.[27]

Although their travels provided leadership and social opportunities, which both Helen and Owen enjoyed, the early years of their marriage were also marked by their worry over their inability to conceive a child. As Owen recorded in his journal:

> The past two years have been the most eventful, substantial and best of my life. My good, faithful Helen has been the chief factor in the hands of God in making the past two years the best of my life. She has always been full of faith and equally anxious with me that I may be successful in the service of my God and fellow men. We have as yet not been blessed with children, but the Lord has heard our united prayers and at last blessed us with "good Prospects." I am contented, happy and thoroughly satisfied with my Helen.[28]

Their fears proved unwarranted, and the "good prospects" to which Owen referred — Wilford Owen Woodruff — was born to Owen and Helen on

October 31, 1899, after a very difficult labor. Owen noted later that day:

> Fordie — 10 2 lbs — 5:25 pm
> Prest. Richards made a promise about 10 months ago regarding
> my son and therefore we regard him as a child of promise.[29]

Busy with a new baby, Helen remained at home while her husband continued with his church business travels in Wyoming, Mexico, and Utah. Owen recorded an example of the extensive travel requirements of his apostleship in a December 31, 1900, journal entry:

> In the year just closed I have attended 317 Meetings
> Travelled 3555 Miles by team
> Travelled 10570 Miles by R. R.[30]

The bulk of Helen's letters correspond to the frequent and lengthy periods of time during which Owen was away from home. Initially, Owen's absence and Helen's increasing familial responsibilities troubled her. Two early references in Helen's letters demonstrate her love for, dependence on, and need for Owen:

> The way I feel sometimes I am afraid I will not hold out until
> you come but hope I will. . . .(Letter 7)

> Only two more weeks. I can scarcely wait that long to see you.
> (Letter 15)

However, as she gained confidence and experience, Helen became a more independent woman.

The Woodruffs moved in an elite social circle. Owen's position as a member of the Quorum of the Twelve Apostles, albeit the youngest, aligned him with the prestigious and powerful of Salt Lake City. Owen's letters, for example, include his correspondence with Senator Thomas Kearns, Senator-elect Reed Smoot, and various leaders of the LDS Church. Within this influential group, Owen associated most closely with apostles Mathias F. Cowley and John W. Taylor, both strong advocates of polygamy, even after the 1890 Manifesto. Because of his relationship with these two men, which grew closer as the three traveled together to Wyoming's Bighorn Basin, he must have been aware that secret, officially sanctioned plural marriages were still taking place. Eventually, apparently after much soul-searching, Owen determined to embrace post-Manifesto polygamy because he must have believed that the laws of God would eventually supercede those of the government despite the Manifesto's promise of the church's legal compliance.[31] Indeed, Hardy quotes Owen from the clerk's record of a November 1900 quarterly conference in Colonia Juárez as stating "no year will ever pass, whether it be in this country, in India, or wherever, from now until the coming of the Saviour, when children will not be born in plural marriage. And I make this prophecy in the name of Jesus Christ."[32] This prophecy underscores both his philosophical and practical commitment to plural marriage, as he was engaged to Avery at the time.

Owen's travel stemmed mostly from a new assignment he received from his father's successor, President Lorenzo Snow, in December 1899 to be a colonizing agent for the church. In January of 1900 President Snow gave Owen a mandate:

> You are a committee of "one" and I want you to go right ahead to organize your Co. for your work in Wyoming and I want you to be Prest. of it. You know you have been sustained to do this work by me and the Twelve Apostles.[33]

Owen enthusiastically accepted this assignment, stating that "I have had a desire all my life to be of use to my people in this line."[34]

While this assignment came to Owen as an ecclesiastical responsibility, it was primarily an economic development task. The Bighorn Basin project developed partly out of the Carey Act. LDS Church leaders had been impressed by the Carey Act of 1894, whereby settlers had irrigated arid lands in the Greybull River area of the Bighorn. The original act stated that any person twenty-one years or older who intended to become a citizen of a western state such as Wyoming was entitled to land. Settlers in the Bighorn Basin purchased a perpetual water right from the Cincinnati Canal builders for the number of acres wanted, but not to exceed one hundred and sixty. After the canal was ready, the settlers had one year to cultivate at least one-sixteenth of their acreage and within three years to have cultivated no less than one-eighth. Having met these requirements, the settlers could then buy their land for twenty-five cents per acre. The opening for the church to become part of this settlement opportunity occurred when the Cincinnati Canal builders abandoned the project. Because William F. (Buffalo Bill) Cody owned most of the land and water rights near the Shoshone River and envisioned successful agricultural settlement in the area, he supported the church's interest in the canal project:

> If the Mormons want to build a canal and irrigate the land down lower on the river I will relinquish both land and water to them, for if they will do this I know they are the kind of people who will do what they agree to do. . . . Now my dream will be realized, for I have thought that I should live to see this country developed into a great agricultural region and now the Mormons will fulfill my dream.[35]

While Cody's approval of the project served his own dream, it also facilitated LDS expansion and settlement into the Bighorn Basin. With Cody's backing and the support of Wyoming's governor, DeForest Richards, the Big Horn Basin Colonization Company met April 6, 1900, with Elder Franklin S. Richards, attorney for the church, who drew up the articles of incorporation. The company was organized as follows: Abraham Owen Woodruff, president; Byron Sessions, vice president and head of canal project; Charles Kingston, secretary; Charles A. Welsh, treasurer; and Jesse W. Crosby, Brigham L. Tippets, William B. Graham, Hyrum K. North, and Charles A. Welch as board members.[36] After the organization of the company, recruitment began in earnest through personal contacts and *Deseret News* advertisements. Settlers began to arrive in the Bighorn Basin in May of 1900. Owen dedicated the land and the canal on May 28, 1900, promising the settlers, "If you keep the commandments of the Lord this shall be a land of Zion unto you and your children."[37]

He organized the first stake in May 1901 with Byron Sessions as the stake president. As Kurt Graham notes in his thesis, "The Mormon Migration to Wyoming's Big Horn Basin in 1900,"

> The three [Sessions, Crosby, and Welch] shared general supervision of the spiritual activities of all the Mormons in the area and were influential in all of the matters until they were released from their church positions in 1910. All three were men of influence before coming to the Big Horn Basin, and they had more in common than the leadership of the stake. They were three of the wealthier individuals to migrate to the Basin, and like their esteemed leader Apostle Woodruff, all three were polygamists.[38] Crosby and Welch both had their second wives join them once they were established in Cowley, and Sessions entered into a plural marriage after he had settled in the Basin.[39]

Although the local stake leadership was comprised of polygamists, the LDS communities in northern Wyoming were primarily monogamous.

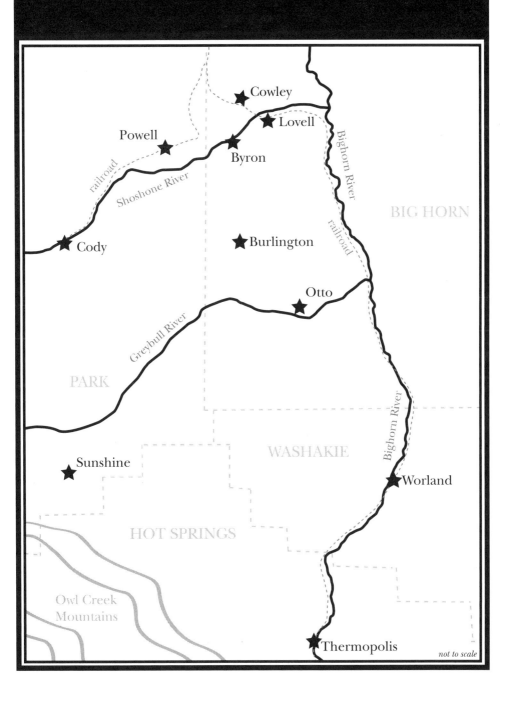

Mormon Colonies in the Bighorn Basin, Wyoming

Cowley

Lovell

Powell

Byron

railroad

Shoshone River

Bighorn River

railroad

BIG HORN

Cody

Burlington

Otto

Greybull River

PARK

Bighorn River

WASHAKIE

Sunshine

Worland

HOT SPRINGS

Owl Creek
Mountains

Thermopolis

not to scale

There is little evidence that the Bighorn Basin settlements, unlike those in Star Valley, Wyoming, were intended to harbor church members still practicing polygamy.[40]

Owen's most significant contribution as an apostle came as a result of his supervision of the settlement of Wyoming's Bighorn Basin. Working closely with fellow apostles Cowley and Taylor, Owen negotiated water rights and land purchases to establish this important LDS colony, and he directed the settlers in their material as well as their religious needs. A May 27, 1900, journal entry illustrates this secular/spiritual mix in Owen's administrative responsibilities:

> I spoke about an hour to the saints and told them some things I wanted them to do in this new colony. Said if there were any dissatisfied they had better go home at once. I told them as an Apostle of Jesus Christ I wanted to call them on a mission to remain and make homes in this land that I would tell Prest. Snow what I had done and if he disapprived would come back and rectify my mistake.
>
> We had a good spirit present and I felt that the Lord was with me and the assembly.[41]

Owen's journal suggests that as early as 1899, Elder Cowley encouraged Owen to join him ideologically and practically in supporting post-Manifesto polygamy. The subject of polygamy weaves itself cryptically through Owen's early journal entries in 1900, and in August of that year he writes of presenting his dilemma to the future president of the church, Joseph F. Smith, who would succeed Lorenzo Snow in 1901:

> A subject has been troubling me of late so I have made it a matter of prayer and asked the Lord to reveal his will to me through Prest. Joseph F. Smith to whom I will present the matter at the Temple tomorrow.[42]
>
> I talked with JFS and he counsiled me to follow the impression I have had. The matter is clear to me now and I mean to do it.[43]

In this frame of mind, Owen traveled that month on church business to the Bighorn Basin, stopping in Star Valley on the way, and there met Eliza Avery Clark, an eighteen-year-old woman spending summer vacation at home with her family while on a break from her university studies in Logan, Utah.

Eliza Avery Clark Woodruff

Eliza Avery Clark Woodruff Lambert

According to Avery's autobiography, written fifty years later, she remembered being impressed with Owen's "charming, magnetic personality . . . angelic as Mother often said afterward."[44] Avery, who was tentatively promised to a young man named Fred Dixon, began comparing Fred and Owen, finding the latter more "handsome and intelligent, and thinking what a lucky girl his wife was."[45] Avery's romantic young mind fantasized about what it would be like to be married to someone like Owen. It was thus a pleasant surprise when Owen later joined her family at home for an informal visit.

The Clark family assumed that Owen's visit concerned a possible church calling for Avery's father, Hyrum D. Clark. With these thoughts, the Clarks welcomed Owen into their Star Valley home. Hyrum drove Owen to his destination the following day, expecting to hear the specific purpose for Owen's visit. He was not expecting, however, Owen's awkward request for Avery's hand as a polygamous wife. According to Avery's autobiography, Hyrum later recounted the conversation to her, his shocked and tearful daughter:

> I was just as shocked and surprised as you are Dot when I learned of this new Polygamy and I asked a lot of questions about it. . . . He [Owen] said that while he was speaking it was made known to him that the girl sitting before him would be his wife. . . . It was as if a voice had said the words. . . . "Not being able to throw it off my mind, I've prayed about it, feeling that my impression is from the Lord. . . . Would you be willing for her to marry me in case she wanted to"? I said, "Not unless it can be sanctioned by the Church." Bro. W. pointed out how several of the brethren in high positions had been advised to take plural wives which justified his [Hyrum's] confidence in the matter.[46]

After contemplation and prayer, Avery consented to Owen's proposal and, after four brief and secret meetings over a four-month period, Owen and Avery married in January 1901, probably on January 18.[47] No official LDS Church document records the polygamous marriage or who performed it, although Hardy's Appendix II indicates that Elder Cowley officiated at the ceremony.[48] This makes sense because, not only was he close to Owen, but also, according to Hardy, he was probably the "most frequently employed of the church's high leaders in performing polygamous marriages for his brethren."[49]

Avery had had little immediate experience with polygamous families, having been raised as the eldest of a very large monogamous family. She was born March 9, 1882, to Hyrum Don Carlos Clark and Ann Eliza Porter. She moved to Star Valley with her family when she was six. They took over a squatter's claim of a hundred and sixty acres, including a two-room log house with a dirt floor. Meeting with some economic success there, her father eventually bought out his neighbors. Avery explains this development in the following way: "As father expanded his meadow land — eventually buying out his neighbors on three sides, the work on the ranch multiplied, he had more live stock to care for, more machinery, more money and more children, more worries, more blessings."[50] The Clarks eventually moved from the log cabin into a twelve-room ranch house, the largest and most imposing in all of Star Valley. Two rooms were also added to the back of the cabin and the dirt roof was replaced with wooden shingles. The family used the cabin as a kitchen, and one of its bedrooms was often occupied by extended family members.

Although polygamy was quite common in Star Valley, Avery's youthful sexual and spiritual attraction to Owen seemed to push her resolve toward polygamy more than her personal experiences in observing "the principle." She writes of her interaction with Owen in her autobiography with an emphasis on the spiritual:

> Always I felt sure he was as perfect as mortal man can be. He treated me as if I were a queen, tenderly touching my hand. There was no love making, just beautiful, lofty words of devotion to the principle we were contemplating living and for each other and Helen.[51]

Further, after their first discussion of marriage, Avery wrote to Owen on October 25, 1900, in spiritual terms:

> I can say that I feel as you do in regards to the matter and think it is all right. I believe too that we have been guided by our Father in Heaven. Do not see how it could possibly be mistaken.
>
> A happier hour of my life was never spent than was during the conversation. It filled me with joy and gladness that has not departed from me, and I thank God that I am so highly favored for I feel that I am. (Letter 3)

Both Avery and Owen considered their impending post-Manifesto polygamous marriage to be sanctioned spiritually according to the "new and everlasting covenant," which they must have still interpreted as referring exclusively to plural marriage, and they comported themselves during their courtship after the pattern established years earlier by Joseph Smith. Whatever sexual and emotional attraction they may have also felt toward each other, their focus was on the spiritual aspect of their relationship.

The Woodruffs' Post-Manifesto Marriage

That Owen entered into a post-Manifesto polygamous relationship in 1901 is ironic, of course, because it was his own father who had issued the 1890 Manifesto proclaiming the end of plural marriage. This contradiction may be understood best in light of the belief held by some members that the LDS Church had adopted a public stance against plural marriage while maintaining a private stance supporting it. According to D. Michael Quinn in "LDS Church Authority and New Plural Marriages, 1890–1904," local church leaders quietly performed undocumented post-Manifesto plural marriages in the 1890s, probably with the church's tacit approval both outside and within its temples.[52] Indeed, Hardy's Appendix II lists 262 post-Manifesto polygamous marriages (October 1890 to December 1910) involving 220 different men, 59 percent of whom served as missionaries, branch presidents, bishops, stake presidents, or apostles, reinforcing the notion that polygamy continued to be practiced mostly within the male hierarchy of the LDS Church.[53]

Family letters and journals do not indicate that any of Owen's siblings entered into post-Manifesto polygamy, but his father's belief and practice in plural marriage, combined with Owen's own childhood experiences in a polygamous household, helped establish his affinity with this way of life. Hardy suggests that Wilford Woodruff's close relationship with Owen demonstrates that his actions were "at least indirectly representative of the sentiments of his late father."[54] Although polygamy proved difficult to practice personally, it was a marital and familial arrangement that grew out of Owen's own experiences. After a confrontation about polygamy during a quorum meeting, Owen recorded the following defense in a journal entry dated January 11, 1900, a year before his own plural marriage:

> I owe my exhistance to the principal of Polygamy and I have some intense feelings regarding the sustaining of that principle. I am indebted to that principle for my life and anytime my Father wants my life to defend that principle (and those who practice it in righteousness) God being my helper it is at

his command. . . . I pray God to give me light on this matter as I feel almost sick about it. I want to and intend to be loyal to my belief.[55]

No documentation exists to substantiate whether Owen was given official permission to enter into polygamy. However, Quinn suggests that "[i]f Joseph F. Smith did not authorize Apostle Owen Woodruff's plural marriage . . . he gave it after-the-fact sanction as Church president."[56]

After Owen and Avery's marriage in January 1901, she moved with her sister, Mary, back to school in Logan. Owen wrote Avery often and sent money on a regular basis. Following Owen's instructions for protecting their secrecy, Avery wrote to Owen in November of 1900 during their courtship:

> I must not forget to tell you that I have burned all letters and will continue to do so, although it seems like destroying valuable literature. . . . I will keep all secrets in my heart and ask God to guard my words and actions. (Letter 10)[57]

Secrecy presented a difficult situation for Avery; only her immediate family and a few close friends knew of her plural marriage to Owen. Publicly, people still referred to her as Miss Clark, and Avery's correspondence from Owen was either communicated in code, using different names for people and places, or written mostly about trivial matters from a detached viewpoint. Avery remembered crying over her difficult marital situation, longing to see her husband for more than a few minutes, and being scolded by her sister for not being thankful.[58]

In addition to living with the complex logistics of a secret polygamous marriage, Avery had to face the world as a single woman. She recorded an incident that sheds some light on the emotional complications the secret marriage arrangement had for both her and Owen in terms of jealousy, particularly related to Avery's would-be suitors:

> Russell [a companion in Owen's group] and I took little lard buckets and strolled down to the meadow to pick wild strawberries. Owen sat on the front porch watching just how close our heads came together while we were fairly rooting for the tiny wild berries. He said to me later on: "Make sure he behaves himself I can tell he likes you, just give him the cold shoulder or do you want to?" It was an aggrivation to me to not be able to announce to the world that I was happily married to a grand

person whom everyone admired. I had moments of resentment, when I may have used indescression in acting naughty.[59]

Pregnancy further complicated the issue of marriage secrecy for Avery in
1902, but that pregnancy ended in a miscarriage after just a few months.
Except for the support of her sister, Mary, Avery struggled alone through
this sorrowful time, unable to explain her illness or receive immediate
emotional support from others. Owen's support at this time came mainly
through letters.

As Avery struggled with the difficulties of living within a post-Manifesto marriage from her situation and perspective, so Helen struggled
with it from hers. Because post-Manifesto polygamy remained a secret,
even within the church, there were only a handful of people in whom
Helen could confide her feelings. Some of the pain Helen experienced
stemmed from a natural sense of jealousy and also from her own deterio-
rating self-confidence given Owen's frequent absences and the necessity
of sharing his marital affections. From a contemporary perspective, it is
difficult to understand how she persevered so earnestly to help make this
polygamous union successful. The motivation behind her determination
may be found in an essay she wrote for the *Young Women's Journal* in 1903
entitled, "Be Ye Not Unequally Yoked." The following excerpt from this
essay, combined with Helen's devotion to God and to her children, clari-
fies the foundation on which she built her life as a polygamist's wife:

> Parents who are united in their belief in the Gospel of Jesus
> Christ and who by their works show that they are striving to
> serve God and keep His commandments furnish for their chil-
> dren a corner stone upon which may be built a structure of
> faith that cannot be shaken by the powers of adversity.[60]

In a November 1900 letter to Owen, two months before Owen and
Avery's marriage, Helen reported an incident that had just occurred
which gave her some comfort in anticipating their entering into post-
Manifesto polygamy:

> You ask how I am feeling. Some days I feel fine and at other
> times I am "blue" as "Indago." Yesterday I had Aunt Zina and
> Aunt Bathesheba down and we spent a splendid afternoon.
> They gave me a lovely blessing and made me some beautiful
> promises which I firmly believe will be answered if I am hum-
> ble and faithful.[61] (Letter 7)

This blessing, administered by women who understood very personally the doctrine and practice of plural marriage, strengthened Helen's faith and restored her courage. Again, even though she drew sustenance from her few apprised friends, Helen still felt isolated, both physically and emotionally. Helen drew strength primarily from her children, from her role as a mother, and from her personal connection with God. In March 1904, two months before her death, Helen wrote a moving letter to Owen that demonstrates her depth of character and devotion:

> I have my precious children and I am wrapped up in them heart and soul. They give me joy and comfort every hour. And I have so much to be thankful for the Lord knows my heart and He knows how grateful I am for all my many blessings although it would seem sometimes to others that I am ungrateful. The one fact, that God knows my every thought, hope and desire, is one of my greatest sources of happiness. I keep nothing from Him. . . . there is only One who can judge me, and He is merciful and I feel will be charitable with me. (Letter 76)

Helen's isolation also led her to more independence, and Owen's confidence in her abilities increased as did her competence in rearing a growing family. She attended parties alone and began handling financial and delicate religious matters for Owen, such as his August 5, 1902, request to "Please drop a note to Sophronia Tucker. . . . Tell her I have no authority to release them from any covenant they have made with the Lord. You know the case dear & I can't trust it to anyone but you" (Letter 41). These additional responsibilities occupied Helen's daily life and altered her tone in letters as shown in entries two years later:

> I have been so extremely busy since you left that the time has passed so rapidly I scarcely know where it has gone to and you will soon be home again before I get half done that I anticipated. (Letter 54)

> Now I do not want you to cut your visit short on my account for I will get along some way as many women have to do. (Letter 61)

Three baby girls — Helen Mar (1901), June (1902), and Rhoda (1903) — quickly followed the birth of Wilford Owen, so home and family responsibilities threatened at times to overwhelm Helen. She hired a young immigrant girl, Anna Rosenkilde, to help care for the home and the children, and she also employed "young Heber" (probably Helen's nephew Heber Bennion) to do chores. In addition to this help, Helen could rely on her mother-in-law, Emma Woodruff, and Owen's sister, Winifred Blanche Woodruff Daynes, who lived nearby. Furthermore, Helen traveled to Pleasant Grove for visits with her parents in Owen's absences, as she relates in an August 1899 letter:

> Mother says it seems like old times to have me at home again and says she can't let me go again, she has been trying to persuade me to stay here until you come but I have nearly finished all the work I brought with me and have so much to do at home I feel as though I must go and get some of it done before your return. (Letter 2)

Although Helen was not completely alone, she felt increased personal responsibility during Owen's absences and expressed her discouragement in a letter to Owen, dated February 1904: "I feel more keenly all the time the great responsibility of the children's rearing and am at a loss to know how to deal with them always. I get discouraged in this every few days" (Letter 68). To cope with discouragement and loneliness, Helen immersed herself in friends and church activities. Her letters to Owen often recount social events which she attended, such as parties at the splendid McCune Mansion near the state capitol building, church meetings, or Woodruff family gatherings.

At times Owen sensed Helen's frustrations and insecurities. He did not share his letters from Avery with Helen and did not speak frequently about the other family unless questioned.[62] Owen mentioned several times to both women that he was thankful for their sisterly love and feeling of friendliness. He also emphasized the importance of unity for the success of their family. However, one glimpse of a more vulnerable Owen surfaced in his July 12, 1902, letter to Helen, in which he may be alluding to a personal questioning of the wisdom of his decision to enter into post-Manifesto polygamy:

> Write me often dear, I so love to hear from you and nowadays you seem more like my own, sweet Helen in letters than you do when I am with you; for when I am with you I try you and when I am away you think of me as your other self, struggling and trying to do my duty just as you are trying. How much

easier it is when we sustain each other and struggle together. I love you my darling Helen and for my life I could not have you alienate yourself from me. I feel that if you were to I could not live. I may have been unwise but God who knows me best knows I am as loyal to you in your position as I am to Him in his. (Letter 38)

Owen's possible second thoughts about entering into post-Manifesto polygamy and his concern over maintaining a good relationship with Helen demonstrate his own difficulties in managing to be a good husband to both wives. Obviously, plural marriage presented difficulties for all participants, not just the women.

However, as the second, secret wife, Avery was perhaps in the most difficult situation of all. As the first wife, Helen held more familial authority than Avery, following the established tradition of LDS plural marriage. In addition, Owen appeared to be deeply in love with Helen. While his letters to Avery express kindness and love, albeit sometimes with a slight touch of condescension, Owen's letters to Helen declare his deep devotion, even passion. Becoming the third partner in such a strong relationship undoubtedly presented particular challenges for Avery, who was ten years younger than Helen and Owen. However, she always spoke of Helen with gratitude, even admiration, as in her October 1900 letter to Owen: "I am also thankful to her who gave her consent and sacrificed that she all ready has for my sake and for principle's sake, for it must be contrary to the natural feelings, which we all have" (Letter 3). No documents exist that give direct evidence of Helen's consent to Owen's polygamous marriage, but her letters document an emotional change prior to the marriage date, which seems to indicate that Helen and Owen had discussed it. Helen's assumed consent thus placed Avery in her debt. Also, Helen's general church position with the YLMIA, advanced schooling, maturity, and guardianship of Owen's growing family could have left Avery feeling subordinate and even inferior. Perhaps these factors contributed to the idea that it might be easier for Avery to carve out her own space in the Mormon colonies of Mexico.

In 1903 Avery graduated from college in Logan, but Owen's travels on church business kept him away from the ceremonies. Because she had prepared herself to become a teacher and because she was pregnant again, Owen arranged for her to travel a second time to Colonia Juárez, Mexico, to teach at the academy there. Colonia Juárez and other LDS Chihuahua colonies had been founded in the mid-1880s as a place to expand polygamy outside the United States' borders. For a time after the Manifesto, no plural marriages were performed there. However, in June

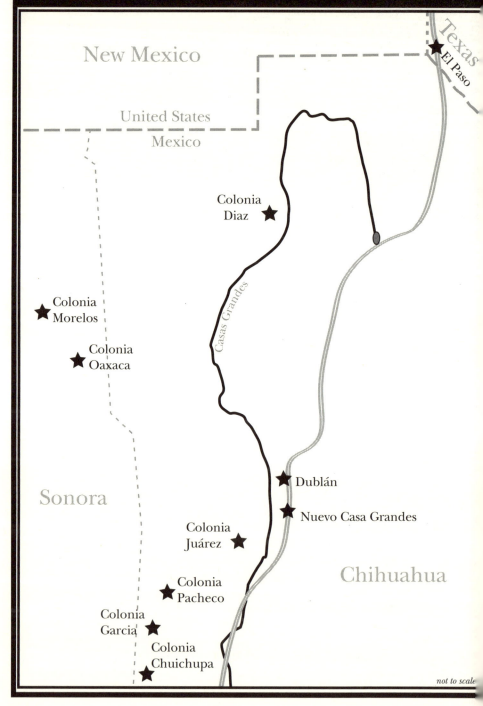

Mormon Colonies in Northern Mexico

New Mexico

Texas

El Paso

United States

Mexico

Colonia Diaz

Casas Grandes

Colonia Morelos

Colonia Oaxaca

Sonora

Dublán

Nuevo Casa Grandes

Colonia Juárez

Chihuahua

Colonia Pacheco

Colonia Garcia

Colonia Chuichupa

not to scale

Avery Woodruff's house in Colonia Juárez. On the porch are Mr. and Dr. Farr, to whom Avery rented one of the front rooms. Avery lived in the house for over a year, leaving it in May 1905.

of 1897, holding to a narrow interpretation of the Manifesto prohibiting plural marriage only in lands where the law forbids it, the First Presidency authorized President Anthony Ivins to perform polygamous ceremonies in Mexico, even though, as Hardy argues, "polygamy had been against the law in Mexico ever since they [Mormons] first entered Mexican territory in the late 1840s."[63] Many polygamous wives and families from the United States sought refuge in the LDS Mexican colonies, protected against prosecution by Mexican laws that indirectly sanctioned male adultery to preserve Mexican marriages.[64]

Avery lived initially with President Ivins and his family, close friends of Owen's, and taught at the academy until close to her due date. A few months before the baby was born, Avery moved in with Rhoda and Roxie Taylor, sisters and wives of John W. Taylor, another pro-polygamy mentor-apostle to Owen. Owen and Avery made plans to build a home in Mexico, which they discussed in detail in their correspondence. Both Owen and Helen mention the importance of Avery obtaining a "home of her own." In Owen's January 1902 letter to Avery, for example, he places this desire in the context of turn-of-the-century gender roles and, accordingly, subtly affirms his authoritative status in her regard:

As woman's highest aim and noblest mission is wife-hood and mother-hood all men appreciate any of these qualities which goes to make home the dearest place on earth. My dear girl I want to give you every possible advantage of education and practice to become a model house-wife and that means that you must be an excellent cook (which qualification I think you already possess), a good seamstress, a lover of house plants, a good washer, and possessing originality in the draping and decoration of home that it may be tasty and cozy. I will feel glad for some reasons when you have a home of your own so that you can take pride in keeping it according to your own ideas. (Letter 30)

Avery's autobiography, however, suggests her more negative feeling toward their new Mexican home, especially because it would represent a permanent settling so far from her home and family in the United States:

From the moment the first load of beautiful white stone was delivered to the building site I was filled with apprehension fear of the financial struggle it would involve and the feeling of permanency that a house in Mexico would bring. This feeling increased as the solid foundation took shape. Then as the walls arose high and higher under the mason's skill I projected my thoughts ^in^to the years ahead when I should be left in this far away land with my little family my husband on tours for the church most of the time and the folks in Wyo. I would seldom see. Loneliness enveloped me.[65]

When Avery questioned Owen about whether her status in Mexico would be permanent, he replied, "This is our home as long as we are in the flesh or not another dollar goes on the place." Owen's words struck Avery like a heavy blow.[66] Having a home of her own, however, would facilitate Avery's full acceptance within the Colonia Juárez community, for other polygamous wives had settled in Mexico to escape a new national probe into Mormonism and polygamy, finally giving Avery an open support system. Owen made the long trip from Salt Lake City to Colonia Juárez to see her several times, allowing the couple to enjoy a more public marital relationship together. The birth of Owen and Avery's daughter, Ruth, in February 1904 seemed to signal this emergence of normalcy in their marriage and family relationship.

Most of the time the two distinct families led separate lives from each other; however, situations arose when Helen, Owen, and Avery met together. The few letters that exist between Helen and Avery and from Avery to both Helen and Owen offer a first-hand view of post-Manifesto "sister wives" and the curious relationship derived from sharing the same husband. Although both strived to be generous and kind to one another, a slight tone of jealousy and insecurity sometimes colors their rhetoric of love and friendship, as evidenced in Avery's account of a visit Owen and Helen made while she was still living in Star Valley:

> Owen and Helen came for a week's visit enroute for the Big Horn. My family made their stay pleasant as possible, especially were we careful to guard Helen's feelings against any strain of sharing her husband's time with another woman on this vacation trip. Mother kept me near her coaching me very frequently on how to play my part heroically. "Be happy about it and don't expect Bro. W. to give you much time or attention" mother said, "not in Helen's presence. Remember she is our guest." So I was thrilled when one morning while I was running the "separator" in a back room and Owen rushed in, taking me in his arms for an instant told me how sweet and brave I was. This lifted my spirits — primed me for the day ahead — reassured me of my husband's love.
>
> As Helen said of herself — "It is as natural for me to be jolly as for the sun to shine" proved to be a fact to all observers. She had hours and days of feeling blue she told me and had to struggle with self discipline. It worried her that I took life so seriously, and she often asked me if she had made me unhappy — she didn't mean to.[67]

As might be expected, Helen's occasional insecurity expressed itself in her letters to Owen more than in her letters to Avery. However, in the following excerpt from an October 1903 letter to Avery, Helen demonstrates her understanding of how Avery might take her suggestions in a negative way that possibly could damage Avery's sense of self-worth:

> I have gone off on a tangent that sounds very much like preaching and you do not need preaching to one bit; you are just doing fine, it is myself that I need to labor with. (Letter 59)

Sometimes when Helen wrote to Owen, perhaps for validation, her fears and jealousies seemed more obvious, such as in the following from November 1900 and then later from July 1902:

> You won't need my letters so much now as of old as you will get encouragement and strength from other sources and it seems when I read over what I have written it will surely fail to interest you. (Letter 8)

> Now you might think from the tenor of my letter that I am dissatisfied with my lot, but believe me dear Owen, when I say such is not the case. I am contented as can be and would not change one thing in all my circumstances. The only thing I would have changed is "<u>my self</u>," my <u>stubborn selfish</u> nature. But this can not be done in a day. I must struggle & wait. I am not a bit like I want to be. (Letter 39)

As evidenced here, Helen tended to be self-critical in terms of her role in her polygamous marriage and worked at not making others responsible for her personal happiness. Owen and Avery demonstrated similar self-critical, self-reliant attitudes as well. At almost every turn, the three sublimated any emotion or criticism that could undermine their relationship.

To complicate the personal struggles felt by Helen and Owen and Avery, outside forces combined to create a growing hostile environment both locally and nationally. LDS apostle Reed Smoot publicly announced his candidacy for United States Senator at a meeting of the Ladies' Republican Club of Provo on May 14, 1902.[68] This announcement infuriated an already angry anti-Mormon faction in Utah and also drew unwanted attention from national anti-Mormon political figures. The *Salt Lake Tribune*, for example, listed the four main anti-Mormon arguments against candidate Smoot, all revolving around his ecclesiastical position.[69] On January 21, 1903, the state legislature voted him in as a United States senator, and five days later a Salt Lake City citizens' group and a ministerial group filed protests directed to the president of the United States stating that senator-elect Smoot should not be seated.[70] After much wrangling in the Senate over his being seated, Senator Smoot was officially seated in March 1903 with questions and protests to be raised later. As he noted in a letter to Owen, dated January 21, 1904:

> I am not worrying about the investigation of myself, the only thing that is troubling me is the inclination of many, and the determination of some, to go into a never-ending investigation of the Mormon Church and charge me with being responsible for the sayings of every man, and the actions of every member of the Church.[71]

Senator Smoot, himself a monogamist, was correct in his prediction that he, along with the LDS Church, would go on trial when the Senate committee had collected its data.

Through the summer of 1903, anti-Mormon articles and publications filled the nation's newspapers. Two incidents in November intensified the committee's search. First, Heber J. Grant, Helen's brother-in-law, just returning from his mission to Japan, spoke at a University of Utah fund-raiser. Milton Merrill notes:

> Heber J. Grant . . . always a vigorous, outspoken, and enthusiastic man, he was extremely popular with gentiles as well as Mormons. . . . In 1903, however, his exuberance was not appreciated . . . he made statements which brought down a storm of abuse on his head, on Smoot, and on the Church. He was in the process of giving a gift of one hundred fifty dollars; fifty dollars for each of his two wives and fifty dollars for himself. This evoked loud laughter among the students and stimulated the speaker, who added, "yes, I have two wives and the only reason I haven't got another one is because the government won't let me."[72]

The national public saw this incident as a flaunting of polygamy. Charles Owen, an enthusiastic anti-Mormon from Salt Lake City, charged Grant with cohabitation and issued a warrant for his arrest, but Grant was quickly sent on another mission to Europe before it could be served.[73] Senator Smoot commented on Grant's unfortunate speech and its dramatic consequences in a letter to John Henry Smith:

> You state that Heber's case has created a stir in Salt Lake City, I can assure you that it is not to be compared to the sensation that it has created in the East. Heber is lost sight of as the person making the comment, and the whole criticism is laid at the door of the Church and myself.[74]

In a letter to his close friend, James Clove, Smoot reveals an even more candid response to Grant's actions:

> Heber J's little episode . . . has caused an immense amount of unpleasant criticism against myself in particular and against the church in general. . . . I guess Heber is on the water, and we

can all take a long breath again. Oh, what an immense amount
of trouble would have been avoided if he had remained in
Japan a couple of months longer.[75]

The second problem rose out of Idaho's rabid anti-Mormon Fred T.
Dubois's desire to travel to Salt Lake City on a fact-finding mission regarding his suspicions that post-Manifesto polygamy was on the rise.[76]

While official church statements denied the charge of increasing
post-Manifesto plural marriages, a study of Helen and Owen's close circle of friends and relatives clearly supports its occurrence. Again, Quinn
suggests that the church hierarchy was divided and ambiguous about the
post-Manifesto polygamy issue and argues that while President Lorenzo
Snow mildly opposed it, instructing the full Quorum of the Twelve to
stop performing plural marriages, he probably gave individual approval
for some of the apostles, including Owen, to marry plural wives. He also
argues that Joseph F. Smith, as counselor and then as president, privately
promoted post-Manifesto polygamy.[77] Helen's sister, Susan, for example,
became Heber Bennion's wife in a monogamous marriage in 1885. She
had given birth to ten children by 1900 and, shortly thereafter, about
the time of Owen's polygamous marriage to Avery, her husband married
two additional wives, Mary Bringhurst in 1902 and Emma Jane Webster
in 1900. In addition, Edwin "Teddy" Bennion, Heber's brother, married
Mary Clark, Avery's sister, in a polygamous relationship in April 1904.
Interestingly, Avery's father, Hyrum D. Clark, also became a polygamist
on December 3, 1903, marrying Mary Alice Robinson. Heber J. Grant
also recorded that President Snow told him in 1901 to "take the action
needed to increase my family." The timing of these post-Manifesto marriages within the same circle of family and friends implies an attempted
renewal of plural marriage as advocated by apostles Cowley and Taylor.

Post-Manifesto polygamy carried the same significance as earlier
polygamy: compliance would qualify one for eternal salvation. As Carrie
A. Miles argues in "Polygamy and the Economics of Salvation," "Many
questions that polygamy raises for us today were simply not a problem
in early Mormonism, since the basis of plural marriage was salvation, not
love, sex or material production."[78] This basic belief, however, became
more emotionally difficult to practice at the turn of the century because
companionate marriage — the union of two approximate equals, based
on mutual respect, affection, and the close companionship of husband
and wife — was becoming the American social norm.[79] Thus, according to
Miles, the substance of comments like the following from Brigham Young
in 1856 made less sense to the husbands and wives of 1900:

Wives should put aside all desire for the exclusive and romantic company of their husbands. Rather, they should simply "receive, conceive, bear, and bring forth" in the name of Israel's God. They should not be concerned with whether they were loved "a particle" by their companions. That was not what the principle was about.[80]

When Helen wrote to Owen in November 1900, just two months before his marriage to Avery, that "we will not shrink from duty whatever it may cost for that in the end will bring true happiness in the Eternal World and that is what we are striving for" (Letter 13), she was referring to the founding principle of plural marriage: eternal salvation. Nevertheless, Helen's conflicting feelings between polygamy and companionate marriage are demonstrated in another, earlier November 1900 letter to Owen:

How very selfish and mean it is for me to want you all for my own, and all your love and affection just for my own comfort and happiness, and still when I think of it, this is all I have been grieving and suffering in my feelings for. (Letter 9)

This excerpt shows Helen's personal conflict with Owen's impending marriage and her growing anxiety over losing her exclusive, companionate marriage. Post-Manifesto polygamy was conflicted at the personal level and at the general church level while being increasingly opposed at the national level.

In December 1903, the Committee on Privileges and Elections laid out its plan: 1) they would attempt to prove Smoot a polygamist; 2) they would prove that Smoot had taken an oath against the State of Utah and the government of the United States (in the Mormon temple); 3) if 1 and 2 failed, they would show that such an oath would be administered by the LDS Church and that Smoot would comply; 4) if 1 through 3 failed, they would try to expel Smoot because Utah flagrantly violated its contract with the United Stated by permitting polygamy.[82] The hearings began the following March with subpoenas sent out to Joseph F. Smith, M. W. Merrill, John W. Taylor, George Teasdale, Matthias F. Cowley, John Henry Smith, and Dr. J. M. Tanner. Apostles Merrill and Teasdale could not appear due to illness while apostles Taylor, Cowley, and Tanner simply disappeared. President Joseph F. Smith took the stand on March 2, 1904, and testified for three days regarding polygamy, church involvement in business and politics, and LDS doctrine and practice. Smith's testimony angered many people, who interpreted it as a validation of the charges and petitions. The following excerpt of his testimony, which was distributed nationally, illustrates both the substance and tone of his testimony:

MR. TAYLER: Is there not a Revelation published in the Book of Covenants here that you shall abide by the law of the State?

MR. SMITH: Yes, sir.

MR. TAYLER: If that is a revelation, are you not violating the laws of God?

MR. SMITH: I have admitted that, Mr. Senator, a great many times here.

MR. TAYLER: But do you mean to say, at your pleasure, obey or disobey the commands of God Almighty?

MR. SMITH: Yes sir [. . .] I obey or disobey at my will.

MR. TAYLER: Just as you please.

MR. SMITH: Just I please.

MR. TAYLER: And that is the kind of a God you believe in?

MR. SMITH: That is exactly the kind of a God I believe in.[82]

While this publication may have been construed to incite anti-Mormons, it nonetheless represents the view received by non-Mormons of President Joseph F. Smith and the LDS Church's view of the dilemma between obedience to temporal laws and ecclesiastical commandments.

Apostle Francis M. Lyman's testimony followed, which, combined with President Smith's, outraged the national public. As president of the Quorum of the Twelve, Apostle Lyman admitted to cohabitation and his intention to continue the practice, even though it contradicted the laws of the land and the law of God as articulated in the Manifesto.[83] The committee asked for President Smith's assistance in encouraging the other subpoenaed witnesses to appear before the committee, but Smith responded that "As this is a political matter and not a religious duty devolving on them or me, I am powerless to exert more than moral suasion in the premise."[84] The missing witnesses and the church's uncooperative attitude plagued the Smoot trial and the LDS Church's national reputation for several years.

During this period the *Deseret News* reported that the committee intended to subpoena Owen; however, a letter to Owen from Reed Smoot indicated that no formal subpoena had been made:

I see by the papers and also learn by telegraph that you have not been subpoenaed as a witness in my case. This coming

Courtesy of the Lambert and Woodruff families

Avery Woodruff and her daughter Ruth, 1905

week, if all is well, we will have a quorum of the Twelve here, and, I suppose, if we should happen to meet, the papers of the country would immediately howl that the Presidency of the Church and the Quorum of the Twelve had held a meeting for the purpose of plotting against the Government of the United States. I hope that most of the Senators will have a chance to meet our brethren; if they do, I am positive that their visit will have a good effect.[85]

To ensure his safety from testifying, Owen traveled to Mexico in March 1904 to visit Avery. He had planned to remain with Avery during this turbulent time, especially because Avery was due to give birth to their first child in early April. However, shortly after Owen arrived in Mexico, he received a telegram from President Smith requesting his immediate return to Utah for an important meeting during the LDS Church's April General Conference. In this meeting, President Smith presented a proposal to the full Quorum of the Twelve stating that "any violators of the Manifesto regarding plural marriage would be severely dealt with by the church."[86] Midway through April Conference, President Smith told Owen to "stay in retirement. . . . You would not make a good witness."[87] So, to avoid a subpoena, Owen immediately prepared to leave Utah for Mexico and then possibly to preside over an LDS mission in Germany.[88]

Avery gave birth to her only child, Ruth, in Mexico on April 11, 1904. Although unable to be present for Ruth's difficult delivery because of his assignment at General Conference, Owen visited Avery and Ruth four days later. Owen's arrival surprised Avery, for she did not expect him; nor did she expect Owen to be accompanied by Helen and her four children. Helen dismissed Avery's nurse and proceeded to care for her. Avery later recalled that "this may have been distasteful to her taking care of her husband's other wife and child and I wondered why she chose to come at such a time."[89] Avery subsequently learned that President Smith had sent Owen and Helen to Mexico to avoid the threat of arrest and the possibility of testifying in the Smoot polygamy trials.[90] Fear of prosecution may have sent the Woodruffs to Mexico, but they determined to have a good time anyway. In spite of Avery's postpartum condition, Owen and Helen planned to leave three of their children and their maid, Anna, with her while they traveled to Mexico City. In addition, Avery learned that President Smith advised Helen and Owen to travel to Germany later that summer to escape the law. Hurt by these new decisions, which did not include her and Ruth, Avery somewhat resentfully bade farewell to Owen, Helen, and baby Rhoda on May 5, 1904. Little did she know then that this would be the last time she would ever see Owen and Helen.

Death and Burial

Before their trip, Helen and Owen had been advised to vaccinate themselves against smallpox, which infected many in Mexico at the time. According to Avery's autobiography, Owen refused vaccinations, saying that he was on the Lord's errand and God would protect them.[91] This attitude, however unfounded it would turn out to be, proved consistent with Owen's preference for faith and obedience in spiritual as well as material matters. Helen fell ill first, contracting a serious case of black smallpox on May 23. Alonzo Taylor, an LDS missionary in Mexico, helped care for Helen and kept a daily record of her treatment and Owen's bedside devotion. Taylor described Helen's horrific condition in a journal entry dated June 3, 1904:

I decided at his suggestion to return to the sick room and help wait on Sister Woodruff. The eruption had developed so much that I was about frightened when I saw her. Great white blisters

Courtesy of the Lambert and Woodruff families

Grave of Abraham Owen Woodruff (AOW) in El Paso, Texas

filled with pus were standing out all over her body and wherever they had broken were sores it was a terrible sight.

After suffering so severely that she even asked her husband to pray for her death, Helen died on June 7, 1904. Her final moments were detailed by Taylor:

[A]t 3:45 a.m. Bro. Henning came rushing up the steps to where Bro. Woodruff and I were sleeping on the roof, and told us to come at once for sister Woodruff was dying and scarcely had we reached her bedside when she passed peacefully away after having suffered since May 23 with a most loathing and virulent form of smallpox. Her suffering has been something fearful and for her, death was surely a relief.

Taylor continued his narrative with a detailed account of Helen's burial. He concluded:

There we all surrounded the grave and sang "O My Father." Bishop Johnson dedicated the grave . . . and the grave was covered while a sorrowing band of brethren and sisters looked on in silence.

It was a terrible blow to Bro Woodruff but he stood it bravely and manfully and reconciled himself to the ordeal.

Because of feared contamination, Mexican law prevented moving Helen's body to Utah for twenty years, although Owen had planned to bring her home to Salt Lake City. Unfortunately, he was also afflicted with smallpox just after Helen's death. To get Owen better medical attention, his companions privately and unlawfully moved him to El Paso, Texas, where he seemed to regain his strength and move toward recovery. However, on June 20, 1904, Owen died suddenly, shocking friends and family. Family members today recall the promise reportedly made to Helen in 1896 by President Woodruff: Owen and Helen would not be separated in death by more than two weeks.

Countless memorial services, letters of condolences, resolutions of respect, and commemorative articles appeared immediately in honor of both Helen and Owen. Owen's mother, Emma, received an outpouring of love and support from friends, family, and church leaders. However, symbolic of the public/private conflict of post-Manifesto polygamy, Avery and her daughter, Ruth, received no public consolation. Initially left with three orphaned children, a newborn baby, and her private grief, Avery struggled as might be expected. She later wrote in her autobiography:

> The sorrow that filled my heart can't be described. It seemed I wept buckets of tears in the days that followed. Two wonderful people who left me well and happy never returned and their four children made orphans. My own child fatherless. I was now a widow.[92]

Strongly encouraged by church authorities to remain in Mexico for another year, Avery worked to make a new life for herself and her daughter. The other Woodruff children traveled to Salt Lake City to be with their grandmother and other relatives, while Avery and Ruth's existence remained secluded.

Helen's friend, Ruth May Fox, memorialized her in a sentimental, overly wrought memorial poem:

Helen

Pure as the fragrance of lilies,
Fair as the roses of June,

Sweet as the breath of the valley
Where zephyrs with peach-blossoms dally,
Where the birds and the honey-bees rally,
Was Helen — our sister, our friend.
Simplicity's mantle adorned her,
Humility haloed her brow;
Veneration for all that is holy
For the good, the meek and the lowly
(Ah, blessed thy friends were to know thee!)
Was Helen's — our sister, our friend.
A flow'r from the hand of the Father
She descended to gladden the earth,
To blossom and bud for a season,
Then return to the gardens alysian.
O God! do Thou grant us submission
Like Helen's — our sister, our friend.[93]

Rudger Clawson likewise praised Owen in a 1904 letter to his mother, Emma Woodruff:

He accomplished a work of great magnitude, and his memory will ever be green in the hearts of the Latter-day Saints. His life and labors, his devotion to the Cause of Truth, his purity of life, his winning manners and lovable ways will continue to exert a power and influence in the earth when other things are forgotten.[94]

Admirable character traits were shared by Helen and Owen and Avery. However, at the reburial of Owen and Helen in 1993, church leaders once again voiced high praise for Helen and Owen, while Avery remained absent and unmentioned.[95]

After Owen and Helen's death, Avery communicated from Mexico frequently with Emma regarding the Woodruff children. She even attempted to live with Emma as a co-caregiver, but Emma's strong personality eventually drove her away. The LDS Church, especially Elder Cowley, may have supported Avery initially, but Avery independently raised her own daughter for ten years before remarrying. She met and married George Lambert, a widower with one child, in 1914. Avery died in El Cerritos, California, in 1953 and is buried alongside her second husband in the Cyprus Lawn Cemetery. Ruth grew up in Avery's care and

Courtesy of the Lambert and Woodruff families

Wilford Owen, Rhoda, June, and Helen Mar Woodruff

eventually married her stepbrother after attempting to sublimate her own complex feelings of romance.

Owen and Helen's children stayed for several years with their grandmother Emma. Other members of the Woodruff family desired to care for the children, but Emma remained determined to care for them herself. It was during Emma's care that baby Rhoda, then three years old, died unexpectedly. Family members consoled themselves with the thought that Helen and Owen could be reunited with their baby. At Emma's death, Heber J. Grant and his wife Augusta (Helen's sister) "adopted" Wilford Owen, Helen Mar, and June. The children remained in the Grants' care until adulthood. Wilford, the eldest and perhaps the most affected by his parents' life and death, led a troubled existence. He served the LDS Church on a mission and married in the LDS temple, but later felt compelled to enter into plural marriage. The LDS Church, by then totally estranged from the practice of polygamy, excommunicated Wilford, and his first wife divorced him. Wilford was later rebaptized in the LDS Church, remaining with his second wife and their seven children but almost completely abandoning his first family of five. Both Helen and June also married, each having five children. Wilford died in 1986, Helen in 1990, and June in 1995.

Shortly after Owen and Helen's deaths, apostles Cowley and Taylor were removed from their leadership positions in the LDS Church, and their membership was tenuous. President Joseph F. Smith issued in 1904

Helen Woodruff

what became known as the "Second Manifesto," calling for a complete end to public and private polygamy. Some Latter-day Saints speculated that Owen's death had spared him from church punishment, while others felt his death represented a punishment itself. Although the first Manifesto had enabled Utah to achieve statehood, national fears of lingering polygamy left Utah politicians powerless, as evidenced in the 1904 Smoot hearings. President Smith's Second Manifesto solidly set the course for the LDS Church's increased social status and political power in the United States and for the Latter-day Saints to become supportive, patriotic Americans.

The Abraham Owen Woodruff family story reflects national public dramas over post-Manifesto polygamy while also revealing private internal dramas. Viewing the relationship between Helen, Owen, and Avery offers an unusual, if not unique, opportunity to see how polygamous first wives dealt with insecurity and jealousy, how additional wives struggled to measure up and find their own place, and how the logistics of managing two families presented challenges for the polygamous husband, both financially and emotionally. The letters and autobiographical reminiscences that follow present three distinct individuals who desired to demonstrate their faith in God by following the counsel of LDS Church authorities to participate in an illegal but privately sanctioned relationship. Their trials and sorrows and the faith and courage that sustained them command our respect.

So it was against this backdrop that, on July 17, 1997, in the Salt Lake City Cemetery, the Woodruff family gathered for an affirmative, unifying reburial ritual. Descendants from Owen and Helen and from Owen and Avery attended the ceremony. Both lines of descendants honored their ancestors and conveyed a love for them. It was Helen's grandson, Bruce, and Avery's grandson, Richard, who directed the reburial project, reuniting ancestors and descendants in a common purpose. Perhaps it was in this quiet, shaded Utah cemetery that Helen, Owen, and Avery's vision of what faithful LDS families could become, if they remained united, finally became a reality.

Woodruff Letters and Supporting Documents

1899

[Letter 1: Helen to Owen]

[LDS Church letterhead, handwritten]

July 17, 1899

My Darling Owen: —

This morning I sent you a telegram informing you of the sad news about our darling little Florilla.[1] Owen dear, we are all heart sick this morning. Blanch[2] is just frantic they can do scarcely anything with her. It all happened so suddenly that we can not realize the real truth. Last night I was sleeping over at mother's and about twelve o'clock the electric bell rang <u>furiously</u> and we all jumped up and ran to see what was the matter, little Florilla was having a convulsion, she had two in a short time and then she came too and seemed perfectly natural, she talked about her dolly and seemed cheerful and bright. Will Mother,[3] Sister Lambert and Blanch and Joe[4] sat up nearly all night and she slept all night until six o'clock this morning, when they called us all again and the little darling just gasped twice and never breathed again. We all watched and prayed for nearly an hour thinking every minute she would come back and it was not until the Doctor came that we could believe the sad truth. Oh, my dear I wish you were at home now, I know you will fell so very sad as we all do, but I do not know whether to look for you to come home for a few days or not. The rest of the folks are all as well as they can be under the circumstances.

They have telegraphed for Asahel[5] and Van[6] and also Bro. Daynes[7] who is at Rd. [Richfield, Utah] attending the dedication of the Sevier Stake Tabernacle.[8] Nellie[9] and I went out and spent the day with Susie[10] yesterday and Susie and her children are going to Pl. Grove next week and I will go with them.

My Dear Husband I hope you are well and I know you will pray for Blanch if you can not be here to comfort her.

With constant prayers for your comfort and welfare I remain as ever

Your <u>Own</u> Helen.

[Letter 2: Helen to Owen]

[*no letterhead, handwritten*]

Pleasant Grove
Aug 14, 1899.

Dearest Owen: —

Your letter written at Ft. Bridger [Montana] Aug 10, is the last one I have had. Was real disappointed that I did not get one this evening as I thought after reading your "whole pack" of mail you would have made a beginning at answering some of my letters sent there.

Yesterday I received a letter from your Mother and will send it to you and then it will be needless for me to repeat all she says. Isn't it terrible that the Scarlet Fever has broken out again? I am very much afraid it will go through all the families; and also the whooping cough, oh, dear I am afraid of that Mother[11] is beginning to worry about it all ready, she had such an experience with Susie's baby and the poor little fellow isn't over it yet.[12]

Van's case was very light, he was only at the Hospital seven days and is getting along nicely; but poor Clara what an ordeal it was for her. I don't know who had the worst of it she or Van. It was <u>terrible</u> for both.

Doesn't Eugene write to his Mother? I think he ought to she hasn't heard from him only through my letters to your Mother.

Have almost decided to go home [Salt Lake City] next Friday, but do not know how I shall go. Ray[13] is thinking of taking a load of fruit in and I could go with him and take my fruit with me. Mother is trying to persuade me to go on the train. Says she thinks it would be much better for me but oh, I do dislike going on the train and will have to take the car home; but I'll decide about that later.

Got a letter from Gusta[14] to-day. She is still at Soda [Springs, Idaho] having a fine time. Will no doubt return in time to see the "boys" come home. I wish you were going to be here for the occasion and then I could ride out and see the parade anyway, but as it is, think I shall have to content myself with reading about the <u>grand</u> <u>affair</u> same as you will.[15]

Mother says it seems like old times to have me at home again and says she can't let me go again, she has been trying to persuade me to stay here until you come but I have nearly finished all the work I brought with me and have so much to do at home I feel as though I must go and get some of it done before your return.

Shall probably write one more letter to Vernal [Utah] before leaving here and then one to the farm, but hardly see the need of that as you will be home the next day. Oh, how delighted I shall be to see you once again, it seems <u>ages</u> since you went away, and I am afraid the remaining time will seem ages too; but I keep busy all the time and that helps to make the time seem short.

Did you read the account of the Wasatch Stake Conference?[16] Le Roi and Ma Belle accompanied papa and mamma and had a glorious time. I hope Ed and wife attended the meetings and got the instructions on tithing. "Most undoubtedly" they were there.

Delia[17] came over Saturday and stayed until to-day. She also came while Susie was here so Ma had four of her girls home at once. Mami gets a little stronger every day but very slowly.

Well, my dear boy you will soon be home and I fear I shall talk you blind I have so much to tell you. Am well and happy and trust you are. With bushels of love and constant prayers for your safety and success I am as ever Your devoted wife

Helen Winters Woodruff.

[Avery's "Autobiography and Recollections": Excerpt A (pages 32–42)]

[*handwritten*]

1901 [*in left margin*] "After fifty years" As I remember it January 17, 1951. The question has often been asked me, "How did you come to know Owen Woodruff"? It's a unique story.[18]

Mary[19] and I were home in *Valley for our summer vacation having attended B.Y.C.[20]

Conference was scheduled for Auburn Ward announcement had been made in church the week before when a committee was formed to clean up the rock church for the occasion because one of the "authorities" from Salt Lake City would be present.

But when Mother,[21] Mary and I went to choir practice Saturday night we noticed the church in much the same condition as of last Sunday. The committee evidently had not functioned, where upon mother decided to take things in her own hands. So early Sunday morning Old Grey and Minnie were hitched to the old carriage and off to a good start went Mother, Avery and Mary with an ample supply of brooms, scrubbing brush soap cleaning cloths galore and a ladder.

We arrived at Auburn a self made committee of three. Soon the activity and speed with which we moved our equipment drew the attention of Johny Walton and Nate Putnam who had come to Henry Harrison's store across the street. These boys soon joined our force and with good spirit helped to transfer grimy windows, benches and dirty wooden floors into sparkling steaming surfaces — which left a strong "wet wood smell." After wiping the last foot print dry — doors and windows were left wide open in hopes the summer sunshine would lend her hand in drying out the place before the morning services began at 10 a.m.

The three of us rushed home driving the two and a half miles in about twenty minutes. After a quick bath we changed dressed in our best togs — pure white summer sheers — "transforming the scrub women into lovely ladies" as we jokingly put it and were soon on our way back to town this time in the white top carriage.

Promptly at 10 a.m. our whole family arrived en mass with father[22] driving his favorite high spirited team of horses.

Immediately on entering the church we sniffed the "wet wood odor" and took a quick glance at each other — Mother, Mary and I — as we spied damp spots on the floor. During the fifteen minutes delay — waiting for the visiting brethren the spots almost completely disappeared and we inwardly were glad they were late.

Mother, Mary and I took our accostomed places in the choir on the front bench, facing the pulpit. The little church was filled to capacity little over 150 souls when suddenly all eyes turned to the front door as the visitors were entering. Mary and I sat stoically watching our manners since we remembered our tutoring at B.Y.C. on the rudeness of turning one's head and staring at late comers, and too we spared no criticism of the country folks' carless habits. We were all the more circumspect in contrast perhaps to the degree that we put on city airs.

Bishop Hyde and Father his first councelor stood immediately and greeted the guests and all were seated on the stand.

The services began as usual — singing, prayer, singing. Then bishop Hyde introduced Apostle Owen Woodruff and Joseph McMurrin[23] to the audience. At bro. A. O's request brother McMurrin was the first speaker. I recall not a word he said, but I do remember that according to instructions I received in my English class at B.Y. that he spoke with more gusto and in larger voice than the size of the audience and Church warranted. Mary and I voiced this observation in the privacy of our room afterward. Most everything in our immediate life was measured by B.Y. standards.

Elder Woodruff followed elder McMurrin in a soft conversational tone yet quite as affective as his companion. As we arose Mary nudged me and I pressed her hand — we were both impressed with this charming, magnetic personality — angelic as mother often said afterward.

I heard only part of what he said — my mind wandered — I thot of Fred Dixon, a young man I called my sweet heart tho I hadn't seen him for almost a year. He had moved away from *Valley with his family to a farm in Burly Idaho. He and his brother Jim attended B.Y.C. the first year Mary and I were there and Cynthia Davis, a girl who lived with us, and I went to College dances with the brothers, Fred and Jim. This last year our letters were infrequent and very brief, he had not come to *Valley to see me in the summer as planned. I began to wonder if Fred and I really cared for each other altho I wore a ring he had slipped on my finger before he went away.

I found myself comparing the younger man with brother Woodruff as he stood speaking — I had never seen bro. W. before, but he at once captured my admiration and respect — I felt that he was a great man — pure and holy. I questioned my love for Fred — if only I could see him I would know! My frustration mounted during the rest of the service.

After the meeting Father introduced Mother and all of us children to the guest speakers and we waited while the brethern and the "bishop rick" administered to Money Welch's boy who had been spitting blood for several days — a slip of June grass lodged in his lung. Brother W. was mouth and he promised that according to the faith of the parents and the will of God the boy would be healed. In not many hours we were told the boy coughed up the cutting grass and very soon recovered. Note: Money Welch had never before been seen at church except to attend dances and other recreations. He and his family were known as "Jack Mormons."

On our way home from church, I sat quietly absorbed in my thoughts, wiping a tear now and then refusing Porter's peanuts and candy the others were gaily munching. Mother said: "Avery what's the matter"? I said: "Nothing." But once inside the house I dashed into my bedroom clamped down the leaver on the lock of my door and dropped to my knees and prayed: "Dear Heavenly Father if Fred and I are meant for each other please make me feel assured of our love. May I have for him the same admiration and respect I feel for brother Woodruff." Amen.

I quickly unlocked my door, tied an apron around my waist and went to the kitchen to help with lunch. There was no time to waste if we were to be on time for the two o'clock, meeting.

Now my tention was relieved with the assurance that God understood what was in my heart and instead of tears I was able to smile. Prayers if sincere are always answered.

On our way back to conference Mary and I commented that the old meeting house certainly looked a lot better for our efforts especially when the benches were filled with people and the spotless white cloth was laid for the sacrament. The silver service added much. It had been purchased from E. D. Harrison of Pocatello [Idaho] when I was Pres. of M.I.A. It consisted of a beautiful pitcher, two goblets and two plates. All the people sipped water from the two goblets which was customary in the church at that time. There was a good spirit in our conference and we were glad we had in any way contributed to its success. Afterall this was our town, our people and we were proud of any obvious virtues and we lamented our deficiencies.

We greatly enjoyed the afternoon session of the conference — again listened to services by our guest speakers. It was announced that the evening meeting would be held at Grover [Wyoming] a small town a few miles East of Auburn. O yes, we wanted to go to this meeting too and were willing to help with the chores such as ^the boys^ milking cows after supper so we might get an early start. Father enumerated the many things that would have to be done. The girls helped mother with an early supper.

Again Mary and I slipped on our white dresses and white straw hats with pink roses and feathers. Our shoes and stockings were black — these were worn with any and all dresses by all girls and women in 1901 so we were in good style tho it seems funny as I write about it in 1952. The little church in Grover was very dimly lighted and with a huge cylinder shape stove in the center of the room there was a somber atmosphere. We felt a bit strange as we glanced about for familiar faces. Finally we took seats midway between the awful stove and the wall, wondering how it was we had become so very religious as to go to the third meeting in one day. But on second thought realized our church contacts furnished about all the social enjoyment we had in *Valley in the summer time and we should make the most of the opportunity.

We listened to ward officers reports and again talks by the two visiting brethern — Woodruff and McMurrin. At the close of the meeting brother W. stopped to shake hands with Mary and me and asked if we intended going to B.Y.C. in the Fall — remembering that Father had mentioned proudly that his two daughters were home on vacation. We were pleased to tell him we expected to go on to College. This made us feel so important as we related to Father and Mother every single word that passed between us [and br *in left margin*]other Woodruff as we said good bye. We still raved on about his good looks intelligence and personality wondering why there weren't more of his kind to be passed around so more deserving girls could get a worthy husband. His wife — what a lucky woman!

Monday morning mother decided if we were to pick wild currants this season we better waste no more time — the birds were taking them fast. "Which of you girls want to go with me"? Mother asked in her cheerful tone. "I want to go" I said. Mary was glad she was to stay home with the younger children. She never liked getting all scratched up picking wild fruit.

In short order Mother and I were off to a good start with our small buckets wearing our broad brimmed straw hats for shade. We followed the banks of Stump Creek to our familiar spot where for several seasons we had gleaned the precious fruit. Mother was used to the horses she often hitched to the old carriage to go to Primary and Relief Society and it was no trick for her to detach the team from the carriage and stake them out to graise while we picked our berries.

Disregarding burs, bites and scratches we scrambled thru brush finding the gleaning tedious. But we were enjoying ourselves busy with out chatter about the wonderful conference of the previous day — the friends we met. We agreed that our family had contributed a good share in making the conference a success with father in the bishoprick, two of us in the choir and the older boys Hyrum T. and Heber[24] passing the sacrament.

Then mother asked me: "what was the matter with you Avery on our way back home yesterday." Then I told mother about my frustration over Fred. Mother was so comforting and understanding and she loved romance even in her own children. After I had finished my story she said "Avery I'm sure if you continue to pray about it you will be sure to find the right companion or he will find you. There's no question in my mind but that your father and I were meant for each other and that the Lord brought us together."

When we reached home in late afternoon Father was at the kitchen table eating alone. Mary had fixed his meal. Mother inquired why he was all dressed up in his Sunday best? Father said: "Charley's boy (on horse back) came with a message from Apostle Woodruff to come to Fairview [Wyoming] to get him." Mother said: "Do you mean you are to bring him to this house." As she spoke she surveyed the humble appearance of the four log rooms with the meager furnishings. Father said: "I guess that is what it means" and he left in the white top carriage on the ten miles trip to Fairview.

While putting our house in order Mother Mary and I speculated on the purpose of bro. W's visit to our house deciding he was putting Father in a higher position in our church probably to make him a high councelor to Pres. Osmond.

I chose to scrub the kitchen floor prefering this to most other tasks. However this time I made short work of it since the strong homemade soap suds caused my scratched hands and arms to burn and smart. Remembering the "wet wood smell" of the church the morning before I wiped the floor as dry as I possibly could with the hope that there would be no wet spots showing by the time Father and our guest arrived. We three women laughed about the similarity of the two occasions.

In due time Father returned with bro. W. The evening meal was eaten leisurely with no comment as to the purpose of his visit to our home. As Mary and I washed the dishes we fabricated reasons of our own.

Later in the evening after the chores were done all the family gathered in the front room where we sang several gospel songs with Avery at the organ struggling with the accompaniment. We had family prayer and retired for the night. Mother fixed a bed for brother Woodruff in the front room. After all we had only two bedrooms. Next morning as I was drawing water from the well bro. W. came and took hold of the rope to help me. As he poured the water into my bucket he asked me how I spelled my name. I said: "A-v-e-r-y" He said: "A very good girl."

Shortly after breakfast Father took bro W. to Fairview where he joined bro. McMurrin and they left the valley for Salt Lake City. On Father's return we quizzed him getting little satisfaction. But the following morning he asked if I would like to ride to Afton [Wyoming] with him. He had to take some machinery to a shop for repair. "Why not take Mother" I said. "I'll stay home and do the work" or else take Mary if mother wont go. Mother took me to one side and explained Father wanted to talk with me, that I should go. My heart thumped against my chest as my thoughts flashed over my past conduct. What ever had I done to displease Father and I thot of the time he called me to account on the red parlor carpet.

At that time I had broken a rule laid down by the presidency of the Stake and high councilors which was — that they and all their families hence forth cease "round dancing" . . . [25]

I went to Afton with Father as he requested. From the moment we left home until we reached the Leavett Hill — half mile to the South he hardly spoke a word but seemed deep in thought. I sat rigidly beside him still waiting for to tell me the purpose of our trip.

Then he said: "Dot how would you like to swap Fred for brother Woodruff"? Puzzled I said: "What do you mean"? Isn't bro. W. married? I thot all the apostles were married." "Yes he is married and has a family." What then do you mean — polygamy"? "Yes, Dot" Then I burst into tears — cried hard and long. Father tried to comfort me realizing the terrible shock that brought the tears and he began to tell me of bro. W's conversation as he rode along with him from Fairview. Father said: I was just as shocked and surprised as you are Dot when I learned of this new Polygamy and I asked a lot of questions a bout it. Bro. W wanted to know the first thing if you had any impression regarding him at Auburn conference. I said: not that I know of." He said ~~that~~ while I was speaking it was made known to ~~him~~ that ~~I would be~~ the girl sitting before ~~him~~ would be ~~his~~ wife. Then after the service bro. Clark you introduced her to me as your daughter Avery." It was as if a voice had said the words. It was with effort that I continued with my talk, so strong was the impression. An angel from heaven could not appear more pure and perfect as she sat there all in white. Not having seen her before I wondered as I took my seat what to make of it. Not being able to throw it off my mind I've prayed about it. Feeling that my impression is from the Lord I sent word for you to come and take me to your home so I could get acquainted with your family and especially your oldest daughter." Would you, be willing for her to marry me in case she wanted to"? Father said "Not unless it can be sanctioned by the church". Bro W. pointed out how several of the brethren in high positions had been advised to take plural wives which justified his confidence in the matter.

After his visit to our home Father took Bro W. back to Fairview to join Bro. McMurrin. En route bro. W. explained that he would write to

Father but not to me until he learned the facts of how I felt about the matter. On our ride back from Afton I told father about my impression of bro. W. while he was speaking at Auburn Conference that it had caused me to question my love for Fred, about the relief and comfort I got thru prayer. Father then said: Dot do you feel happy about it now after I've given you bro. W's explanation"? I said: It is more than I can fully comprehend I still feel frightened and puzzled but I believe if I keep on praying I will know in time what is best for me — what is right.

1900

[Letter 3: Avery to Owen]

[no letterhead, handwritten]

Logan Utah
Oct. 25, 1900.

Dear Bro. Woodruff: —

Yours of the 22nd reached me yesterday. It filled me with joy to read its contents.

Sister [Mary Clark] is at school this hour and I choose to write now.[1]

I can say that I feel as you do in regards to the matter and think it is all right. I believe too that we have been guided by our Father in Heaven. Do not see how it could possibly be mistaken.

A happier hour of my life was never spent than was during the conversation that we had.[2] It filled me with joy and gladness that has not departed from me, and I thank God that I am so highly favored for I feel that I am. I feel more and more inclined toward you and have more affection and a higher respect for you than have I ever had for any other. I am satisfied with my lot as yet and think I alway shall be. I am also thankful to her who gave her consent and sacrificed that she all ready has for my sake and for principle's sake, for it must have been contrary to the natural feelings, which we all have.[3] I do not worry about the financial part of it and think you need not. I will try to be a help meet, any how you know I have not been raised in great luxuries and don't expect them. I will not delay going to the Temple and will be careful, be as you said true as steel. Will be pleased to see you at any time.

I humbly ask God's blessings upon us in all. From One True and Sincere,

[no signature]

[Letter 4: Helen to Owen]

[*LDS Church letterhead*]

November 4, 1900

My Dear Owen: —

This is Sunday and fast day too, and naturally enough, I am wondering where you are and what you are doing and I am wondering too, if your <u>thoughts</u> are with me, as mine are with you.

This is a perfect day as far as weather can make it. Your Mother and I went to Temple fast meeting[4] and although we had a splendid meeting, I was a <u>little</u> <u>disappointed</u>. Neither Prest. Snow[5] nor his Councilsor[6] nor any of the apostles were there, and I wanted to hear some of them speak so very much. Your Mother and Eliza have gone to fast meeting in the Ward and Ruby[7] has taken the baby out for a walk so I am all alone, just as I <u>want to</u> be so, I thought I would sit down and talk to you.

Last night we were all invited up to Prest. Frank Y's[8] to supper and Alice & Will[9] insisted on my going with them but as Asahel [Owen's brother] had room for one in his Surrey I rode with them. We spent a pleasant evening. Bro. and Sister Kelch[10] were to have been there but their little girl has Scarlet Fever and they are quarentined. Br. Kelch will not be able to go East for some time on account of this. I was invited to Sister Empey's[11] to a lovely dinner yesterday and I went for I am determined to keep cheerful if it is possible. Sometimes I long to have some one to talk too to sympathize with me but I must wait until you get home for that. <u>Dearest</u>, I do not want you to worry one instant about me for it will unfit you for your labors, which I know are many and arduous. I want you to have a good time and come home looking better for it grieves me to see you looking pale and worried.[12]

I coppied the piece you wanted mailed to you and will send it with this letter.

Have received two letters asking questions about the Big Horn.[13] Think I can answer them O.K. One from Bro. Crosby,[14] nothing particular.

With my hearts purest love I am as ever

Your affectionate Wife,

Helen.

P.S. Kind regards to Bro. & Sister Ivins[15] and all whom I may know.

[Letter 5: Avery to Owen]

[no letterhead, handwritten]

Logan, Utah
Nov. 7, 1900.

Dear Brother Woodruff: —

Yours of 31ˢᵗ and 2nd have come to hand. It indeed delighted me to hear from you, and although there is not much of any thing to write thought it would be a pleasure if nothing more to drop a few lines. Was very sorry to hear that you were not feeling well and my prayer is that the Lord will give you health and strength to preform your labors. We are well and enjoying our school as ever, one would think so any how by the stack of books that we have been studying to night.

I must say I enjoyed going through the Temple and appreciate it too and think if I could alway feel like I did then I would be a better girl. Called on Bro. Merril today who gave kind and encourageing words.

It is not certain whether we will go home holidays or not but think likely we will. Any thin that is for the best suits me, I am not dissapointed but have no doubt that it would have been a pleasant trip.

We are having a spell of good weather now. Expect the climate is delightful this time of the year where you are now.

I will try to patient and contented for truly I have cause to be happy.

Thank you for the asistance you have offered, we are getting along all right at present.

I am as ever with love —

[no signature]

[Letter 6: Helen to Owen]

[LDS Church letterhead, handwritten]

Nov. 10, 1900.
Salt Lake City Dec 3rd.

My Dear Owen: —

It is quite late and all the folks have gone to bed so I thought I would take this opportunity to write you. Your two letters written at Thatcher [Arizona] reached me to-day and I was so glad to get them but sorry to know you have been suffering from a cold. Why did you not tell me before? You say you will start home Monday Dec. 16. Well look at the date of Monday again and you will find it the 17th. You must have lost your "calender." I thought you had planned on purpose to hold your Conference at St. Johns [Arizona] on Sat. & Sunday so you could get home one day sooner.

You no doubt know that Prest. Cannon has gone to the Sandwich Islands.[16] He took Carlie and three children with him and expects to be gone two months.[17]

Prest. Snow's wife Sarah[18] died yesterday and so he is at Brigham City. I suppose you get all the news in the "Semi-weekly," where ever you go, so I scarcely know what to tell you. Van [Collins] brought the canon wagon home and they dumped your wagon out doors. I got Heber[19] to put it in Mr Doxey's barn however so it is all right.

Our little darling[20] does not walk entirely alone but he could if he would. He takes a streak sometimes and walks all around and then will go for several days and not try to walk. He tries to talk but its rather difficult to tell just what he says. He makes you understand just what he wants any way. He fell off the bed to-day and got a terrible bump on his forehead but he did not cry very long. He knows papa's picture on the wall.

The way I feel sometimes I am afraid I will not hold out until you come but hope I will. Will write a few more words in the morning. I love you dearly and want to live to be really and truly your helpmate, and hope I shall never be a burden to you.

Goodnight dearest, goodnight.

All our board is invited to Sister Dougall's[21] next Monday night and to bring our husbands but as I can not take mine I will remain at home. Will try to follow out your instructions but the oil is so hard for me to take, oh, my. But I think it will help me.

[Letter 7: Helen to Owen]

[*LDS Church letterhead*]

Nov. 10, 1900.

Dearest Owen:

Yesterday I received your letter written at El Paso [Texas] Nov. 4. I wrote to you the same day, (Fast Day) and told you how I had spent the day and suppose you have received it ere this. You said it seemed a long day to you, well that is just how all Sundays seem to me, I like any day better.

You ask how I am feeling. Some days I feel fine and at other times I am "blue" as "Indago." Yesterday I had Aunt Zina and Aunt Bathsheba down and we spent a splendid afternoon.[22] They gave me a lovely blessing and made me some beautiful promises which I firmly believe will be answered if I am humble and faithful. We could not get the Surrey as

Asahel was going to use it, so Asahel took Aunt B. home and I took Aunt Zina. It was dark when we left here and quite dark when I got back home again. But I did enjoy the ride with dear Aunt Zina. She talked all the way up and gave me some good council. Your Mother and Grandma Grant[23] were here and they got to talking about Navoo times and of course drifted on to the subject of Pologamy. It seems strange dear, but the spirit of it seems to be broadcast. I have thought it was my condition that made me think of it so much but I made up my mind that I would not speak about it and see what other people had to say, and invariably someone starts it up. The day after you went I had all the girls here to sew and while I was out in the kitchen getting dinner they were discussing the subject. Up at Prest. F. Y. Taylors, Asahel started it and they kept it going the whole evening, and Bro. Taylor said that he and Bro. Kelch were at Bp. Atwoods a day or two before and they talked it all over and got out revelations and read them. Bro. Cowley,[24] it is said, preached a Pologamy sermon at the funeral of Sister Hickman, Van's aunt who lived at Provo.[25] Since your Mother received your letter yesterday I think she surmizes something. But she doesn't ask any questions.[26]

To-day they are going to hold services at the cemetary. The setting or unveiling of your dear father's monument and I wish you were here for I know how well you would like to be present at the exercises.[27] Prest. [Lorenzo] Snow is not very well so they are going to have it at One o'clock the warmest part of the day. I am going to drive up and take little Owen. Will write you all about it to-morrow. Your Ma has gone to Taylorsville to attend Relief Society Confrence and will drive back for the exercises at one o'clock.

Alice & Will were over here to supper last night and are very kind and thoughtful of me. Asahel also came in to see me one night this week.

You will no doubt be as much surprised as I when I tell you that Blanche & Joe [Daynes] sent us one of their nice Photos. I must write and thank them for it. Blanche wrote a lovely letter to your Mother. It was full of love for everybody.[28]

Our baby has a very bad cold in his head and coughs all the time. Last night he nearly had croup. I was up for or five times to doctor him in the night. He doesn't look thin nor pale but he is so cross and peevish. I just tell you a few thinghs he did yesterday to amuse himself. He took the key out of the kitchen door and dug about a square ft. of plaster of the wall with it. I got the big bath tub ready to put him in and went to get a towel, when I got back he had put one of his shoes & stockings in to soak, and was in the act of putting the rest of the clean clothes in. Then while I was in the tub he got the coal oil can and spilt coal-oil all over himself. He plays in the coal bucket all the time. I do not care for these triffles if he will only keep well.

Ida Smith's[29] baby is quite sick and all the babies around here have bad colds.

Well my darling I love you still and pray God to bless you in your labors and may you come home happy and well.

> Your loving,
> Helen.

[Letter 8: Helen to Owen]

[*LDS Church letterhead, handwritten*]

Nov. 11. 1900

My Dear Husband:

You don't want very much do you? Two letters for every one I receive. I think it ought to be the other way about and you write two to my one.

Will McEwan is going to buy a cow so does not want the brown cow. Bro. [Hyrum K.] North wrote that he could not get any one to bring her in for your price so I suppose it is all right. Will says he knows a man who will take your farm. He has thirty head of cattle of his own and he is very highly recommended by Tate, your neighbor, and also by Mary Price's father. Will says he will come and see me about it but I told him I could not tell him much about it. He will have to wait until you get home Xmas.

We went to the Dedicatory Exercises at the Cemetary yesterday. The day was beautiful, sunny, and warm but Prest. Snow was not there. There were very few present. Will send you a clipping from the news and so will not write the particulars. In the afternoon I went to Sister Writters to dinner. She invited just a few and had it on purpose for me she said. Wasn't it kind of her? There was just Sisters Empey, Harker, [Gusta] Grant, Talmage,[30] Hyde,[31] and Dr. Maggie [Shipp] there and we spent a very pleasant afternoon. I think every day I will not get out again and then some one coaxes me to go and you know that a little coaxing will get me to do almost anything.

Well dearie, this is Sunday again and the day is fast drawing to a close; and for this I am thankful. This makes two Sundays since you went away and only five remain until you will be at home again. It seems a long long time.

The Y.M.M.I. of Granite Stake are holding their Conference to-day. They met in Farmers Ward this afternoon and this evening will meet in Sugar Ward. Will is going to be set apart. Heber and Eliza have been away all day. Ruby [Freeman] went to the Matinee with Mary and has stayed up there all night & all day so Baby and I have been alone all day. He is a great deal of company though. He is never idle one moment. He lets go of chairs now and takes two or three steps alone and it pleases him so he just laughs about it. He tries to talk and just jabbers away.

When I got this far Mrs. Wallace, Miss Chambers, and Mrs Doxey came in so I scarcely know where I am at.

Bro. Crosby has written you a long letter telling you all the news in camp. I wrote him that you had gone away. What did you tell me to do with the letter from Huber? It has come and I can not remember for the life of me what your instructions were.

You want to know how I am. I feel better than when you left, and am trying not to worry about things of the future, but they will come up before me all the time and it is a constant battle for me to keep cheerful, but I am doing it any way. If you had made different arrangements about your trip I think I would have been a mere shadow when you returned. But as it is, I can make two shadows standing once, instead of having to "stand twice to make one shadow."[32] However I don't want you to worry about me I am all right and will try to keep my little worries to myself for it is the better plan I'm sure. You have enough to worry you without me pouring my troubles into your ears constantly. So dear, do not think about that any more but have a good time and come home looking ten years younger than when you left. We are all getting along nicely at home, baby's cold is a little better to-day and hope he will be entirely over it in a few days. You won't need my letters so much now as of old as you will get encouragement and strength from other sources and it seems when I read over what I have written, that it will surely fail to interest you.

You did not leave me a program of your Conferences, so I can not write to the Arizona Stakes until you give me the dates of your Conferences and the place in which they are held.

May God continue to bless you in all your travels and labors is the constant prayer of your loving Wife,

Helen.

P.S. The man mentioned as wanting to take the farm is a Mr. Midgley. Relative to the one who lives down below us.

[Letter 9: Helen to Owen]

[*LDS Church letterhead, handwritten*]

Nov. 12, 1900.

My Dearest Owen: —

Your <u>dear</u> <u>beautiful</u> letter, written at Juárez [Mexico] came to-day and it was so full of loving words of comfort that it gave me new hopes and new ambitions, and I have resolved to be a better girl-mamma for I feel that I do not merit all the love and kindness you bestow on me. But deep in my heart I am grateful for it all and I do truly appreciate all the comforts and blessings I enjoy but my actions make you think at times I do not. If I could receive a letter like the last precious one every day, I would be all right but you see I need you all the time, for, left to myself a time, I get discouraged and faint hearted; I know I must get braver and more independent but just now I cannot be, so I must have your good letters very often or I cannot live.

Your prayers, dearest, in my behalf have been answered. I do feel better than when you left me but still I do not feel exactly as I used to. I love just the same but there is something that tries me all the time and I think it will always be so, perhaps in a less degree. But we cannot expect a reward unless we make a sacrifice, and if it were no trial or sacrifice for me, where off would be the blessing. In the course of my life I expect many trials and hardships and I am not shrinking from it in the least, and you must not let my worries trouble you so much. It is my intention to make the best of it and live the best I can but how well I will succeed the future will decide. If we could only continue to live as we have the past three years it would be Heavenly to think of; but ~~chan~~ circumstances must change and we change with them. And in this I think we are improving, we are bringing our spirits into submission to the will of God, in doing so I have selfishness & stubborness to overcome. I can see now that I have spent my whole life in the gratification of my own selfish pleasure, but in the future I live for others, for you, my nobler purer self, for that's what you are to me, and for my children, precious spirits whom God has entrusted in^to^ my care. I must rise above self and conquer all that is selfish or coarse in my nature.

How very selfish and mean it is for me to want you all for my own, and all your love and affection just for my own comfort and happiness, and still when I think of it, this is all I have been grieving and suffering in my feelings for. Why I ought to want to make others happy and want you to make others happy, and to make others happy I must be happy myself. Now after all this preaching to you, I am just the same little, weak, selfish Helen that you left two weeks, still with a strong determination to become like my ideal a true wife and mother in Israel. This I know means a great deal, years of battles with self; successes one day and total failures another.

Don't think me eccentric, for if you should drop in this minute you would find me the same as when you left not one bit better.[33]

When, in looking over this letter, I see that it is all about myself I am reminded that you may be getting weary and would like to hear something of some body else.

Mrs. Doxey was just in and says that Tom Seevey and his new bride are staying with them for a few days. They were married on Election Day. I called in to see Ida and Hyrum[34] this evening to see how their baby is. He was feeling much better. Prest. Smith[35] and Bro. Seymour B.[36] start for Mexico to night. The papers giving the election returns were all destroyed before your letter asking me to send them came. Perhaps it will satisfy you to know that the Republicans made a clean sweep. So you were wrong when you thought Bryan was elected.[37] Jake ~~made~~ won a thousand dollars by the election going as it did, he showed Asahel a check for Three Hundred and said the rest was coming. Prest. Smith will be able to tell you all about the Election I am sure. Sunday School Convention is in Session, will send you the report of to-day's proceedings.

All members of the family are well I believe. Your Ma wrote you yesterday. To-day the Relief Society sisters went and sewed for Emeline all day. Poor girl she is so miserable.[38] Aunt Delight[39] was there and is looking and felling better. John[40] is in Virginia and feeling fine.

Well, my dearie, it is real late so I must say Good night. Will take your letter under my pillow to dream on. God bless you Owen dear and keep you well and happy Is the constant prayer of

> Your loving Mamma-Girl.
> Helen.

[Letter 10: Avery to Owen]

[*no letterhead, handwritten*]

> Logan Utah
> Nov. 17, 1900.

Dear Brother Woodruff: —

Yesterday I received your very welcome letters, I thought there would be no use of my calling for my mail very often by the way you wrote and so put it off for some time. But ⊖ I was so pleased to hear from you I could not express in words the joy it gave me.

We just returned from a lecture at B.Y. given by Pres. Paul of L.D.S.[41] thought it was fine good music in attendance too.

Now I am going to finish my letter this being my third attempt at it, friends have called or I have been interrupted in some other way and although the hour is late thought it my best opportunity.

You must not have heard from me, I wrote to Colonia[42] about the 4th. We are well, and was glad to hear that you were. I expect you are having an enjoyable time on your hunting tour about now hope you have success. Yes I think I am not so well skilled in the art of using a gun but that I could stand a little training which I might get on our trip to Yellow Stone?

We have had a long spell of pleasant weather but it is stormy now looks like winter was coming. I like to hear the geography of countrys their civilization and so on and expect you will have a great many interesting things to tell me when you return. I happily look forward to the time when I can be in your company again, would like to have been with you on that lonesome Sunday, we count those days as long ones too. O Brother Woodruff I shall never regret our having met and will always be contented.

Interrested in school as ever and especially this week we have had a feast; the Utah Art Institute has had use of our gymnasium hall showing us many beautiful paintings, drawings and designs and some of us have a notion to become artists. Think we will go home holidays. I enjoyed going through the Temple and will go again if I can.

I must not forget to tell you that I have burned all letters and will continue to do so, although it seems like destroying valuable literature.[43] Thank you for that pretty little present you sent me. I will keep all secrets in my heart and ask God to guard my words and actions and to bless us in all.

From loving
[*no signature*]

[Letter 11: Helen to Owen]

[*no letterhead, handwritten*]
Salt Lake City,
Nov. 19, 1900.

My Dear Owen: —

More than a week has passed since I heard from you but still I am not alarmed since you gave me fair warning that there would be a dearth of letters while you were away in the mountains [Mexico], but I shall expect you to make up for lost time when you get back to civilization.

You will not get this until you reach Thatcher Ariz. You did not tell me whether you were going there with Prest. Smith or whether you and Bro. Ivins would make another trip visiting the far off districts in Mexico.

Your mother has a new "<u>domestice</u>." A Sister Smith who was converted to our Faith in California. She has two sons one Eleven and one Thirteen. Aunt Delight thinks of taking the older one and the younger will stay at your Mothers. I wonder how long it will last. All parties concerned seem delighted at present, but I fear it will be of short duration.

The LDS College closed on account of Small Pox and Heber has gone home.[44] Arthur Smith does the chores. They think school will start again Monday and I will be glad to have Heber back again. He is one of the loveliest boys I ever new and when he goes away we miss him greatly.

The members of the Sugar Ward S.S. and the Stake Officers surprised Will McEwan last Fri. eve. They had the party at your Mother's as there was a very large crowd present. I went over, but stayed in the kitchen and helped with the lunch. Last Saturday & Sunday was Stake Conference in Our Ward, and they held fine meetings. Apostles Smith, Taylor[45] & Lund[46] were present Heber B.[47] and son Heber came here to dinner. This is all the Conference visitors I had. The Saturday Evening's News gave an exciting piece about an Indian attack upon the Mormon Colony at Pacheco Mex. but as we have had no official report we are inclined to think there is nothing of it or if there is any foundation the story has been exaggerated.[48]

Bro. and Sister Blake of Riverton came to see if their son could board with us. They want to get him into good company and think Heber would be a good companion for him. I told them I did not like to answer them until I had consulted you but he wanted to start right in school now so I told them he might come and stay until Christmas and then if we wanted to make different arrangements we could do so.

I have answered several of your letters that needed a quick reply. One from Walter Graham[49] asking you to get them round trip tickets for half fare to Logan. He and Julia are to be married this month. I telephoned to Dan Spencer and he arranged with the agent at Bridger to sell them round trip tickets. He said it would only cost one Dollar more to come to Salt Lake so I invited them to come and stay with me but do not know what they will decide to do. I also telephoned to Spencer and got half fare rates for Bro. Cuzzen's wife and daughter from Montpelier to Butte which saved them ten Dollars on each ticket.

We are all getting along about as usual. Eliza takes up her daily labor with the stove and the only way we can ever get a fire is to burn wood so Heber's leisure moments are occupied in chopping wood.[50] Baby gets sweeter every day. He learns something new almost every day, and he is such a little comfort to me and I am so thankful for him. I am thankful for all that I have and am trying to be thankful for even trials. Susie had a fine baby boy born last Wednesday and is getting along nicely when I heard last.[51]

I took baby up and had his picture but they are not good so I will have to take him again.

It has rained and snowed for two or three days and is so muddy that the roads are almost impassable. This afternoon I went to my meeting at Sister Taylor's[52] and thought I would never get back through the mud and was covered with snow when I got home. We have made new arrangements for the Journal next year. It is to be Edited and Published by the Genl. Board and all have to help although they appointed a committee of three as the Journal Committee.[53] Sisters Talmage, Grant & Goddard[54] will act as this committee.

Well dear, I sincerely hope you are enjoying your trip and may the choicest blessings of God be ever upon you and keep you well and happy.

As ever I am
Yours
Helen.

[Letter 12: Helen to Owen]

[*LDS Church letterhead, handwritten*]
Nov. 21, 1900.
Dear Owen:

In writing this letter I am breaking a resolution. I declared I would not write to you again until I received another letter from you but this is a business letter.

J. R. Allen called me to the Phone to-day and said that he had bought Buerchart's share of the hay at the farm. 27 1/2 Tons at $450 per ton and if you would sell yours for that price he was ready to buy it and pay cash down. He said he must know within the next ten days as they are going to leave in that time. J. R. Murdock[55] helped him to measure the hay, or it I think he said J. R. did the measuring. I told him I would write immediately to Thatcher and thought we would get an answer in eight or nine days so govern yourself accordingly.

Asahel leaves for New York on the 8, p.m. train and I am going to get him to post this on the train so I must hurry as I have just a few minutes.

We are all getting along about the same as usual. Baby gets sweeter every minute. He is learning to walk and I think by the time you get home he will be able to run and meet you. He sends love & kisses to papa and says he would like to see him very much. He is very good when he's asleep but when awake he is in to everything.

May you always be protected from harm & accident and have the blessings of God to attend you always Is the earnest prayer of your loving Helen.

P.S. I wrote to Blanche to-day for both of us. Your ma got a lovely letter from Joe [Daynes]. Have not had a word from you for a week and a half.[56]

Hurridly
H.

[Letter 13: Helen to Owen]

[no letterhead, handwritten]

Salt Lake City.
Nov. 23, 1900.

My Dearest Owen: —

This is your natal day and I have been wishing that I could be with you to wish you many happy returns and give you some birthday kisses, but you must take the will for the deed this time. It seems a perfect shame that you have to be away <u>every</u> birthday and that we never can spend the day to-gether.[57] I have been working on a little present for you but will not send it to you but keep it until you come home. Gusta asked me to go to the Alice Nielson opera this afternoon, and as I wanted to hear Viola Pratt Gillete sing I ventured out to the matinee.[58] It was just fine. Alice Nielson is such a cute coy little actress then she has a company with some of the best artists in it. You remember Eugene Cowles the Baritone who sang in the Bostonians and several others of that company are members of this one.

Prof. McLellan gave an organ recital in honor of Viola at which she sang. Her voice is not as good as when she was here last.[59]

The News had a short piece in it last night stating that you were among the pursuers of the Apache Indians and was at the burial of the Apache "Kid."[60] I was very glad to get your letter to-day giving the particulars as I felt a little anxious about you. It seems strange you do not get my letters. Have written four or five and hope you will get them. I just about concluded that you had forgotten ^me^ entirely as it has been nearly two weeks since I have heard from you.[61]

Have sent two letters to Thatcher Arizona and will send this to Mesa City [Arizona]. I found a program of your conferences in the News or should not know where to address you. It takes such a long ^ — time — ^ for a letter to come; a whole week from Juárez. Your letter written last Friday just reached me to-day (Friday). The baby is in the bath tub with Ruby. I wish you could see him. He is having such fun. He is the greatest little cut up you ever saw. He pats my face & loves me makes the biggest fuss over me and especially when I have been away for an hour or two. Your Ma thought surely she had found out a secret to-night she came over for me to go over and meet a sister who was going to meet you & go to Mexico with you. She said of course I knew all about it. The lady was from Parawan [Utah] and did not get the letter in time to go. She has been here working in the Temple all this week. I do not see how your ma could suspect such an aged person as she. She looks old enough to be my mother.[62]

I heard to-day that Sister Alice K. is in your company and has two children with her. How ever does she get along with them.

When you get this letter the time will be half gone and I will be so glad to have you back again. Sometimes I feel as though you will not be back in time for the "Tea-party"[63] but Oh I hope you are for I feel as though I could scarcely go through the ordeal without you are here; But suppose there would be no choice about it.

The College will reopen next Monday and I will be glad to have Heber back. The little Smith boy went out to live with Aunt Delight to-day and so I got Asahel[64] to do the chores until Sunday.

Well, Dearest, I love you just the same as ever but there is something changed about me f which I feel will always be so; but we will not shrink from duty whatever it may cost for that in the end will bring true happiness in the Eternal World and that is what we are striving for. Lutie sings a beautifull song entitled "The trials of the road will seem nothing When we get to the End of the Way."[65] I think Bro. Seymour B [Young] composed it but am not sure. It is getting very late so I will not write more to you this time. Hope you will write oftener now you are getting nearer home.

Baby joins Mamma in sending Birthday loves & kisses and in wishing that you may have many more happy and blessed birthdays.

Your Affectionate Wife.
Helen Winters Woodruff.

[Letter 14: Helen to Owen]

[*no letterhead, handwritten, some of the paper damaged*]
Salt Lake City.
Dec. 2, 1900.

My Dearest Owen:

Although I have not received a letter from you for nearly a week I will keep up the practice of writing to you on the Sabbath. This is fast day again and I fully intended to go to Temple meeting but was lame this morning so stayed at home. This afternoon however I felt better and went to our Ward meeting, and the people were so slow getting up that it seemed quite a drag.

You are at Mesa to-day and will have received two letters and baby's pictures which I sent you there. Bro. North wrote me that the potatoes were all gone and they had nothing to feed the pigs but oats and lucern and as oats were rather expensive pig feed he thought you would like to sell the pigs and said if you would set a price on each one he would try and sell them for you.

Now I do not know what to do about it. I thought of asking Bro. J. R. Murdock [*paper damage*] set a price on them & sell them [*paper damage*] But then thought I would wait until I heard from you. Does Bro. North have access to the oats if he does I don't think there will be many left. Will you tell me what to do immediately?

Have received several letters from B.H. [Big Horn] Colony and they were all prospering nicely. Julia S. [Sessions] & Walter Graham were coming to Logan to get married last week. You got a letter from David,[66] he did not get elected Senator. I got a letter from Belle[67] also; they were all well but her.

The Hay man brought two more loads of hay. Said he would like me to pay him for one load. Will [Owen's brother-in-law] and your Mother have a cow. Mother paid for her and Will pays for the feed and they divide the milk. Eggs are 35¢ per doz. and Butter is 35¢ per lb. so I do not know how we are going to live at that rate. Well dearest you will be home in three more weeks and you cannot tell how glad I will be for I do want to see you so much and so does baby.

I expect a letter to-morrow and if I am disappointed, beware. Don't you think I have done fine writing to you. Have written nine or ten letters [*paper damage*]

> Good night my darling,
> With Love and kisses from
> Owen and Mamma

[Letter 15: Helen to Owen]

[*LDS Church letterhead, handwritten*]

> Dec. 4, 1900.

My Dearest Owen.

You did not want to bother me by telling me of your troubles and I was determined I would not annoy you with my grievences; so instead of telling you what a miserable time we have had with our stove ever since you left will just say that I have Brother Burgon[68] here building a new chimney. He came here with Heber one day and examined the flue and stove etc. and said the chimney was altogether to small and volunteered to build me a new one so I acquessed and he and his oldest son are here today doing the job. He says it is the greatest wonder in the world that we haven't had our house burned. The chimney had great cracks in it and the wood work was all blacked with smoke. I think we can be thankful the stove hasn't burned or we would have been homeless.

Bro. North writes me that the wind has blown the top of the hay stack off but says things are going along as well as could be expected under the circumstances. We had bad stormy weather for a week or more but now the weather is perfect, just like Spring.

Sister Lambert[69] is nursing Maud Woodbury; she had a little girl born yesterday. I was thinking perhaps she would not be through there in time for me and think any way it would be better to have Miss Bullock, she is nursing Susie [Bennion] and will stay with her four weeks for $28.00 and I will have to pay Sister L $30.00 for three weeks. I am sure I will have to have her three weeks any way as Eliza has her hands full with the work and could not wait on me much. The post-man will be here soon so I will not write more. I <u>love</u> you <u>dearer</u> than my life and hope you will get home in <u>due</u> time. Only two more weeks. I can scarcely wait that long to see you. I went to Bro. Jack and got my regular allowence but will have to go back and get some more for your debts — $12.00 for hay & $2.00 for Milton North. Then there is the money for Blanche & Nellie [Taylor] so that will make nearly $30.00 from your money. I have had to get a sack of sugar and a ton of coal besides numerous "<u>little</u> thing<u>s</u>."

Well dearest Good bye, God bless you and keep you well and happy.
Ever Your Loving Helen.

[Letter 16: Avery to Owen]

[*no letterhead, handwritten*]

Auburn, Wyo.
Dec. 8, 1900

Dear Clarence [code name for Owen], my very true and esteemed friend:

Your kind letter added so much to my happiness that I have indeed had a joyous holiday. But was again sorry to learn that your health was not the best and hope that you are now feeling better.

We have had some dreadfully cold weather, one of our neighbors tells us that when his thermometer registered fifty below zero it froze up so we can't tell just how cold it was. And I guess it is on account of the change in the weather that so many of the people have such bad colds.

This evening Papa took us for a sleigh ride over to Afton [Wyoming], we called on the Doctor and Mary [Clark] and ^I^ were vaccinated, we are regreting that we did not have it done when we first came home but hope we will take no harm from the exposure going through the mountains. We expect to start back to school about the ninth.

Suit your own convenience and pleasure as to the suggestions in your letter and they will suit me. I feel perfectly satisfied and happy. I am at a loss to express my feelings and appreciation of yours and dear Helen's thoughtfulness of me.

Sister Mary and I have an invitation to attend a party at Afton tomorrow night. I will likely have the pleasure of receiving the package you have sent as Papa has arranged to have it brought in by the Mail.

These things are dear to me but the united affection of you both are is dearer still and I hope to live worthy of it.

The pleasures of home and the association of loved ones makes it hard to leave them again so soon.

May it please the Lord to preserve you all in health and life and bless you with every good thing that you need, is the sincere desire of your loving friend.

Maggie.

[Letter 17: Avery to Owen and Helen]

[*no letterhead, handwritten*]
Logan Utah
Dec. 21, 1900

Mr. and Mrs. A. O. Woodruff.

Dearest Friends

Received letters from both of you yesterday it was a real treat. Just a few minutes remain before I must be on my way to school and I am going to use them in writing to you. Fear if I dont do it now that it won't be done, as we have so much to see to before leaving on the train to night. We have seven hours work in school and I guess the students that go our way will meet here and we'll all go together, and we must prepare for that. Papa wrote and said that he would meet us at Mt. Pelier [Idaho] if all was well, then won't we have a long sleighride. "Have to stop."

Dear sister I think that photo is a beauty, I know I can love you too and think we will have many good times together. When you think of me you must not think of a girl so small, I only weigh 154 pounds. My birth-day was Mar. 9. was eighteen so I guess you got about the right idea in that regard.

Now as to name. How would "Clarence" do.[70] I have no reason for choosing it but thought it would answer the purpose. The name you suggested suits me all right. If you write to me during holidays, think it would be best to direct the letters to Papa as the girls that keep the Office are a little curious sometimes about their schoolmates letters and it is often the case that they are opened. You must excuse this scambled letter for I have had hard work to get a chance to write it. It is now real late and the crowd will soon be here.

I wish you all a merry merry Christmas and happy New Year and my heart is full of good wishes for you. I thank you Bro. Woodruff for that present that is coming. (Think that ring no. eight will be about right)

Yours most affectionately.

Maggie.

Will be happy to meet you.

[Avery's "Autobiography and Recollections": Excerpt B (pages 42–47)]

[*handwritten*]

Come Sept. 15th Mary and I were on our way to Logan and B.Y.C. On arrival we got a list of available room for rent from the College and in a day or so were quite comfortably located in an upstairs room at the Spiermans. This was about five blocks from school — a comfortable walking distance and only three blocks from the main shopping district in main street.

At once we wrote home giving the folks our new address and Father forthwith sent it on to bro. W. In a week or so but without warning I answered a knock on our door. There stood Owen Woodruff as white as a sheet — he was frightened and so was I. In a very few words plans were set to meet that evening after dark on a certain corner of the tabernacle block and O. W. was on his way. This was the first of four meetings with him over a period of about four months when I became his wife.[71]

Always I felt he was as perfect as mortal man can be. He treated me as if I were a queen tenderly touching my hand. There was no love making, just beautiful, lofty words of devotion to the principle we were contemplating living and for each other and Helen. She was forever in the picture as she had every right to be. Before I ever met Helen she was lifted on a pedestal before my eyes and I adored her. Owen painted a true picture of her true worth and charm which in all the years I knew her never diminished. Immature as I was — only two thirds their age I wondered if I could ever reach a status that could be compatible with such splendid persons — Owen and Helen. Their desire uppermost was to do the will of God at all times to live worthily in preparation for the celestial Kingdom. To make any sacrifice in this life for a greater fulfilment in the life to come. It meant unselfish devotion to a cause which would fail unless we were united in heart and mind — humble and prayerful before the Lord. In this respect I needed schooling which only time and experience could give.

(When I was eighteen Owen and Helen were twenty eight)

In the presence of Owen and Helen I felt the power of their great love. It enveloped me giving me strength and security. They made me feel that I was wanted, needed in this higher order of marriage roles. Alone and away from them I often was filled with fear, lonliness, frustration in a world of reality where I was appearing and known to my friends and classmates as "Miss Clark" to camoflage the fact that I was a married woman. I had an urge to shout it to the world just who I really was thus freeing pent up emotions. My honest self rebelled against appearing to be what I was not.

Often Mary would find me in tears and chide me for may lack of gratitude. She would say: "You ought to be the happiest woman in the world." "In your shoes I'm sure I would be, even if I could only see my husband once a year. I mean if he could be your husband."[72]

Owen's special asignment as an Apostle was to take charge of the colonization of Big Horn Basic Wyo. This and his visits to the different missions and stakes of the church kept him away from home much of the time. Weeks went by that I did not see him. Whenever he came to Logan it was to fill a church appointment. I might see him for a few minutes or we spent the night at the house of one of the Stake Presidency. Occasionally I went to Salt Lake or Farmington and stayed the week end with relatives and managed a short visit at Owen's & Helen's house.

I think it was the first summer we had lived in the new, large house in *Valley that Owen & Helen came for a week's visit enroute for the Big Horn. My family made their stay as pleasant as possible especially were we careful to guard Helen's feelings against any strain of sharing her husband's time with another woman on this vacation trip. Mother kept me near her coaching me very frequently on how to play my part heroically. "Be happy about it and don't expect Bro. W. to give you much time or attention" mother said, "not in Helen's presence. Remember she is our guest." So I was thrilled when one morning while I was running the "separator" in a back room and Owen rushed in, taking me in his arms for an instant told me how sweet and brave I was. This lifted my spirits — primed me for the day ahead — reassured me of my husband's love.

As Helen said of herself — "It is as natural for me to be jolly as for the sun to shine" proved to be a fact to all observers. She had her hours and days of feeling blue she told me and had to struggle with self discipline. It worried her that I took life so seriously, and she often asked me if she had made me unhappy — she didn't mean to.

In July 1903 Owen came to *Valley on his way to the Big Horn Basin in Wyo. bringing Frank Y. Taylor, Pres. of Granite Stake, Van Beebe his brother in law, Isaac Russell and George Gibbs.[73] These men were equipped with a comissary wagon to hold their hunting and camping gear. Russell and Gibbs were in charge of this wagon and the two teams of horses. The other three men occupied another wagon.

They all stayed at our ranch several days to visit with our family, to rest their horses and do a little hunting. It was Owen's first trip to the Valley since we were married and now it must be kept a secret from the men with him. As a result I really spent more time with young Russell than I did Owen while Mary and Gibbs seemed very friendly.

The men had been out hunting a couple of days and brought back a fine catch. Besides fresh fish we had great repasts of venison that lasted for days. To furnish the dessert for our fine meal Russell and I took little lead buckets and strolled down to the meadow to pick wild strawberries. Owen sat on the front porch watching just how close our heads came together while we were fairly rooting for the tiny wild berries. He said to me later on: "Make sure Ike behaves himself I can tell he likes you, just give him the cold shoulder or do you want to"? It was an agrivation to me not be able to announce to the world that I was happily married to a grand person whom everyone admired. I had moments of resentment, when I may have used indescression in acting naughty.

It was a busy time on the ranch — father in the midst of haying two of the girls taking turns cooking for the hired men. For two days Mother stayed at the river ranch leaving me and Mary in charge of the meals for our guests. One morning when we kneeled around the breakfast for prayer I called upon Geo. Gibbs to pray. He said: "I never pray, I'm sorry." This really shocked me but I called on bro. Taylor who responded. When we were alone Owen apologized for not having told me that Gibbs who once was a devoted L.D.S. member had his faith upset by attending an Eastern University. That it was the hope of George's father that this trip might help to straighten him out. This episode upset Mary who had become fond of the charming student.

It pleased our guests that Mary and I were such experts at riding tho we were complete novices with the use of a gun or fishing tackle. However, one day when all of us went riding in the "white top" up Stump Creek I picked up one of the guns we had along and pulled the trigger hitting a squirrel perched on a rock a few rods from the road. Every one screamed, the driver stopped the team and one of the boys ran & picked up the dead squirrel. Later on he hung it on the corner of the house as evidence of my skill. It bothered me to know I had taken the life of an innocent little creature just for the sport of it.

To add to the pleasure of their trip one of the men brought along a portable phonograph and a lot of beautiful records. In the cool of the evening we sat spellbound listening to a variety of music. How we missed this luxury when our guests moved on. The one selection which Mary and I have never forgotten — our choice of all the records was: "Your eyes so blue and tender."

1901

[Letter 18: Avery to Owen]

[*no letterhead, handwritten*]
                              Logan Utah
                              Jan. 12, 1901
Dear Clarence:

Have not heard from you since we got back and think prehaps you are waiting to hear whether I have arrived or not before writing. I thought of writing the evening we came and then came to the conclusion not to. We arrived on the 6, after having quite an unpleasant trip. It made us girls sick to ride in the sleigh through the mountains and took us some time to get over it.

We are staying home from school to-day not feeling able to go. Don't know whether it is just bad colds that we have or our vaccination taking its effect. Although our arms are not a bit sore yet, it has been over a week since we were vaccinated.

Few of the students have been vaccinated and they do not seem to inforce it.[1]

The package came the morning we left, so I got to see the presents. I think they are beautiful.

Hoping you are all enjoying the blessings of health and strength I will close.

                              Yours as ever and with love
                              Maggie

[Letter 19: Avery to Owen]

[*no letterhead, handwritten*]
                              Logan Utah
                              Jan. 27, 1901.
Dearest Ivan [another code name for Owen]÷

Although the hour is late I will attempt to answer your so much welcomed letter.

We went to Conference to-day and conjoint meeting to night. The meetings were good and I have come home happy as can be. Dearest, I looked for your blessed face to be among the preachers, yet hardly expected that you would come and think myself that it would have been difficult for us to have met without a little excitement and for that reason am consoled. I am so happy when I think of you and thankful for the grand privelage I have had of becoming what I am to-day and one of my greatest desires is to live worthy of your sweet companionship.

Examinations are near at hand. Am getting along as well as ever in school and enjoying perfect health.

I am glad to hear that you are all feeling as well as you are and hope that little baby[2] is better now.

I got along all right when I came back, as few questions were asked me and all stories connected very well. Was glad to hear of the succes that you had from dealing with those people.

Bro. C. [Matthias Cowley] was to Conference but of course I did not get to see him. Yes I could truthfully say that I didn't see the preformes.

Praying always for the help of the Lord I will try to be careful and patient. Then I feel sure that every thing will be all right.

With love to you all I am

Your own

Matilda [another code name for Avery]

(Over)

[*written on back:*]

Born in Farmington Davis Co.
Utah, Mar. 9, 1882.
Baptized in Auburn Uinta Co.
Wyoming Sept. 20, 1890 by
Barnard E. Parry. Confirmed
by Hyrum D. Clark.

[Letter 20: Avery to Owen and Helen]

[*no letterhead, handwritten*]

Logan Utah

Feb. 16, 1901.

Dear Ivan and Nellie:

Both of your letters did me an immence amount of good. I was so glad to hear how you all were.

After having my head inside my books half of the day, it gives me releaf to talk to you for a short time. I am well and happy and having a glorious time in school. I can see reasons, Nellie, for your longing to be a school-girl again for indeed a school girl's life is and ought to be a happy one. Not meaning of course that married life has not its pleasures.

Yesterday, after our class work was over, instead of devoting the remainder of the day to studying our lessons for Monday we came home and washed and prepared some for Sunday. In the evening we studied a long Sunday School lesson; so that is the reason for my studying to-day.

We are advised to not study on Sunday and I think it is good advice but where girls are keeping "bachelor's hall" there is something more than studying to be done everyday. I am glad to say that our first term examinations are over and that we passed with pretty good marks. You know some of us students seem to think that our lifes depend upon the kind of mark we get in final examinations.

I have just been studying History, Algebra, Grammar and Theology. The latter is a study I take great interest in also Art, and I guess you hope that I will take more interest and learn more about the study of Grammar in the future.

This is surely enough on the subject, school.

Ivan, I am sorry you have been hindered in your work by having a miserable sty, and know how to sympathize with you a little as I was bothered with two of them last year while at school.

I think you did not owe me an excuse for not writing but if you think so I will excuse you. I did not expect a letter much sooner than it came for such reasons as you mentioned.

Nellie I am glad to hear that you and babies are so well and that you are not so tied at home but that you can go out and enjoy yourself. I too hope that the opportunity of our associating together will be given us some time. Tonight I would like to call in and see you all and talk with you instead of writing.

It has been stormy nearly all day and hardly a stir has been made outside. This morning we were told about the sudden death of our beloved teacher brother Mazer.[3] When he spoke to us in school not long since he told us of the few things he would have to accomplish before his work would be ended and I guess it was all done.

I received $ all-right can get along with less next month.

If provisions are made for my coming down at any set time it will be agreeable with me and will not break into my school work enough to speak of.

Kiss the little tots for me. With love and prayer for you all,

I am as ever
Matilda.

[Letter 21: Avery to Owen]

[*no letterhead, handwritten*]

Logan Utah
Mar. 12, 1901.

Dear Ivan: —

I have just returned from school; got supper over with; placed my books back on the table ready for studying. Fearing that I would not get through with studying in time to write afterward, thought I would drop a few lines now. I was very glad to hear from you; little expected to be so thought of on my birthday and thank you ever so much for the remembrance you sent me for it is worth a thousand that could be bought with money.[4]

Yes, my birthday was a happy one I can not say that I ever had a happier one. Little I thought a year ago of being where I am today. I feel that the Lord has blessed me abundantly and with his help I will try to make the most of it. I think I can draw from your letter a good outline to follow; for my greatest desire is to accomplish those things which you mention that is to become an ideal wife and mother; to have the love and approval of God and that of my companion. To know that you have an interest in my welfare is enough to encourage me. You have done all I could ask and I know you are willing to do all that you know is for my best good.

Expect you are where you have to do a great amount of preaching; hope it wont be so hard on you as before.

School goes the same as ever. Today I have been painting on two of those oranges you gave me; they make quite an interesting study.

I never enjoyed a party better than I did the students reception Wednesday night.

Well I have some hard lessons to morrow. If my Algebra were prepared I would be glad.

This leaves me well but sister has a sore throat which I hope will soon be better. Hope that all will keep well at home while you are gone.

Praying for you (the dearest creature on the earth) alway, I am yours lovingly

Matilda

[Letter 22: Helen to Owen]

[LDS Church letterhead, handwritten]
Mar 17, 1901.
Dearest Papa:
Your lovely letter did me so much good although it savored of the blues. I had a good cry and have felt better ever since.

Was sorry you could not spend those lonely hours you spent in Butte [Montana], with me, but must be satisfied with the thought that I occupied a little corner of your thoughts, for I would rather have a tiny corner in your noble, true, heart than to have the whole heart of any other man living, so there!

Clara [Beebe] entertained in honor of Genia and Mrs. Osgood Friday evening, we were all there of course, and had a lovely time. Every body wanted to know where you were and we all missed your smilting face very much.

On Saturday night I took, Clara, Mrs. Osgood and Nellie [Taylor] to see Macbeth and I have had the horrors every since. Talk about the "Hell broth of Macbeth's witches," I saw it all night and wished you were by me to comfort me.

Your Mother is going to have the Scholes girls down to-morrow night. Well, now about house cleaning. I was talking to your ma about carpets etc, and said I was going to make the old ones do but she said I was silly and told me to go and get a new one. She went with me and says she will stand part of the blame for going in debt. She says I ought to pattern after the Grants [Heber J. and Gusta] a little more and enjoy life. Sister Empey & I spent a hundred dollars on their dinning room the other day.

Our house would have looked very shabby all over, the bedroom carpet came all to pieces when Heber shook it, and by getting the one new carpet we can fix up quite scrumptously, and I am going to contrive to save on other things. ^Mrs^ Empey, your Ma and every one who is experienced says it would be folly for me to have my black dress made up now so I will make my other dresses do until fall, so we will say no more about it. I am more interested in house cleaning than any thing else just now. We have three carpets up, all the curtains down and I spent to-day Sunday in the kitchen, with the babies. We eat sit and sleep in the kitchen and you may be thankful you are away for a few days. We will try to be all slicked up when you get home.

It is very late. Will add a few words in the morning. Good night, dear, sweet dreams.

[Letter 23: Helen to Owen]

Owie's finger marks [*in top margin*]
[*LDS Church letterhead, handwritten*]

Mar. 18, 1901.

Dear Owen: —

Will write a few words before the Postman gets here. Nellie is going to start home to-morrow. She talks about going all the time so your "Mar" thinks she may as well go now. Clara is down helping get dinner for your Ma's company to-day.

Prest. Cannon welnt to the Coast last week and the last report was that he was some better.[5] Carol & Willard have a fine baby boy. Emily is going to marry Bro. Willey and they start to Washington soon where they will make their home for the present. He has been appointed to some office there.

Well I suppose you know the Gov.[6] vetoed the Evan's Bill.[7] It has made a great commotion. He said it was the hardest thing he ever had to decide upon. He declared he never told any one he would sign it. Prest. Snow & also Prest. Cannon had a piece in Saturday nights "news" stating that he had never promised them he would sign it. No doubt Mr. Owens[8] will have a great deal of business on hand now.

The day after you left we had Y.L.M.I.A. Conference of Granite Stake in our Wd. House Bro. [Matthias] & Sister Cowley[9] were there and came home with me to dinner between afternoon meeting and evening meeting. Was sorry you were not here to visit with them. Ethel[10] & Hebe [Heber Bennion, Sr] were here also. I was busy getting dinner ready and left them to entertain them selves. Bro. C. filled his fountain pen and wrote letters to his heart's content.

Wrote to sister Sessions[11] a day or so ago. Give the folks my love. My darling boy, I love you with all my heart and pray constantly for your success in your labors and your happiness.

You must have had a good meeting Sunday for I prayed for you all day long. If I could just be as good, thoughtful, and kind to you, as you are to me, I would be satisfied with myself in that regard. Babies are real well, but Owie seems to be getting thin, doesn't eat like he used to. Write and tell me when to expect you as I am anxiously waiting your return.

With my heart's best love I am as ever

Your Affectionate and would be
faithful Wife
Helen Winters.

[Letter 24: Helen to Owen]

[*LDS Church letterhead, handwritten*]
                              Mar. 19, 1901
My Dear Owen: —
     Your letter written from Big Horn arrived to-day, or I should say,
your <u>note</u>, for that is what is was.
     Will send this letter to Burlington [Wyoming] as it will reach there
about Sunday. I am over at Mother Woodruff's to-night sleeping in the
blue rooom up stairs, we are all torn up over home but expect to have our
carpets all down to-morrow and O how glad I'll be, for we have lived in
the kitchen for nearly a week.
     The roads are dry now so I sent to the farm for "Topsy" for I need
to go to town with the buggy. Sent Sioux to the pasture. Her leg was all
swoolen up from standing in the barn so long.
     Nellie went home to-day, she felt very badly on leaving this time. She
wants us all to fast for her next fast-day and she is going to try and go to
meeting in her ward and make things right as much as she can. Poor girl
I feel so sorry for her.
     Sister Frank Y. Taylor[12] is very low, the ward all fasted for her yester-
day and to-day she was a little bit better.
     Sister Doty called to-day, said she did not want to return to the B. H.
this spring if she thought there would be any chance of getting half fare
later in the summer. I told her I thought there would be some one going
during the summer. She said Sister Kelsch's sister had received word from
Chicago [code name for Byron, Wyoming] that Bro Kelsch was called to
go to Japan with Bro Grant.[13] Will take Sister K. [Kelsch] with him.[14]
     The Salts from England are here tonight. They are right from
Blanche and Joe you know. Have not met them yet. They are at Asahel's.
     My <u>dearest</u> <u>sweet</u> <u>heart</u>, I appreciate you more every day and love
you more than words can tell and if you were here this minute could
demonstrate the fact in a manner you would not soon forget. Little Owen
can climb up into chairs. He uncatches the screen door and runs away to
Grandma's forty times aday. The babes are both real well as is every body
else. With fondest love I am as ever
                              Your baby girl wifie,
                              <u>Helen</u>.

P.S.Give my love to Belle, David and all the folks at Burlington.

[Letter 25: Avery to Helen]

[*no letterhead, handwritten*]

Logan Utah
May 16, 1901.

Dear Sister Hettie.

Now have most of my lessons prepared for to-morrow and feel like talking to you a while. I often feel this way and hope that we shall some-time have the privelage of associating to-gether more and comforting each other. If it can always be called <u>comforting</u> what a grand thing it would be.

Our last visit I think was a joyous one; just what we needed. I am sure it greatly benefited me. I have been happier ever since.

The last visit had with Ivan was a pleasant one though quite short. Recd. a letter from him the other day but did not answer it for this rea-son. I did not know his whole address so thought it safer not to write. Tell him I am sorry and will write when I know he is home.

Grandpa did not write to me but Papa has been down and I got a letter from him stating that Grandpa was very ^low^ and in a pitiable con-dition. He told Papa to tell me to come down and take care of him.

Had Ivan been home Papa would have called on him.

Now I'll tell of the kind of times we are having at school. Last week the young ladies of the college petitioned for a holiday on which to remove all the dandelions from the college grounds. The boys also were to assist in improving the grounds by trimming the walks and leveling off the south hill. This kind of petition was of course granted and next morn-ing all students as well as teachers came prepared to work. The girls with their sunbonnets and case knives got down on hands and knees and went at work in good earnest digging the things up. It was an all day's job but we had lots of fun out of it any way.

That night there was a dance at B.Y. but we were all too tired to go. Next morning we were all stiff as boards and disapointed to see the lawn almost as yellow as ever.

This coming Sat. classes 1903–4 are going up in the canyon for a trip and hope to have an enjoyable time.

I guess you say stop. I go at writing about as ackwardly as I do talking and have gotten into the habit of scribbling in taking down notes; so all to-gether makes it bad.

Well dear sister my heart is full of love for you. You have treated me so lovely I can never repay you. My prayer is that the Lord will bless us all in our earnest endeavors.

Love to All
Matilda.

[Letter 26: Avery to Owen and Helen]

[*no letterhead, handwritten*]

Logan Utah
May 30, 1901.

Dear Ivan and Hettie: —

Your dear letters were happily received, and to hear that you were all so well and happy and enjoying yourselves does me good. I am feeling fine.

This being a holiday we are enjoying a rest from our studies and doing a few miscellaneous jobs so as to be ready on the morrow to dive into our lessons in good earnest.

Its being so far to the cemetry we did not go, but went up town, had our "snap shots" and brought back some straw-berries.

The house is building and Mama not being able to do any work leaves much for sister — carpenters to cook for and soon hay men.

I think it is too late for to mention Big Horn to Papa he is pretty well settled and quite contented there. You do give that country a good name it sounds like a little paradise.

Both of you come up to Star Valley on a visit this summer. You would miss warm weather there and find it pleasant out home. I'm sorry a bit that Ivan made one visit there.

It sounds quite tempting Hettie when you mention go home and see the folks. Every letter makes me feel like flying there. Now I expect you laugh at me and say I'm a young thing and cannot leave my Mamy, but nine months is quite a long time to be away from home.

Did not receive a letter from Grandpa but Papa was down not long ago and he said that my cousin and Grandpa's sister were there taking care of him and did not think they would need my help. But he told Papa to have me come. He would do that any way.

The folks at home are very busy now and expect a helper would be appreciated for our dinner. Wish you could have had some with us but us two girls sat here alone and ate them. We do hate to buy and cook things for just us two. But this wont last long. Our examinations come next week and commencement will be on 14th.

Think it will be fine if you can both come. We'll expect you. I feel like saying I would be to the depot to meet you and would entertain you while here but suppose that is out of the question.

You ask what my program was for the summer. Well at the close of school I think I shall be contented to boat rides and drives. I'm sure I would enjoy them with you. Don't miss the trip to Canada if you can help it. Would do you and babies so much good. Don't speak about your non-sensical letter it was just the kind.

Hoping to hear from you or see you soon I remain yours lovingly,
Matilda
P.S. Papa and perhaps Mama will be down to Conference will give them
your address.

[Letter 27: Avery to Owen and Helen]

[*no letterhead, handwritten*]
Logan Utah
June 14, 1901.
Dear Ivan and Nettie: —
You would laugh if you could see me, sitting here in an empty room
alone; using the window for my stationary and my knee for a table.
I will leave for Farmington tomorrow on the 2 o'clock train. Have
plenty to do before I go although I feel quite at rest since examinations.
Our exercises have been fine so far. In half hour I have to be to the
College again so will have to cut this short and get ready.
Was glad to hear from you again and will be happy to see you.
Pardon me for not saying so before but I received the $10.00 and
the $20.00 Thanks for them.
With Love to All
Matilda

[Letter 28: Owen to Avery]

[*no letterhead, typed*]
Oaxaca, Mex. [code name for Billings,
Montana]
Nov. 15th. 1901.
Dear Mattie÷
Think it would be best for you to come down. Will arrange place for
you to stop. Write to me and say what night you will come down. Take the
street car you usually do and get off on IIth. South Street. Go one block
east and if we should miss you by any means, go into the home of Bro.
Kelch, which is on the east side of the Street on the corner and just across
the stree and a little south of where you stopped before. Your "friend"
will meet you there or send his "friend to get you. Would it not be well to
come one day after or before the students?

We are all well and hope all is right with you.
                    May God bless you.
With love and hoping to meet you within the next month,
                    Affectionately,
                    Ivan

[Letter 29: Helen to Avery]

[*company letterhead, handwritten*]
Office of Big Horn Basin Colonization Co.
ABRAHAM O. WOODRUFF, President.
BYRON SESSIONS, Vice-Prest.
CHAS. A. WELCH, Secretary.
BRIGHAM L. TIPPETS, Treasurer.
Charles Kingston.
Jesse W. Crosby, Jr.
John Dickson.
William B. Graham.
                    Salt Lake City Nov. 24, 1901
My Dear Sister:
    Your lovely letter came in due time, and I am ashamed that it has
remained unanswered so long, but when I had the inclination opportu-
nity was not afforded me and when there was time I lacked inclination.
    My dear, I do not merit all the good things you say of me, if it were so,
how truly thankful I would be. It makes me happy to know that you think
those things of me, anyway, for I know you are sincere in what you say.
    Suppose you are well posted on the happenings of the Journey in
the south. I have had two lovely letters and mean creature that I am, have
only written one, but I have been so greatly tried in my feelings lately. Will
tell you all about it when I see you again. I want you to pray that <u>he</u> may
be guided by the inspiration of the Lord in all thing pertaining to our
family connections in future as he has been in the past. I have this faith,
that our course in this life was mapped out for us before we were taber-
nacled in the flesh and if we are in the line of our duty, whatever comes
to us is the right thing, although many things are hard for us to bear
I believe that trials are blessings in disguise. And that some day we will
thank God for our trials if we are only able to stand them and be faithful
to the end. Now you will say I know, that I am preaching again but I want
to say something to help ^you^ and these things when I think them over
help me so I thought likely they might help you so you must forgive me
if it sounds like preaching. No doubt you have heard of my condition at

present.[15] At first I felt very badly, but am reconciled now, for I want to have all the children the Lord wants me to have, but it does seem so soon to go through the ordeal agin. I thought it would be your turn this time instead of mine. Well I want us to pray for the Lord's will to be done in all things and that we may be prepared to accept whatever comes to us as our mission here. I am beginning to realize more fully every day the fact, that we are not living for this life but we are toiling & striving for grand & beautiful blessings in our Eternal home and if we would think more of this fact our burdens and sorrows here would be made lighter and our path way brighter in this life. When I forget this and my thots do not go beyond the pales of this life I am selfish indeed. But we have much to be thankful for. And I am not ungrateful, the Lords knows my heart, and I am truly glad that he does, for if he did not and were to judge me by my actions he would think me bad indeed.

We are all well, busy as can be preparing for Blanche & Joe who returns from England in about one week.[16] I will have near neighbors then and will not be so lonely. Papa [Owen] has never been home to eat thanksgiving dinner with us once during our married life and it does seem hard.

The hour is late so will not write more. Am going to hear Miss Lulu Gates[17] sing to morrow evening. She has been studying in jermany for the past three years and makes her debut in the Tabernacle to-morrow eve. Wish you were her to go with me.

May the Lord bless you in your studies and grant you every richeous desire of your heart.

With love I am as ever
Your friend & Sister
Nell.

P.S. Dec. 8. 1901. You will see by the date of this letter it has been written a long time. Answer soon and I will not wait so long before answering. Got a beautiful letter to-day. If it were not for the lovely letters I get I could not stand to be left alone so much but I feast on them.

1902

[Letter 30: Owen to Avery]

[no letterhead, typed]

Oaxaca, Mex.
Jan 14th. 1902.

Dear Mattie÷ It has been a long time since I wrote to you or since I saw you last. I have been away most of the time for two weeks I was in Wayne Co. Utah for about two weeks, during a very cold spell. The Morning we Left Loa [Utah] to cross Fish Lake Mountain it was 33 degrees below zero. Although we were well prepaired for cold, yet we had all we could do to keep from freezing to death. Have been home but a few days and must start for the B.H. in a few days and will likely be gone about a month. We are going to build another large Canal in that country and I have been given charge of it again.[1] I am going out with the surveyors and will watch the progress of the work pretty closely as I am responsible for it.

I do not intend to let it worry me so much this time as I can profit by my past experience and with the blessings of the Lord in the future as He has blessed me in the past we will get along allright.

How do you girls manage to keep warm this cold weather? Bros, C.[Cowley] & C. [Clawson] have gone out to Star Valley. Say they will have a cold trip will they not? They told me they had called on you for which I thanked them very much. It is very kind and thoughtfull of them to do this. Well dear notwithstanding the cold trips I have had I am enjoying perfect health. I don't know that I ever felt better. Many times I think of the splendid lunch you girls put up for us when we were leaving the [Clark] Ranch and the excellent treatment you gave us while we were there. As woman's highest aim and noblest mission is wife-hood and mother-hood all men appreciate any of these qualities which goes to make home the dearest place on earth. My dear girl I want to give you every possible advantage of education and practice to become a model house-wife and that means that you must be an excellent cook (which qualification I think you already possess), a good seamstress, a lover of house plants, a good washer, and posessing originality in the draping and decoration of home that it may be tasty and cozy. I will feel glad for some reasons when you have a home of your own so that you can take a pride in keeping it according to your own ideas.

I know no one could have acted wiser or have ben more patient under the circumstances than you have been. I feel so thankfull too that all of the folks have been so true and kind to us. I wish I could come see you before I have to go away but for the good of others I shall have to forego the pleasure untill things quiet down a little.

Our Sister next door has a baby boy born this morning. She is doing well. You can address me in the old style if you answer at once and I will give you the next address to write to. The sleighing is fine here for the first time in years, but it is too cold to go sleighing for pleasure only.

I hope this will find all well with you. Excuse my being a little late with the "C". It is on account of my having been absent from home for so long. M—— [code for Helen] and the babies are all well now though our boy has been sick. All send love to you.

Give my kind regards to "the folks".

I pray always for your wellfare and safety. God bless and comfort you and give you success in your labors,

>With love I am,
>Affectionately,
>Ivan

[Letter 31: Owen to Helen]

[*letterhead, handwritten*]
The Billings Club
Billings, Montana

Jan. 17th 1902

My Dearest Helen

Am comfortably located in the pleasant writing room of the Billings Club. Mr Segur the Genl. Agt. of the Burlington RR located me almost as soon as I arrived this morning and I have the best the town affords. Am Mr. Segurs guest here at the Club and he is doing all he can to make me feel at home and happy. Will leave for Frannie [Wyoming] tonight at 11:50 p.m. and should get into Cowley [Wyoming][2] to-morrow. Am feeling well and have got rid of my headache. Felt quite indisposed yesterday but am myself again today. Spent last night up to midnight in Butte [Montana], walking the streets and doing anything to kill time. Did not go along the red-light streets for the reason that I was all alone and I thought it unsafe. There was no theatre or I should have gone. The Elders were not in as usual and so I had time on my hands. Went to a good restaurant and had supper, wrote up my Journal & wanted to write you but had no paper. This is the first letter I have written since leaving home but must write several today.

Darling I wish you would write Bp. Henry W. Esplain at Orderville[3] and tell him how much you apreciate those nice aples. The snow is falling softly and just as straight down as it ever does in Salt Lake; quite unusual I should say for Montana. Up to now there has been practically no winter. Well dear heart I love you more fondly than ever. You are my good Angle girl and I feel so gratefull for you and our little "Lambies". Bless them I should like to see them today. Tell them Pappa sends love and kisses to them. Sweet heart I wish you would send Ma a nice pair of those aples. We can afford to be magnanimous although you feel that you have been wronged. We won't allways have our parents with us and when they are gone we shall not be sorry we have treated them well. I know you are kind hearted and I hope you will be good to Mother as I know you have allways wanted to be.[4]

May heaven bless you dear and may he help us to love the Gospel most of all so that we may have and love each other allways. I want you to be happy darling. You have made my life happy and your sweet, loving influence does so much to help me to do right. You indeed have been and are my Good Angle.

God bless you precious wife. With a heart full of love for you and the darlings you have born me. I am Your

Affectionate
Owen

[Letter 32: Owen to Helen]

[*LDS First Presidency letterhead, handwritten*]

Burlington, Wyo.

~~Salt Lake City, Utah~~ Jan. 21ˢᵗ 189_02.

My Dearest Wife:

We held Conference at Cowley Sunday and yesterday. The Lord was with us by His spirit and we had a time long to be remembered. The new meeting-house at Cowley is just fine and will seat 500 people.[5] It was crowded at every meeting. We have held a ghrist of meetings both religious and business. Woke up Conference with a fire ball last night. I had to attend a meeting and did not get there until about 9:30. Danced the first time with Sister Welch[6] and about three times with "others". David

[Patten Woodruff] was there and enjoyed it imensely we took each other home about midnight and slept together. (When David got through talking horse). Bro. Welch[7] and I drove here to David's house today. We intend to go to Wood River tomorrow, remain at the Ranch two days and then return to Burlington. Will leave for home about 29th or 30th but will go via Cheyenne and could not just say when I shall reach home.

It has been snowing here a little this evening and looks quite threatening. The weather has been just beautiful, almost like spring. They have more beautiful weather here in a year than in any place I know of. Torrey[8] is standing watching me: he says tell Jerry and Aunt Helen [Woodruff] I send my love. All the folks are as well as usual. David went to Conference and feels fine in his duties.[9] Burlington & all the settlements are improving and increasing rapidly. So many people ask about you and want you to come back again. Would like to take a peep into my little cozy nest at home. The weather is not cold but I am well prepared for storm God bless and be with you my darling. I love you fondly as always. Give my love to our parents, babies, Jerry, Anna, Blanche and all.

Affectionately Your Husband
Abraham O. Woodruff

Bro. Welch says: give Helen my kind love and David says: we all join in.

O.

[Letter 33: Owen to Avery]

[no letterhead, typed]

Oaxaca, Mex. Feb. 29th. 1902.

My Dear Mattie÷

Your last letter was received before starting home and was very much appreciated by me. I just returned a few days ago and had the "Grip" two days coming home which completely used me up while it lasted but left me almost instantaniously^,^ as it came on.

Taking all things into consideration I had a very successfull journey but am oh so glad to get home again. My work here has pilled up until I hardly know where to start. Conference is at hand and I can not hope for any let up untill it is over. I want to see you very much and have been wondering if I had best try to come up or get you to come down and have about concluded the latter would be the best plan^;^ what do you think about it? If it is agreeable to you^,^ should be glad to have you come down and stop with Mary as you did before. Write her when you will be down and some of them will meet you unless you think it would be best to come down yourself. But in either event let her know when you can come. Would like very much to have you attend this Conference as if it is agreeable to you we can possibly arrange for you to go on a visit before the next one. This is one thing I want to talk to you about. Was sorry to hear of Heber's trouble and hope he is well before now. I saw Uncles while out on the trip and stayed with them one night. There seems to be some attraction between us but they cannot understand just what it is. Ask father to come down and see us while he is down. I hope this will find you enjoying good health and that we may soon have the pleasure of meeting again. It has been a long time since I last saw you. May God bless you dear and may He guide us in all things. I feel that you have a good excuse now for going to see "Mary" and that it will be alright. Will speak to them about it. With best love to yourself, Mary and H.T. [Avery's sister and brother] and hoping to see you soon I am,

Affectionately,

Ivan

[Letter 34: Owen to Avery]

[*no letterhead, typed*]

Oaxaca, Mexico.

March 17th. 1902.

My Dear Mattie÷

I have thought a great deal about you since I last saw you for I was so sorry you felt bad. I have not been able to quit thinking about it. It is my intention to be down about next Wednesday and hope I can see you. Ask H. to call on the Prest. at the story about four o'clock that day and ask him if I am in town.

Am going away this afternoon and will not be back before calling as I suggest.

I do hope you have been feeling well since your return. It seems too bad that you should feel bad you have been so good and brave. I know the Lord will be good to you and send you comfort.

It is cold and stormy here. We have had so many deaths of late but no doubt you have heard all about them. I would so much rather talk than write I will cut this short and get ready for the trip. All the folks are well M—— [Helen] felt so bad to think you were not feeling happy as usual and hoped it was not her fault.

God bles you dearest. May He comfort and cheer you at all times and may we have a happy meeting in the near future.

With love to the "children" and much to yourself,

Affectionately,

Ivan

[Letter 35: Owen to Avery]

[*no letterhead, typed*]

Oaxaca, Mexico.
May Ist. 1902.

Dear Mattie÷
I reached home and found all well. The storm has done a great deal of good. I hope you got home without any unpleasantness the morning I last saw you.

Enclosed please find the check I mentioned to you. It is my intention to spend a few days over in the section where I told you I was going and will be back some time next week. Did not see anything of M—— [Mary Clark] at the station. Our M—— [Helen] is not feeling well. Poor girl thinks there is something the matter again and she feels very miserable.[10] If you were a little nearer I would be tempted to get you to make "curls" some waists as Mamma feels so miserable and has so much to do it is hard for her to keep up with her sewing and all the other work. Mamma is feeling well in spirits however and that is the main thing after all.

I hope you will be blest in your school and that all may be well with you God belss you and keep you happy and well.

With love,
Ivan

[Letter 36: Owen to Avery]

[*no letterhead, typed*]

Oaxaca, Mexico.
June 7th. 1902.

My Dear Mattie÷
A few days ago, just as I was starting off on a trip I asked Bro. C——. to send you a check which I hope you received alright. He sent it to sister and the check was made to her also.

I think it would be a good thing for you to draw your money from the Bank before you leave as it may save you a trip back there. Get a Cashier's Check in your favor and I will tell you what to do with it when I see you. Please let me know at once when you intend to go home and who you expect will meet you. Will they have a covered rig? If I do not get to go with you I wish you would tell Uncle Wilford[11] for me that I will be along and I should like him to see that I get over without any one knowing where I have gone. How about hired men at the Ranch? Do you think it will be allright to go when you do? Kindly answer these questions at once so I can make my arrangements. If you think it would be better to come over later why possibly I cann arrange that. I should like to stop about a week or ten days.

I do hope you have ben blessed in your studies and been able to accomplish all you desired to do along these lines. I have prayed the Lord would bless you to this end. I have been about used up with a sprained back for several days but am improving and hope to be able to so arrange my affairs so as to go over just when it will please you best.

As I hope to see you I shall cut my note short and hpe we may meet and have a good, long visit. I saw Bro. W——— . he intends to return here before he goes home.

Give my love to M——— [Mary Clark] and accept best your self.

Affectionately,

Ivan

P.S. Address me c/o Box B. I will get it quicker.

[Letter 37: Owen to Avery]

[*no letterhead, typed*]

Oaxaca, Mex.
July 4th. 1902.

Dear Mattie÷

I have just received a letter from Sister Clayson who will accompany you South. She desires to leave this City [Salt Lake] on the 15th. of this Month. We would like it if you will come at least a couple of days before the date mentioned as I would like you to go through the Temple and have a little visit as I suggested.

Come to the place which I mentioned to you and if she should not be at home why come over and someone will see if we can find her for you. I have not received one word from you since I last saw you and have wondered why you have not written. Will try to arrange transportation from Mt. Pelier [Idaho] as I suggested in my last.

It is very warm down here, mamma and the babies [Helen, Wilford Owen, Helen Mar, and June, who was born 24 June] just got home last night from where they have been visiting. We are all well. M——— [Helen] asked me if I gave the "folks" her love and I told I did not remember that I did.

Just like a man to forget the things he should remember. Prest. T. [Edward "Teddy" Bennion] wants to know when you will be down and he wishes Mary [Clark] would come too.

Please write and tell me if we can expect you as the sister will want to know before long.

Address Isaac W. Brown, care of James Cushing, Box B.

Give my love to all the folks. I hope you will have had time to prepare and will be greatly benefited by your visit at home. With love and blessing,

Affectionately,

Ivan

[Letter 38: Owen to Helen]

[*LDS First Presidency letterhead, handwritten*]

Auburn, Wyo.

~~Salt Lake City, Utah~~ July 12th 1902

Mrs Helen W Woodruff.

Dearest Helen:

By my journal you will see what we have been doing of late. We came into the folks [Hyrum Clark family] quite unexpectedly but they have taken the whole camp in and are doing all they can to make our stop pleasant. They have no help and the girls [Avery and Mary Clark] have to work too hard. With ten in family and milking twenty five cows and making butter it almost makes slaves of sister Clark and the two girls who are old enought to be of genuine help have all they want to do and more than they ought to do. You will see by my journal that Van [Beebe], their boys and I have had quite a days sport to-day. I want so much to hear from you and babies. I have been having trouble again and feel almost discouraged with my condition at times but suppose the Lord knows how much He see fit to try me in this way. I shall be disapointed beyond measure if I do not get a letter from you at Vicktor, Freemont Co. Ida. Wish you would also write me next to Wilson, Uinta Co. Wyo. We expect to be there about the 20 or 22nd. Next write me to Dubois, Freemont Co. Wyo where we will be about three days later. Write in good time as these places only have a triweekly mail. Next write me to Sunshine. Please write me often dear, I so love to hear from you and nowadays you seem more like my own, sweet Helen in letters than you do when I am with you; for when I am with you I try you and when I am away you think of me as your other self, struggling and trying to do my duty just as you are trying. How much easier it is when we sustain each other and struggle together. I love you my darling Helen and for my life I would not have you alienate yourself from me. I feel that if you were to I could not live. I may have been unwise but God who knows me best knows I am as loyal to you in your position as I am to Him in his. Write me a dear sweet love letter again, such as Helen knows how to write to Owen. May Gods best blessings be yours dear. With fondest love

Owen

[Letter 39: Helen to Owen]

[*no letterhead, handwritten*]

Salt Lake City, July 20,/02.

My Dearest Owen: —

Have received your two lovely letters and cannot tell you how much they are appreciated. Did not know where to address letters excepting to Vicktor [Idaho].

Josie[12] has been with me a week. Says she will stay until I get tired of her & begs me to tell her when that time comes. She and I are such congenial companions and so thoroughly enjoy each others society that if she adheres to her promise her visit will be a prolonged one.

Am tied hand and foot with the babies and scarcely know what would become of me if Josie were not here. She is such a dear good girl, loves the children & has such remarkable patience with them (a virtue I lack).

We are having such a good visit to-gether. Am afraid the days would be long and lonely without her but as it is the weeks are flying and they cannot go too fast to suit me.

Sisters Cowley, Harker and [Mamie] Thomas came to see me and they talked so much about our baby that Wilma & Ray came down next day expecting to see a "<u>wonder</u>." Well, dear, our little "June" rose-bud is sweet. Every body says she is perfectly lovely. Josie goes into extacies over her, and I can scarcely do a thing but <u>love</u> her. You should see Helen Mar "take on" over her. She simply goes wild over "Junie" as she calls her. Josie went to Tabernacle and to see Bro. McMurrin, and came home feeling so bad it was difficult to cheer her up. And then Lloyd came home with her and she feels sorry to think he likes her for she says she knows just how it feels to love and be disappointed. She is broken hearted but doesnt reveal the fact. If I could only smother my feelings as she does and appear to feel perfectly happy I^'d^ rejoice; but am so weak in this regard. But I am going to try in future to hide my emotions for although I show my feelings so plainly they are never interpretateded correctly. Even you dear, who know me best, don't begin to understand me, i.e. my true motives. For you only have my actions to judge from and your conclusions are sometimes entirely wrong. One thing consols me; the Lord knows my heart and will, I feel sure, make allowance for ~~our~~ my wrong doing^s^

when he sees the motives which promt them. And am sure you would not think me so mean if you knew my heart as well as I know it.

Am sorry, dear heart, that you are having trouble with your throat again, wish I might be with you, but my travelling days are over, then too you know as well as I do that I am not the same comfort to you that I used to bee.

I think I understand you as well as it is possible for one spirit to understand another and perhaps, thro not seeing clearly your true motives for certain acts, have misjudged you, but I am as ready & willing to forgive as I am anxious to have you forgive. Dearest I have never doubted your loyalty to me and I trust you implicitely.

So great has been my confidence and trust in you that, were you ever to deceive me I would never have confidence in mankind again. But, dear I am never fearful on that score for it would be so contrary to your nature. Now you might think from the tenor of my letter that I am dissatisfied with my lot, but believe me dear Owen when I say such is not the case. I am as contented as can be and would not change one thing in all my circumstances. The only thing I would have changed is "my self," my stubborn selfish nature. But this can not all be done in a day I must struggle & wait. I am not a bit like I want to be.

Well I have used up all my paper and haven't said a anything. There is not much news to tell. Alice and Will have another baby girl.[13] Isn't it a shame they didn't get a boy. Just think how disappointed you would have been to have had three girls. Their girl was born on the 9th inst and we have just had the one letter.

We haven't a cow yet. Saw Mr. Walker a few minutes ago and hes said the cow had not "come in" yet. I love you dearest more than you can ever comprehend. More than any one the whole wide world and hope you may continue to love me. Ever praying for your health & happiness I remain as ever. Yours

Helen.

[Letter 40: Owen to Avery]

[*no letterhead, typed*]

Bethel [code name for Salt Lake City],
July 25th. 1902.

Dear Mattie÷

We were very happy tonight to get your letter of the 22nd. I am so sorry it took you a whole week to get to your destination. I cannot understand what could have caused you to lie over so long a LaJara and at other places but at the same time I feel thankfull that you were not sick. I am satisfied that it was through the blessings of the Lord that you escaped this unpleasant part in as much as you are predisposed to be train sich anyway.

We hoped you would drop a line back from diffirent points along the route and were getting quite anxious about you. Am glad you kept up your spirits considering your cheerfull invironments. You are certainly a brick. Possibly you could have been pretty blue for you and still merited some compliments from your companions. You say nothing about the connection at Springville. It must have been alright or you would have said so.[14]

M—— [Helen] and I expect to start for Illinois [code name for Big Horn Basin] in the morning and will be gone at least three weeks. You can catch me with a letter addressed to the Stake Prest. (You know his name) [Byron Sessions] if you answer this at once. Addresse him at Chicago. By the way if you follow out this suggestion or understand this it will give you practice in the use of your "cipher".

Prest. Roosevelt [President Joseph F. Smith] expects to attend the Conference at Chicago and I do so hope nothing will prevent his filling this appointment. It would be such a fearfull dissapointment to the Saints there.

I saw Uncle Marion[15] the other day and he said you hoped he "would send lots of people down." You no doubt will find there are lots of them there as you get acquainted. Brothers Clawson & McMurrin will be down to see you soon. I hope you will be able to keep cheerfull and I really think you will in as much as you did not dispair at the experience through which you have passed in reaching your destination. God bless you dear and keep you well and happy. With prayers for your welfare and best love in which M—— joins me I am affectionately,

Ivan [*handwritten*]

[Letter 41: Owen to Helen]

[*no letterhead, handwritten*]

Lovell, Wyo.[16]
Aug 5th 1902

My Dearest Helen÷
You will see by the field notes I enclose you herewith what we have been doing. Personally I have not been as well as I could wish but it seems the Lord is putting me through a trial in this matter and I will not complain. Am so thankfull that Prest. Young has been able to speak to the people in Conference and in Ward meetings as he has done.[17] He has been

filled with the Spirit of the Lord and last night in a little meeting here in Lovell made one of the speeches of his life. So far thank the Lord he has clinched every nail that I have driven in this country, which makes me feel most thankfull to the Lord. We start for the Natl. Park [Yellowstone] tomorrow and you can answer this letter at Wilson, Uinta Co. Wy. We may remain there a week. Your letter dear which I read at Sunshine was such a comfort to me. It was just like my darling, sweet Helen. It was really the first letter I have received from you while on the trip.

I love you dearest soul and I shall be so happy to hold you in my arms again and love the dear spirit that is not excelled in nobility and sweetness in all this world.

It gives me such joy to love you darling and may God send his choicest blessing and keep you safe and well for me. Kiss my little Lambies. Tell them Papa loves them and I want Wilford O. to be a man while papa is away and be good to Mamma and little sisters. I am better this morning and would be all right if I did not have so much to do. Van is just fine and really the main preacher and stay of the Camp. He has been as good as he could be to me. God bless you my blessed soul. I love you fondly and dearly. Don't worry about things at home. Do the best you can and that is well enough. I have never found fault with you for you have always done well.

Draw enough money to get you a dress for I want you to go out when I get home.

With fond love and kisses to you and the Lambies.

Affectionately Your Husband
Abraham O. Woodruff

P.S. Dearest:

Please drop a note to Sophronia Tucker Genl. Delivery and request her to call on you. Tell her I have no authority to release them from any covenant they have made with the Lord. They ought to have better sense then to ask it. You know the case dear & I can't trust it to anyone but you. You know how anxious they were, now let them sweat it out.

With love
Owen

[Letter 42: Owen to Avery]

[*letterhead, handwritten*]
The Cottage Inn
F. D. McCormick,
Proprietor

Oaxaca, Aug. 8th 1902

My Dear Mattie÷

I have not heard a word from you since the first letter you wrote but am in hopes there will be one waiting me on my return to Chicago. I am out here to meet Prest. Roosevelt and his party whom we expect to arrive here tomorrow from England [Canada]. M—— [Helen] is over in Illinois with our little son [Wilford Owen]. I am very anxious to hear from you and know how you like St. George [code name for Colonia Juárez, Mexico]. We expect to return to Bethel about the 24th. It has been quite cold here but no frost yet and I do hope it will keep off until the President sees what can be raised in this country. We went to the Ranch and found things in better shape than ever before and if it were not for the fact that we owe so much money we could get along just fine now. Will write you about the Conference later. I do hope it will be a success. You must write oftener dear; this makes the third letter I have written and only received one. I earnestly pray God may bless you and make your work pleasant to you. Am very anxious to know if you are <u>alright</u> yet, and am so glad you were not train sick.

God bless you dear and may you ever be precious in the sight of the Lord. With best love and blessings.

Affectionately

Ivan

[Letter 43: Owen to Avery]

[*letterhead, handwritten*]
The Grand Hotel
George F. Bennighoff, Proprietor

Billings, Montana Aug. 16th 1902

Dear Mattie÷

Your very much appreciated letter written from St George was received by me a few days ago while in Ill. I am happy to know you are so pleasantly located and were so kindly received. I feel most thankfull that the Lord is fulfilling to you the blessing I gave you. We have had a choice time over in Ills. with Prest. Roosevelt and party. It has been a joyfull time for the people and also for me. The Prest. spoke so kindly of me and gave his unqualifyed approval of what has been done. This is a great source of satisfaction to me. I feel so thankfull for the love and confidence of the best men in all the world. I know you have prayed earnestly for me and that you will rejoice with us when the Lord crowns my efforts with success. I feel so greatfull to the Lord for I realize that it is He who has brought us success. We will likely go ahead with the large project I spoke to you about. We expect to reach Bethel Friday morning.

Mattie [Helen] and M [Mary Clark] are with me. We did not make the trip we expected to for the reason it snowed about 2 1/2 ft. in the mountains. As soon as we get home we must prepair for our coming Conference and will have plenty of work until it is over. I hope to hear from you soon again. Will be glad to come down as soon as possible and help about the "lot." Am so glad you like it. Will continue to deposit your money until you say you need some. Write often dear as I want to hear from you. What is your condition? May God bless you richly, keep you happy and well. With best love and prayers for your well being.

Affectionately
Ivan

[Letter 44: Owen to Avery]

[no letterhead, typed]

Bethel, Aug. 22nd. 1902.

Dear Wife÷

Your welcome letter of the 14th inst. was received yesterday and I was indeed pleased to hear from you again. It seems to me you still owe me a letter or two. I am very glad you like the school and that every body is good and kind to you. The only thing I fear you are trying to do too much and I would not have you overwork for anything. If you are "alrigh^t^" I want you to be very carefull, especially at the period when you had your trouble before. Remember this is more than school or anything else. If you have so much you feel it a burden you should ask Brother Wilson[18] to relieve you of part of your work. I want you to just do enough so that you feel it a pleasure and not overdo. We had a fine trip and now I am home I find so much to do it will take me some time to catch up. Have got a cold in my head but if it don't go down I will be alright. M—— [Helen] is going to write to you but she has been so busy putting up fruit and caring for our large family of babies that she does not have much spare time. Yes Prest. T—— expects to go south. Tell M—— [Mary Clark] she need not get anxious for I will see that she is well provided for. I saw "Uncles" and "Aunties" up north. They are all feeling fine. We had a glorious time with the good people up there. We had a cold storm which made things disagreeable. I am thankfull you were happily disapointed with the place and your surroundings. I felt sure you would be for I always try to make you expect something a little inferiour to what you will really find to be the case. I am satisfied you have gone among some of the best people in the Church and I want you to thank President Ivins and Sister Ivins for me. They have always been so kind to me I do not hope to repay them only in the gratitude of my heart. You can go with safety to Prest. Ivins for council under every circumstance and I know he will treat you as he would one of his own daughters and will always give you inspired counsel.

I feel so thankfull that these kind hearted folks could give us a place in their home. If we decide to get a place there I wish we could get one with an orchard already on it for it would take so long to get one old enough to bear. I will continue to deposit your check until you say you want some sent down. Will talk with Prest. Ivins about coming down, the hunt and some other things. Do not be too sure about my coming down before the hollidays but will do so if my labors will allow me to do so. If you are sick down there I want either you mother or M—— [Mary Clark] to go down to be with you but as that is a matter of the future we can talk it over when we meet. Some of those good sisters down there who ought to be contented and thankfull where they are seem to be dissatisfied and complain to their husbands. I hope you will not get infected with this spirit and I know you will not. You have been a noble, good, girl and I feel so thankfull for you and the sweet spirit you have ever manifest. The Lord can not help but bless you for your nobility of spirit. God bless you dear, may He bless you richly in all thing. I remember you and pray for you. God bless and preserve you from every evil and harm. With love and blessings

Affectionately, Your husband,
Ivan

[Letter 45: Owen to Helen]

[*LDS First Presidency letterhead, handwritten*]
Victor, Ida
~~Salt Lake City, Utah~~ Aug. 25th 1902

Dearest Helen÷

We have just ended a splendid Conference and I shall start homeward this forenoon.

Prest. Young left here Saturday in a very critical condition and unless the Lord does something for him can not last very long. The last talk here made (at Lovell) was I consider the talk of his life. The way in which he bade me "good bye" has worried me considerable.[19] If all is well I hope to be home about Saturday.

Have only abbreviated my journal. Will you kindly get it up in good shape. By bye until we meet. God bless you with love to you and "the Lambies".

Affectionately
Owen

[Letter 46: Owen to Avery]

[*no letterhead, handwritten*]

Detroit, Mich.
Sept. 30th 1902.

Dear Mattie÷

I was much grieved on getting a letter from home to learn that you have passed through so serious a period but hope and pray that all may be well with you by this time. It is a great dissapointment to me as I know it is to you for I had hoped that all might be well with you and this would mean more to us than school or anything else. You must not feel bad that you made an innocent mistake the next time we shall be more carefull. God know your good true heart and he will bless you and when you get that way again you must not wash and do other hard work. I want to have that done for you. But never mind dear it could not be helped and you must have an extra one to make up for the one lost.[20] The Lord is blessing me on my Mission but about the time you were passing through your ordeal I felt very much depressed in spirit, which may have been partly the result of conditions at home. I feel so thankfull that M—— [Helen] went to see you. Bless her dear, good soul she is a noble hearted woman and I appreciate her interest in you so much. I am so thankfull for our unity and for the feelings of love you show towards each other. I want to live worthy of you and pray God you may be blessed in your lives during my absence. Unless I am held longer than I now expect will be home in about two weeks and will take advantage of the first chance to see you. Wish we could all be together to spend the hollidays but do not know how that can be. Unless I come when I expect to will write you when to find me by mail. Don't spare any means to make you comfortable as by writing M—— [Helen] she will send you what you need. Do be carefull dear and take the proper care of yourself. Don't lift things that are too heavy and when you are able give your physical culture considered attention, to make you strong when you are weak.

I regret that it is impossible for me to be with you when you need me so much. This is one of our trials. God bless and heal you and comfort your dear heart is the constant wish of your

Affectionate Brother
Ivan

Letter 47: Owen to Avery]

[*no letterhead, handwritten*]

St. Paul, Minn.
Oct. 18th 1902.

My Dear Mattie÷

Your much appreciated letter was received. Was happy to hear that all is well with you and hope you will realize your desires in connection with your years studies. Tell Father I want him to keep the horse if he will. I have two at home and that is one more than I need. If you will accept it I will give you that animal and we can pay Father for keeping it and raise some colts: as she is well bred and cost me about $130.00. Father can say he has bought her of me and of course use her as his own. She is a fine driver and not bad under the saddle. She had a swelling resulting from an abserated tooth that can be taken of I think by blistering and will get Father some medicine to treat it with when I see him.

Was sorry to hear that everything is "all right," but the Lord will overrule all for the best. Am enjoying my Mission very much but do not expect to be released until at least the middle of next month. A letter will catch me anytime at the same address, only write the first name in full as my initials are so much like my brothers we sometimes get "mixed".[21]

Will have many things to tell you when I am released as it will have been a long time since we last met and I have seen many new places of interest. I feel very anxious to do my work well and to enjoy the spirit of my calling which I fear at times I do not do to the fullest degree. I want you to pray for me and that I may allways do my duty and be kept clean from sin. This is my great desire.

We have had beautifull weather until today but not it is foggy and I am not as fond of foggy weather as I am of sunshine but then we appreciate the one by experiencing the other.

The Lord has been good to us and we ought allways to remember that, though He may occasionally send us cloudy weather. May God bless you dear and continually fill your life with sunshine and His choice blessings.

Accept of my love for you and M [Mary Clark]; also W.

Tell me where you have moved to.[22] With love and prayers for your wellfare.

Affectionately
Ivan

[Letter 48: Owen to Avery]

[*letterhead, handwritten*]
Cosmopolitan Hotel
Bourbon & Royal Sts. Near Canal
Jos. Voegtle, Prop.
European Plan

New Orleans, Oct. 26th 1902
My Dear Mattie÷
I hope you get the little package mailed to M [Mary Clark] and that you will enjoy looking at that strange fruit: if you do not enjoy eating it. It will no doubt keep some time. Have not heard from you for a long time but hope you are well.
This is the most Frenchi City in the U.S. It is very beautifull too and has a population of 300,000, made up of Negros, French and American. I fancy I hear you say: oh what a mixture but not so badly mixed after all as one would suppose, for the Whites hate the Blacks too much to mix with them very much: at least in marriage. If you are with me in my new field you will find me right at the mouth of the "Father of Waters" — the Mississippi River. None of this country is more than about ten ft. above sea level and if sometime she rolls her great banks over the City I shall not be surprised. Hope to be home by the 10th of Nov. if I get my release you know. Wish you were here to attend the Theatre tonight and take in the many interesting sights of this Sunny City. Will send you a rose, they are blooming everywhere here and it is almost like Summer. This may possibly be my last letter for some time. Am enjoying myself and feel well. With best love to you and Mary and with a prayer for your welfare and happiness.
                    Affectionately,
                    Ivan

[Letter 49: Owen to Avery]

[*no letterhead, typed*]
                    Oaxaca, Mex.
                    Nov. 9th. 1902.
My Dear Mattie÷
Have just returned home and am anxious to know how you are getting along as I have not heard from you for so long a time. I rather

expected to get a letter from you at the last City I visited but was disapointed. On returning home I find that just at the present time a terrible stir is being kicked up about some of our bretheren's affairs and on this account we will have to be most carefull fore a few months and I fear it would hardly be wisdom for me to make you a visit just at this time although I should like to see you very much indeed.[23] However unless we can arrange it for you to come down and spend the hollidays I will try to visit you if it is only to have a talk. What would you think about coming down to spend the hollidays? We have two people in the house that I should not like to trust but think I cann̄ arrange for you to stop somewhere I could see you and where you could go out to diffirent places, thus giving you a change from what you have had so long. I must see you as I have some plans to talk over with you. If you think you would like to go home for the hollidays why then I shall see you where you are before that time. I am anxious dear to have you do that which will make you most happy. I sympathize with you in that we are able to see eachother so seldom; but I hardly know how it can be otherwise untill we are out of school and then I have a plan which may be better in some respects.[24] I don't want you to feel bad dear but be patient. I fear that if you were to get into the condition you were in again you would have the same trouble if you continue in school. I feel to that it is quite important that you remain in school now as if you were to quit at this time it would attract more attention than it will for you to continue. I want you to do as you feel impressed however for I would not spoil our "prospects" for all the schooling you will get.[25]

M—— [Helen] said she feared you did not like your school and was sorry to find you feeling just a little blue. Now I don't want you to take one study you do not want to take but to suit yourself absolutely in these matters. Please write me at once what you would prefer to do during the hollidays and then I will lay my plans. May God bless and comfort you dear and in his own time send you some little comforts. With kindest love and wishes for your well-being, love to M—— [Mary] and T—— .

Affectionately,
Isaac W. Brown

[Letter 50: Owen to Avery]

[*letterhead, handwritten*]
Headquarters, Southwestern States Mission,
Church of Jesus Christ of Latter Day Saints.
P. O. Box 493. Office 1421 Locust St.

Kansas City, Mo. Nov. 21st 1902.

My Dear Mattie÷

Although I have not heard from you for a long time I trust all is well with you. If you had my address all the time I know you would write me as many letters as I write to you, but while we elders are travelling without purse or scrip, going from place to place we do not know what our address will be very far ahead. We came here to Austin, Tex. this morning to hold the Conference with the Elders and Saints of South Texas. We feel very much honored in having with us Apostle Woodruff and Prest. Duffin of our Mission. We called on the Governor of the State to-day and bore our testimony to him and had a very pleasant visit. Just as we were leaving Genl. Fred Grant called at the Capitol and we got to see him. He is you know a son of Prest. U.S. Grant. As the general and his party came into the Grounds some negro soldiers fired a can and then proceeded to load it again and while one poor fellow was ramming in the load it exploded and blew off his right arm and knocked him a great distance. We were among the first to get to him and found him unconscious and bleeding at the ears. I do not think he can live. Of course a Nigger is not considered worth much in Texas but I thought it a most pitifull sight.

I expect to be released at this Conference and If I am hope to accompany Apostle Woodruff and Prest. Duffin back to Kansas City in Galveston and New Orleans. Get your map and go with me. This is a very beautiful City with a population of about 30,000.

Down here it is still warm and many nice flowers are yet in bloom. Will enclose you one from Nauvoo. The people in this part of the Lone Star State are much superior to the ones I wrote you about last. Will try and mail you a "Persimmon." It would be nice to paint but will be better to eat: just cut it open and eat it, if you get it all right. We get any amount of Hazel nuts here; also Pecans, Hickory and Wallnuts. If I am released will be home about 5–10th of the Month. I hope you are feeling well dear and doing fine in your school. This will no doubt be your last year at school; though you may be able to attend Summer School. I don't want you to work too hard and get ill. What would you like to do for the hollidays?

I wish we could all be together yet that may be impossible. I would be pleased if you could enjoy this balmy Southern air for a time and hope that when you get out of school we may then have the pleasure of a trip together.

Am enjoying my labors just fine and know it must be because those I love are praying for me.

God bless you dear I love you and want to be as good, true and kind to you allways as you have ever been to me. Give my love to M [Mary]. Hoping this will find you comfortably located in your new quarters.

Affectionately,
Ivan

1903

[Letter 51: Owen to Avery]

[*no letterhead, typed*]

Chicago, Ill. Jan. 19th. 1903.

Dearest Mattie:

Your very welcome letter of the 7th. inst. reached me at this place yesterday and I assure you I was happy to hear from you again. It is pleasing to me to learn of the kind interest our good friends are taking in the erection of our dear little home. It is so kind of them but just like them for they are full of good deeds and my heart is full of gratitude to them to think that they look after my dear wife in my absence. My programme for the immediate future is rather uncertain until I get word from headquarters at Bethel and learn the wishes of our Chief [code for President Joseph F. Smith] about some things. It is my intention however to start from here to the Big Horn Basin next Friday and then will return to Bethel if there is no danger but if there is you may get a call before you expect it. I should not like to come down without Sister and without going to Bethel to get the things and if it is left to me to decide will come immediately after Conference instead of before. If I did this It would become neccessary for Sister to go down alone and take the things so as to be sure and be on time. Please find out the date Prest. I—— expects to be in Boise on his way up and if M—— [Mary] must go alone I shall arrange it so that she can be there on that day and I will then ask the prest. to see her safely through the C—— House.[1] Will write you again just as soon as I know something definite. I shall trust all things pertaining to the house to you and our friends. Do not depend on me one bit I will try to come and enjoy it and leave you to do all the work. Yes have the orchard trimmed if you can find someone who knows how to do it. I only want the sprouts cut away from the roots of the trees and little trimming outside of this done until I am there to see about it. Also the plowing you and the Bishop just manage this matter to suit you and I know it will be right. It has been very cold here and I have been on the go almost day and night. The weather has been beautiful today and for several days past. I want you to be very

104

carefull of yourself and I am sure if you follow out my many suggestions to you^,^ you will hardly have time to sleep.

Just adopt what you want and discard the ballance. I am very anxious for your welfare and do so hope and pray the Father will send us a perfect little darling, with a choice and beautifull spirit to make us happy in it's little life.

I often go out alone and pray for you girls and ask the Lord to care for you in my absence from home which I know he does.

God bless you dear, may sweet influences ever surround you for you are a brave, good girl.

> With much love and prayers
> for you always I am
> Affectionately,
> Your Husband,
> Ivan

[Letter 52: Owen to Avery]

[*no letterhead, typed*]

> Bethel, Me. Jan. 29th. 1903.

Dear Mattie: —

I leave tonight for Chicago and will likely be away for about one month. Enclosed you will find a draft for $150.

Hope you will keep account of the amounts you pay Pres. I—— for I will depend on your doing this.

Tell Brother [Junius] Romney I would prefer to have him use the "ballustrade" on the porch unless he can got the plain posts ten inches or one foot in diameter.

I think the square posts at the bottom and turned about would be alright if the railing is used but it would not look well without.

Was very pleased to hear from Brother Romney and I am satisfied he will do us a good piece of work.

Mary comes down quite often, she has gone to Farmington for a few days. She went Thursday morning to attend the funeral of "Aunt Mary Lizzie" of whose death you may have heard. She died of cancer and it is really a xxxxxa great blessing that she did not linger longer to suffer.

Brother J. [Joseph] M. Tanner's little daughter LeRue is reported to have consumption and the Doctor has taken her to St. George for her health. This seems very sad as she is her mother's only child. When we have health we have much to be thankfull for.

As only a short time is left me to get ready and I have been so busy today I hardly know where I am at I wil have to make this "note" short. It was H——— [Helen] who sent the collar I failed to tell you this before. We are all well and hope you too are enjoying the blessings of the Lord. H———joins me in love and says she will write you in a few days. Remember me kindly to the girls. God bless you dear and preserve you as sacred that you may have great joy in contemplating the blessings of the Lord to us. With love and blessings,

Affectionately,
Ivan

[Letter 53: Helen to Owen]

This letter went to Great Falls. [*handwritten in pencil in top margin*]
[*no letterhead, typed*]

Salt Lake City, Utah. Feb. 4th. 1903.

Dearest Owen:

For the last three or four nights I have tried to write you but something has happened to prevent my doing so. Last evening as I was getting ready to write^,^ Prest Bennion[2] and wife[3] came in. She came to stay with me while he went to meeting, thinking M[4] stayed here and she wanted to get better acquainted with her. Suppose she was very much disappointed at not finding her here. I sent for Sister [Elizabeth Campbell] Taylor to come over and we had a good talk until about ten o'clock when the brethren came from meeting and stayed until twelve and we had a warm discussion on a certain subject. Mary has made an impression all right I think but is as innocent of the fact as can be. Our ^""^little^"^ friend with the "big heart" has made arrangements for M. [Mary Clark] to come down to our house Saturday night to a little sociable of a few of the "select." I do wish you were at home, you are missing lotsof fun. Monday night Bros. [Frank Y.] Taylor and [George M.] Cannon telephoned me to go out to Edwin's with them that evening and be sure and bribg Miss "C" [Mary Clark]. We left here at six and went in a bob sleigh. There were thirteen of us and [*illegible stricken out line*] we were afraid something would happen on account of the unlucky number and sure enough a great many things did happen but nothing bad. Sister T.[5] said that ^"^it^"^ happened the next day in their family. She said some mean things that were uncalled for and she felt so badly about it that she sat up all night repenting. I told Bro. T. [Edwin "Teddy" Bennion] yesterday that I had not written to you yet I just hadn't had time so he wrote for me. He said he told you all about our sleigh ride and who went.

I went to the theater last Friday night and the play was fine. Your mother went with me and we enjoyed it immensely. Yesterday Lutie had Bro and sister Taylor, sister Kelch, Ray and John and Gusta and I up to her home to dinner and we missed you very much. Naomi[6] had her sewing club at her home yesterday all the MacDonald's you know and I went over for awhile.

Owen has just come in with his feet sopping wet and I have had to whip him and with all the noise there is here at present I fancy this will be a jumbled up letter and I beg you to overlook all mistakes and I will try a write a better one next time.

It seems like I miss you more than ever this time and I wish you would write often and I will try to do the same. If we must be separated so much we shall have to resort to writting to make up for it. Now did you ever hear such a clumsy sentence as that last? I was just in the middle of it when Naomi came in and asked me if Emma Rose[7] could come down and stay while she goes to meeting and I forgot just what I had planned to say.

Don't you wish you were here? We have all our own children and Emma Rose [Butterworth] and Ruby [Freeman] besides. You have tried to write under similar circumstance and can sympathise with me. I will not try to write more but will write again when conditions are more favorable.

I love you most ardently, my dear and pray God to bless you every day that all the desires of your heart may be granted unto you and that you may be successful on this trip especially.

I am as ever yours Ioderly,
Helen.

[Letter 54: Helen to Owen]

[*LDS Church letterhead, typed*]
Mar. 5th. 1903.

My Own Dear Husband: —
Your letter asking my advise on the business proposition, came about fifteen minutes ago and I take, or rather make, this opportunity of a answering. While I feel rather dubious about giving my ^"^yes,^"^ or "No^,^" to your question I have every confidence in the business firm you mention^,^ and feel that while we may feel weighed nown for awhile with the debt^,^ that we will come out all right in the end.

"Nothing ventured nothing gained" [*underline added later by hand*] says the old addage, I feel that we cam make this venture and if we should find that we have made a mistake later on^,^ I will bear my share of the blame. Now you know that I am answerin^g^ on the spur of the moment^,^ not having time to think very much on the question and it is not usually my way of doing, but I feel safe in saying^,^ I <u>know</u> [*underline added later by hand*] you have been praying that I might give an answer that would meet the approbation of our Heavenly Father. I feel impressed that it will be all right for you to go ahead and borrow the money. I like the idea <u>very</u> [*underline added later by hand*] much of your getting interested in things of this kind^,^ where you feel that competent men have the business in charge, than to unbertake farming or stock raising when you cannot have your eye on the business personally. I feel gratified over the results of the "Logan Knitting Factory,"[8] investment, as there was a check came a few days ago for ~~$120.~~ $120.50 One Hundred Twenty Dollars and Fifty cents and I am going up to pay the interest at the bank this afterno^on^. I went up yesterday and forgot to take the check and told George M.[9] that ~~In~~ I had come eXpressly for the purpose of paying it. He said not to bother about it until you came home but as long as the check is here I will take it up to-day. Susie [Bennion] and I are going down to Provo to-morrow night and I will stay a week. Be sure and tell me in your next letter when you will be home. I am taking a lot of sewing down with me and expect to get it all done. Anna[10] is so home sick to see her folks in Eden [Utah] that she was determined to go up there so I thought it would be better for me to go than to stay at home alone, then I will be saving her wages and coal and food for a week and I hope to get out of debt this month by managing this way. The two boards meet at Sister Dougall's next Wednesday. You will not be here^,^ neither will I.

The cow and calf are doing fine, the latter is a little beauty, I hope we can raise it. I did the feeding for about a week myself^,^ and then Will [McEwan] came over and insisted on doing the chores. I think they want the milk and and do not feel like taking it without helping in this way. Will and Alice have bought a building spot in Sugarhouse ward and are going to build soon. It is raining, haling and blowing furiously to-day and how I do hate to go up town^,^ but I <u>must</u> [*double underline added later by hand*] or this letter will not go until to-morrow night and I want you to get it as soon as possible. You will not wonder at the number of mistakes I make when I tell you that Emma Rose [Woodruff] has been here playing with our three <u>noisy</u> [*double underline added later by hand*] little tots all the morning and I am trying to write in the midst of it all. You know from your own experience that it is next to impossible to do so.

I have been so extremely busy since you left that the time has passed so rapidly I scarcely know where it has gone to and you will soon be home again before I get half done that I anticipated.

We are all well <u>dear</u> [*underline added later by hand*]^,^ and doing the best we can with everything at home. I love you with all my heart and hope you love me as much in return. I am proud of you and always glad that you are my husband and cannot get away from me if you should want to. You have my full confidence and I appreciate the fact that you show by your acts that you have confidence in me. Well darling goodbye, if I keep on writing I will not get up town before the bank closes. Ever praying God to bless you in all your labors^,^ keep you <u>well</u> and <u>bring</u> you <u>safely</u> [*underlining added later by hand*] home ~~is~~ I am as ever,

Yours Hopefully,

Helen Winters Woodruff. [*signature handwritten*]

P.S. We get five or six eggs every day that is when Ford [new nickname for Wilford Owen] and Donald[11] don't get ahead of us and break them. [*added later by hand*]

[Letter 55: Owen to Avery]

[*no letterhead, typed*]

Oaxaca, Mexico
May 2nd. 1903.

My Dear Mattie÷

I hope it will be disapointing to you as I assure you it is to me that I shall not be able to come up to the closing exercises of the College. I must leave for the Basin today and will be gone for about two weeks then I will have to go to Idaho for about two weeks more. After returning from my last trip which was quite a hard and long one I hoped to be able to come up but we have been in our Conference eversince until last night.

Was very sorry you did not get my letter for so long a time but I was very glad indeed to finally get a letter in return from you.

I feel most thankfull and pleased that you will be able to graduate as we have hoped. You did just righ to conclude to take the Summer School work. I have talked with Bros. T and Wilson about the proposed plans for next Winter and Brother Wilson has kindly consented to go up with Bro. T to see you and give you any aid he can by way of suggestion for your Summer School Work. Brother Guy C. Wilson is the principal of our Juárez Stake Academy[12] and I am sure you will like him very much when once you becom acquainted with him. He is one of the choicest spirited men in all the Church. I want to arrange to have an out with you and then to have another visit with you in this southern land. Will see you just as soon as possible. Bro. T. [Edwin "Teddy" Bennion] has invited M—— [Mary

Clark] to go to L.[Logan] with him and I think she will do so. Will send
something to you by her.

Ever since I received you letter I have prayed for your success and I
know the Lord will bless you.

Hoping your graduating exercises may be most happy for you and
that God may bless you richly I am with love and blessings,

Ivan

P.S. Enclosed find Check.

[Letter 56: Owen to Avery]

[*no letterhead, typed*]

Oaxaca, Mexico.
June 29th. 1903.

Dear Mattie÷

We arrived home after one of the most pleasant outings we have
ever enjoyed. We voted the outing a therough success.

On the way over to Mt. P. [Pelier] we caught about fifty fine trout
which we brought home. While catching them however we got a glorious
soaking but found refuge from the storm under the hospitable roof of
Bro. & Sister McGavern at the old Cozzens Ranch. We changed our clothing and enjoyed the ride ver very much as it was so cool and delightfull.

I only spent one night at home and then had to start for another
Conferce. The folks who stopping down south are all well though I have
not seen v much of them.

I received a letter from Bro. Wilson to the effect that he would start
south today. I knew it would rush you too much to be here in time to go
today so I saw him and arranged for you to accompany a Sister Teacher
who will go in about two or three weeks.[13]

I will arrange for you to get a reduced rate and will either notify Uncle
Wilford or have the Agt. instructed to sell you a reduced ticket to this City.

I hope you will enjoy your visit and make the most of it as it will be
hort. Have not yet received the check. Be sure and settle with your Father
for "Jane".

It is frightfully warm here and I long for a cooler clime especially in
the middle of the day when the sun pours down with such intensity. Give
my love to the folks and tell them that both of us had a most enjoyable
time while we were your guests.

With love and blessings,

Affectionately,
Ivan

[Letter 57: Owen to Avery]

[*no letterhead, typed*]

Bethel, Sept. 2nd. 1903.

Dear Mattie÷

You are again delinquint in writing to me as this is the second one I have written you since I last heard from you. When you went away I resolved I would write you more often than I had done before and when it is possible for me to do so I do not want to break my resolve. A few days ago I wrote Mary [Clark] inviting her to stay at our home when she comes down to conference and to bring father ofcourse. Have not heard from her and cannot say whether they will come or not but I hope they will.

It is very stormy and cold here just now.

It is the intention of Uncle J.M. [Joseph M. Tanner] and I to make a tour of the country now lying between us and arrive in Germany [code name for Mexico] about Nov. 1st.

A great deal of extra labor has been placed upon me in connection with our new Canal project in Ill. The scheme is to irrigate some 50,000. acres and the Canal will cost $200,000. this is one of the extra little things which your husband has to look after just now.

I do hope you will not make the acquaintance of some of those disaffected "widows" in that country. People who should naturally be most greatfull for some priviliges oft times are the most ungreatfull and I do not care for you to get too well acquainted with people of this character.[14]

Am thankfull to the Lord that you have something to occupy your mind for I am satisfied you feel happier for your work and the time will pass quickly. Brother C—— [Cowley] who has just returned with Prest. Mc. [McMurrin] says he almost envies me. You made quite an impression on him and he has quite got the spirit of the principle. You may have more company. Let us hope it will be of the best variety. What would you like me to bring you?

I forgot to ask Mary to bring anything down they might wish to send you but she will likely think of it. It makes me happy to know that you dear are contented and happy in your labors. God bless you dear wifie, may you always be favored with His holy spirit to make you happy.

With best love and prayers for your welfare always,

Affectionately,

Your husband, Ivan

[Letter 58: Helen to Avery]

[*no letterhead, typed*]

Bethel, Oct. 4th. 1903.

My Dear Sister.

It will soon be two months since you left here and I have not written you yet.[15] I hope you will forgive me for this negligence and I <u>will</u> try to do better in future.

I am so glad to know you have found such warm friends and are so pleasantly surprised with the place. I think you made up your mind that you would be contented when you left home, and that I know, has a great deal to do with your present spirit of peace and happiness. We can make our lives just about what we will and if we are continually looking for something to feel badly about and for some body to treat us unjustly we ~~can~~ can always find plenty to worry about and make ourselves miserable. On the other hand if we look for blessings and look to the future for the realization of our hopes we can be contented wherever we are. I have gone off on a tangent that sounds very much like preaching and you do not need preaching to one bit; you are just doing fine, it is myself that I need to labor with, however I will leave that for some other time and proceed to tell you some ^"^<u>bits</u>^"^ of news that may or may not interest you, but trust they will.

We had a very pleasant tripp to Illinois and all the way from here to Pueblo I thought of you^;^ for you had such a short time before gone over the same route. Wasn't the scenery sublime? I enjoyed the whole trip but ^got^ homesick for my baby girls the last week and that marred my peace of mind somewhat. The people treated us perfectly lovely and some times I am "a bit" suspicious that it is not on my own account that it is so^;^ but on account of the great love & respect they have for my husband. They simply adore him out there and he merits it too, and it pleases me when I see that the people have this great regard for him, knowing so well how earnestly and prayerfully he has worked for their interests.

We came home and found the "little uns" well and very glad to see their parents again. It must have seemed <u>ages</u> to them but they were so well taken care of that they did not mind it so much after all. One of my neighbors actually had the audacity to say that they were cared for better while I was away than when I am at home. How would that strike you?

Conference started this morning and I have my full quoto of visitors. I have two young ladies ~~fro~~ and one Bro. from the Big Horn and three others making their home with us and Anna and I are going to get supper for about a dozen people. Am not going out myself to conference as I take up too much of the sidewalk and the streets are crowded anyway.[16]

We expect Mary down to stay with us during conference, that is Papa wrote for her to come but knowing your mother's present condition[17] and realizing just how she feels I will not be surprised if she does not come this time and if not we shall try to have her come in April. Bro T. thinks a great deal of M. and if he would only send her to Germany it would be fine for you. M. is a sweet girl I think a great deal of her.

How is your health? Write and tell me all about yourselffor I am very anxious to know. I am feeling fine with the exceptions of a great many aches and pains that are perferctly natural to my condition. I am very thankful for the health and strength that we are all blessed with for there is no blessing that I prize more greatly that health, and I have been blessed exceedingly in this respect during my lifetime.

Bro. and Sister Grant returned from Japan last Sunday a week ago to-day; and to say that I was glad to see them is putting it mildly.[18] Sister is not feeling a bit well but think perhaps It is due to the long journey home think she will be better soon. Our good Bro. from your locality has not arrived yet that is, we have not seen him but suppose he will be here later. We are anxious to see him to hear from you as he will tell us all about you.

Now write to me often , just open your heart to me any time and I want to prove to you that I am your sincere friend and will always comfort you and help you when ever I can. I want you to keep all in your heart that I tell you^;^ and we must all stand by each other and be a unit in all things. We must uphold the one at the head and do his bidding. This is hard for me some times for I have such a strong will of my own, but whenever I do as he says I am always in the right and although I can not always see it at the time I see it afterwards.

Now good bye dear and may God bless you,

I am as every yours Sincerely,

May.

[Letter 59: Helen to Owen]

[*no letterhead, hand written*]

Salt Lake City, Oct. 27, / 1903

My Dearest Owen: —

Your dear letter written at the "Alvarado" came to-day and could you have seen the tears course down my cheeks as I read and re-read its contents you could perhaps understand how truly I appreciated it and value the love of the dear soul who penned it. It came from your true heart I know and found quick responce in my own. The thots and emotions you have expressed are identical with my own. Our Souls are so closely allied with each other that it seems impossible for one to have a thought or feeling that the other does not experience. I know that when your dear heart is tried mine aches from sympathy if not from the same cause.

You want me to write you how I feel since you left me. Well, dear, my feelings have been so many and so varied that were I to depict them all you would think me a queer mortal indeed. You know well enough I am moody and the moods have changed with the days. I've had <u>blue</u> days and bright days, and days when my heart has been a stone. With my independent spirit and my will power I builded a wall of reserve about myself until it seemed almost adamant but when your sweet love letter came the wall <u>fell</u> and great was the fall thereof. I was humbled to the earth and was ready to don sack cloth and ashes. To think you could be so forgiving and so generous as to write your recreant naughty girl such a beautiful letter when you had received such undeserved ill treatment from her, made me feel how mean I really am.

Well, dear since the arrival of <u>that</u> letter I have thought and thought of the many sweet experiences of our lives together and have lived again those happy days when first you took me to your heart and then to "<u>our</u>" home. How free from care and sorrow those days. We were children then, boy and girl together. I remember how I used to watch and wa^i^t for your home coming and when you came would always welcome you with a smile and a "bebe kiiss" (I can't spell German). How we used to sit for hours and never tire of telling each other of our love for each other. And that same love still lives in my heart for you dearest, only increased ten fold by the cares and burdens which come to us and made more pure and holy by the heart aches and sacrafice our Father has required at our hands. I would indeed be faint hearted to turn away from you now when as, you say, you need me most. Almost any one can be true while all is sunshine and gladness but it takes a stout heart and great faith to remain devoted when the storms of life come. I want to be a <u>strong</u>, <u>brave</u>, woman and I mean to be with your help and the blessings of the Lord. I want to love you and stand by you in all the trials and labors of your life. The first is <u>easy to love you</u>. But to give you support when I am tried is ^not^ so easy. I am ashamed that I should cause you one moments pain or sorrow when I realize better than any one else the great load you have to carry and the many responsibilities you you have to bear. I do want to be a true help meet to you that you may always love and trust me. Then I ought to be happy. I ought to know your heart by this time, having lived so near to it, but Satan tries to make me think that because of a change in circumstances our hearts must also change. Only yesterday I said to Mother that my happiness for the first three years of our married life was so complete that were I to have no more in this life I ought to feel satisfied; for truly it was a foretaste of Heaven. Well dear I wrote this far last night and it was ten o'clock. Anna came in from Ogden just then and June started to cry with the ear ache. The spell was broken or I do not know how long my letter would have been. Was awake nearly all night with June and my own aches, and don't feel extra bright this morning. The children are well but into more mischief. Naomi is doing fine. Dr. Allen[19] called yesterday and said she could stand on her feet now and go for a ride the last of the week and the next time he saw her he wanted her to come to his office. Its the only time he has called. I will write you once more at Juárez and tell you the news this is a love letter. The children talk of Papa every day. Ford says tell him I want two sacks of marbles when he comes and tell him [I love him and I love mama too. *written sideways in upper margin*] I will not write more to-day. I love you with all my heart and ever pray for the rich blessings of Heaven to attend you in all your labors.

I am as ever your affectionate
Helen.

[Letter 60: Helen to Owen]

[*no letterhead, handwritten*]
Salt Lake City Nov. 1,/03.

My Dearest Owen: —

This is Fast Day and on account of the starving condition in which I find myself I'm fearful that this letter may not prove satisfactory to either of us. Last night Prest. [Frank Y.] Taylor brought a letter over for me to address to you. He asked me to read it before sending it and after doing so am certain it will give you great joy to read it as it is written in such a kindly spirit and exhibits such true brotherly love that I know you will appreciate it thoroughly. I'm afraid you will not be pleased that he read your letter before the Priesthood meeting tho, for I know it was not your purpose to have it known of men, but that it was a desire to do good eminating from your generous heart, like unto none other in the world.

Bro. Taylor told you that we were all at his home to dinner yesterday. Sister T. gave us one of her lovely dinners and we all thourroughly enjoyed it. Bro. Grant and his two wives [Gusta Winters and Emily Wells] and mother [Rachel Ivins Grant] besides your wife, son, and mother [Emma Smith Woodruff] were all the invited guests. It being Wilford Owen's birthday he had a fine time. He says to tell you Grandma gave him a Dollar and he wants you to take him up to the Bank when you come home, so he can deposit it. Sister Taylor and I went up town for a ride last evening and we had a good talk. She was feeling fine. Says its the first day she has felt natural for a long time. But my, she is frail and meek in her body. She is a good noble woman I only wish I could be as good but that is entirely out of the question.

Aunt Naomi is getting along nicely, it is surprising how well she looks and feels. Yesterday she went out for a ride and was mending stockings when I went in in the morning. Clara [Beebe] is down at your mother's to-day. She's so afraid Van will not get back for her "Tea party." I am trying to think how I could fittingly and appropriately celebrate your birthday and have about decided to have my contemplated Xmas party on your natal Day. Wouldn't that be all right?

I went to the matinee last Wednesday to see "Ben Hur."[20] I think it one of the finest plays or the best one I have ever seen. The public nearly went wild over it. Anna and William went Friday night and although it was the eighth performance they had to pay a Dollar each for standing room in the 2nd circle.

Delia, Lide Brown and Anna Rose came up for the Theater. Poor Delia, I feel so sorry for her. She has so little enjoyment or happiness in this life and to add to her trouble, Mr. Booth scolded Milton for something which Milton thot he did not deserve so he has left home and gone to Idaho.[21]

Sister Minnie Robison has a fine son all doing well and especially Joe. Wilma thinks she may add to the list again too. Nabbie Spencer is up to be married next Wednesday and wishes you were here to perform the ceremony.

Gusta is feeling so much better and looks just fine. Oh dear, I wish I were over my trouble. I'm so worried and still there is no cause for alarm more than usual I suppose, only it seems natural for a mother to dread it more every time. Bro. Grant gave me a lovely blessing a few nights ago but it seemed more for you than for me.

Well my dear heart, I wish I could say something to encourage you but do not know ^what^ it shall be more than that I love you with all my heart and soul and want to be a help rather than a hindrance to you, but I fail so many times. But I intend to keep trying and perhaps some day I'll succeed, at least partially, in reaching the standard I am aiming for. Give my love to M [Avery]. Tell her I was pleased to get her letter and will answer soon. Tell her not to send my letters to Helen Winters any more, it caused more excitement at the Prests. Office. Jimmy C. would hardly give it up. And Bro. Winter asked Gusta if she knew of any body by that name and sent the letter to her. I made explanations to Gusta and she wasn't the least bit surprised. Well dear hear I will not write more this time but send you bushels of love and kisses from Mamma and babies.

Affectionately,
Helen.

[Letter 61: Helen to Owen]

[*no letterhead, handwritten*]
S.L.C. Nov. 11, 1903.

My Dear Owen: —
As it is not quite time for the Postman to call thought I would add a few more lines.

Bro. Grant leaves to-day "for sure," so they say; but he has been going every day for a week so I'll not believe what they say until I hear he has gone.

I never saw such people to change their plans. Every day Gusta telephones me about their new program. They have bought and sold two or three homes for Lutie and also for Gusta. They first bought Bp. [Nelson A.] Empey's corner and were going to tear down that house and build a new one for Gusta, and Lutie was going to buy (?) Aunt Emily's home. Next thing Gusta bought and had the deed made out in her name a lovely little house on the corner of 2. and 1st Street just above Sister [Maria Young] Talmage's. Now she has sold that to Lutie and she and Grandma will move in this week and Gusta will remain in the old home until Heber returns and then she will have a house built on Bp. Empey's lot between his place and Sloans. They have had so many more plans that I can not tell them all. Gusta says Heber's scheeming machine works like a "<u>buzz</u> <u>saw</u>."

You say send the cow away when I get tired of her, but I feel that we cannot afford to do that as milk has raised in price now. You only get 16 qts. for a Dollar. Our cow gives just a little more than a qt. each ~~d~~milking, but that is better than buying it. The girls have milked until lately I have learned and do the milking myself. I don't mind that part of it at all but it is taking care of the cow I dislike. I put her in the barn at night of course have to clean out the stable every day and ^my^ taste as you know doesn't run in that line. I always thought it a small chore until I have had actual experience and now I have sympathy ~~with~~ ^for^ any body who has it to do. I will continue tho until all my "labors" are over.

Now I do not want you to cut your visit short on my account for I will get along some way as many women have to do I would of course appreciate your being here but fear you will be a little late.

Ford and Helen Mar say to tell Papa they love him and when he comes home the will kiss him all away. When Ford gets angry he ~~say~~ says he doesn't love Annie nor Mama nor any body in the world, but Papa and when you get home he is going to tell you how mean we have all been to him.

Well my dear I shall continue to pray for you and love you I can't help doing the latter even if I try. It is just as natural as breathing.

Give my love to Avery and all the other people that I know. I haven't seen Zina since John left and do not want to for fear I would not lend her much cheer.

The children and Mama send love and kisses to Papa.

> Yours Affectionately
> <u>Helen</u>.

[Letter 62: Owen to Avery]

[*no letterhead, typed*]

> Bethel, Me. Nov. 14th. 1903.

Dear Mattie÷

Yours of the 6th. inst. was received night before last and was very glad to hear from you again and to know that you are well and happy. M—— is still on deck.[22] It beats all I ever heard of and now I do not believe she will be sick until X-mas.

I have been laboring around the country near by so that I could get in soon if it became necessary. Up at Grandpa's old place of residence "our friend" with whom we travelled on our tour through the Stake gave a fine party to the widows of that settlement. He invited Mother [Emma Woodruff] and I up and we enjoyed ourselves very much. I Met Grandma, Uncle J—— and your Father there. He came down partly to see me and learning that I would be up we had a fine visit. We talked over everything from A to Z, and I am most pleased that the "folks" feel that our de~~xx~~cision was a wise one and feel to help us all they can. I appreciate very much the kindly feeling expressed toward me by Father and hope I will live so that he will never be disapointed in me.

When we decided to build[23] I felt assured that the Lord would open up the way for us to get the means to pay for it and the way is opening up gloriously. Notwithstanding I told him I felt capable of providing for my own Father said he desired to help us at this time and will make arrangements to do so. The payments will be made right along I feel confident and I only wish I could be there to watch the progress of the little home and superintend it myself but at any rate I am sure we will appreciate it when it is done. About the change I want it to suit you but by making this change it will neccessitate the building of another chimney and somewhat interfere with our roof plan and besides it would bring the window so near the grate that there would always be danger of lace curtains or other drapings catching fire. My choice would be as we originally planned but you are the one to be suited first and if you are pleased I am sure I shall be. Please tell Brother Romney I would prefer to have large round pillars for the front porch instead of the [*illegible*]. And in useing the round posts or pillars I think I would prefer them without the ballistrade in between them. I fancy this will show the front windows off to much better advantage and be quite an improvement.

This ballistrade which I refer to is sometimes spelled balustrade or called the bannister. Brother Romney will know all about it. Am glad they have finished the foundation and I hope it is a good solid one and I know it must be if it is according to the specifications. How does it look to you? You know you must be a woman of affairs now.

Brother Peart & I have invested in the Union Mercantile Company and I expect we will get most of our furnishings from Dublan. I did this with the hope that it will prove a blessing to us in getting our supplies in that land. They carry about fifty thousand dollars worth of goods down there and it seems to me that from this stock we may be able to find what we need to furnish our humble little home. Just as soon as I get this matter straightened out I will let you know so we can save money and use credit.

Father says Mary will come down to be with you when you are sick [childbirth] and if possible I shall be there also.

Your Father is to be ready to go on a mision to the Southern States on Jan. 6th. but I am about to get the President to change his mission to the Illinois to aid me in our great undertaking there. His practical experience I am sure would be of great help to me and his labors will be a great blessing to that land. Am glad you got an extra $30. It was like finding it. Every little helps. Am awfully glad you have taken those ugly drawings down and hope you will pattern after the Madona child. Take care of that lariat. Well dear this will reach you about Christmass time. I hope it may prove a happy one for in contemplation of the little new home and other good things. I saw Aunt Phoebe the other day tell Rhoda.[24] She is well. Give my love to the dear girls and wish the President [Anthony Ivins] and family, the Bishop and his, Prof. Wilson and our other dear girls and friends a Merry Christmass for me. Tell Brother Wilson to be "kind to the [*illegible*]. Will send some more money on the next payment about the first of the month. God bless you dear and keep you well and happy.

Keep busily employed all the time in something for the home or something which will benefit you in some other way and you will continue to feel alright.

Wishing you God's blessings on your Christmass day and hoping that you may be happy and well I am,

Affectionately,

Ivan.

[Letter 63: Avery to Helen]

[no letterhead, handwritten]

Saint George
Dec. 22, 1903.

Dear Sister May÷

Yes, I was surprised to get a letter from you but extremely glad. Your letter reached me 20th and I wanted to get one off to you next mail, but did not have my money in the form of a check so that I could send it and am wondering what you have done. Nothing could suit me better than to help you get Ivan a present and I know he wants a stud. I have heard him say that he would have to get one several times. It is lovely of you to consider me in this, I think we ought to get a good one but can not send any more than $25.00 now. You pay what you want to for one and I can send more later. Am glad that you wrote as you did about presents as I have been worrying as to what in the world I could send you from here. It is not safe to send things through the mail and I had concluded to not do anything but think some right good things about you on Xmas. At odd times I have made a few little doilies that don't amount to a pinch of snuff, these together with some candy we girls are going to make will make up my presents to my friends.

School is about out for me and I will soon put all my time on making some tiny things for that baby you had such a pretty dream about.[25] That will make me happy wont it? These girls and I, (ask Ivan who they are) had a great discussion this morning on women going out under certain conditions, I declared that I was not going to show this town my wrapper and they said that I must. Maybe I will change, but I have been out so much, that these few days at home seem a real treat.

Can you imagine how glad I will be if Mary can come down to my "party." The dear Sis, I will be glad to see her. I do hope she can go to the L.D.S. after holidays.

I want to say a word about the weather we are having now and if you are cold prephaps it will make you think you would like to spend next winter farther south. Really we have had but one day of storm for two months and it is so warm that we feel comfortable most of the day without a fire and we wear our winter hats and wraps because the delineator says we ought to.

The babies have been crying ever since I began this and I have a shameful looking letter. I am perfectly well and happy and want to work every minute.

Am sorry that you are feeling so miserable and believe a rest is all you need. I hope the next news is "a boy" that sounds good to me.

May the Lord bless you through your sickness and grant the desires you have in your heart is my earnest prayer. Wishing you all a joyous and happy Christmas and New Year. With love
Mattie.

[Avery's "Autobiography and Recollections": Excerpt C (pages 47–51)]

[*handwritten*]

After four years at B.Y.C. plus a six weeks in Summer School I accepted a position to teach in Juárez Stake Academy Mexico. I introduced Domestic Art in the school and most of the girls signed up for my course in sewing. Owen had arranged with brother and sister Ivins for me to live in their home and they were the only folks that knew that I was married and going to have a baby other than Guy C. Wilson, Pres. of the Academy. I still was called Miss Clark. Generally I felt quite well but terribly sleepy due to the change in climate and my condition. But I was able to continue with my classes until Feb 22 '04 when became so uncomfortable in my tight fitting clothes.

The Ivins family had treated me royally. Their house was by far the finest most attractive house in the colony with beautiful flowers & shrubs grapes apples and peaches. The vegetable garden provided the greens I so enjoyed. I hesitated to leave this large family with the many diversions and activities that kept life interesting to me. Roxie & Rhoda Taylor[26] had invited me to live with them and do my sewing for the baby on their sewing machine. They would help me. Having a child each they knew my needs. Also by living with them I could watch the conscrution of my house across the street.

John W. Taylor had given Owen the property on which to build. It had all 100 feet frontage and ran back up the hill side to about 300 feet. The slope had been terraced and planted into an orchard of young fruit trees. The house was to be built in sand stone similar to bro. Taylor's home and by the same masons — the Romneys.

On one of Owen's recent trips to Mexico he and I had planned our home in such a way that additional rooms could be added later on if desired. From the moment the first load of beautiful white stone was delivered to the building site I was filled with aprehension — fear of the financial struggle it would involve and the feeling of permanency that a house in Mexico would bring. This feeling increased as the solid foundation took shape. Then as the walls rose higher and higher under the mason's skill I projected my thoughts to the years ahead when I should be left in this far away land with my little family — my husband on tours for the church most of the time and the folks in Wyo. I would seldom see. Loneliness enveloped me.

The walls were up to the square ready for the roof. In a few more weeks the house would be ready for occupancy. Bro. Ivins & Bro. Taylor had made frequent inspections and said the job was being well done. Of an evening I sat with bro. Taylor's family in their font porch in full view of my little home. On one such evening Mary Bennion had taken dinner with us & bro. Taylor invited us all to the front porch. The night air was cool & delightful carrying the full tones of our gospel hymns as we sang on and on. Then we went inside and knelt in family prayer as was the custom of most Latter Day Saints. In his prayer bro. Taylor asked the Lord to make it possible that sister Bennion be provided with a home in "this fair land," to add to her contentment." After we arose Mayme said: "Bro. Taylor please don't ever pray for me to have a home in Mexico — I don't want one. All I want is to leave this place as soon as possible as soon as it is safe to return to Utah. No home is going to keep me tied to this forsaken land."

Mayme's speech made me tremble for I saw in that hewn stone that built my home the very quality of permanency. (Moved into new home 2 weeks before Ruth born) In a few days after Owen moved me into our home I told him about Mayme's reaction to bro. Taylor's prayer and that I had told her that no home would keep any of us girls in Mexico when it was safe to leave. Owen's reply to that was forceful and direct — I shall never forget his words, "This is our home as long as we are in the flesh or not another dollar goes on the place." This fell on my ears like a heavy blow, neither of us made further comment. He left on an errand across town. Again I looked at the hewn stone that formed a structure — my home that could last a thousand years!

There were yet no windows finished — sheets pinned up waiting for the glass when Owen rec. a telegram from Pres. Smith to return to April conference. This was disappointing to both of us since he had made the trip to Mexico especially to be with me when the baby came — due any day now. He had been with me less than a week when the call came, had made a trip to Dublan and bought the bare necessities with which to start house keeping — besides a few groceries we had a stove, a bed, also springs on a frame that fold up, a rug for the one front room, two navajo blankets, a table bro. Romney made from oak, round and highly polished extension table and four chairs dishes and utensels.

Left Mexico May 1st 1905 with Mayme Bennion.

Owen left for Salt Lake as requested by Pres. Smith to attend April conference. Mayme Bennion (with her baby Susie) moved in with me that same day and stayed to take care of me during my confinement. Ruth was born April 11, 1904. Mrs. Saville a "midwife" made the delivery with the help of Mayme, Roxie and Rhoda. Apostel Taylor gave me a blessing while I was in labor after ordering the men who were laying shingles to go home. I think my screams might have f rightened them away. The ordeal was terrible — bungled — resulting in later operations.

When Ruth was four days old Owen returned bringing Helen and their four children — Fordie, Helen Mar, June & Rhoda, also Anna Rosenkilde the maid. Mayme went back to the Harris home and Helen took over the nursing job. This may have been distasteful to her taking care of her husband's other wife and child and I wondered why she chose to come at such a time — a total surprise to me. However, I learned later on that she came to get away from the threat of being arrested & brot into court to testify regarding pologamy. And that also was the reason that Owen attended only one meeting of conference after making the long trip home. Pres. Smith told him to stay in retirement after the one session. It was strenuous and difficult times for all of us because of the Federal investigations that were in full swing.

While in Salt Lake Owen attended a meeting of the Presidency and Quorum where a vote was taken and carried to up hold the "Pres.' Official Statement" that was presented to the conference which was to the effect that any violations of the Manifesto regarding plural marriage would be seriously delt with "by the church." Owen voted to uphold the Pres. "contrary to his personal feelings" so says his journal.[27] A few months after this declaration Apostles John W. Taylor and Mathias F. Cowley were excommunated from the Church. Less than three months after casting his vote Owen died of black small pox — June 20, 1904 following Helen's death June 7.

Because of my weakened condition Owen & Helen with held from me their plans for the future however, it was only a few days after their arrival that Fordie came to the side of my bed saying: "Daddy and Mama are going to the City of Mexico and I am going to stay with you, so is Helen and June and Anna, but not Rhoda cause she's going too." I asked: Am I going" And when Daddy & Mama come back from the City they are going to Germany, all of us are going but you and Ruth. Yes, Anna is going too." I took it all in and said nothing to the others. Then one day after I had been up and taken a few steps Owen came into my room and repeated Fordie's very words to me. He was quite surprised when I told him how I came to know and he waited for my reaction. Of course, I said, I think its grand for you and Helen to go to Mexico City but I don't understand "why Germany"? He explained that Pres. Smith had told him at the late conference that he might send him to Germany very soon to preside over that mission. Owen had previously filled a mission to Germany and spoke the language fluently. He & Helen would likely get the final word on their return from this first trip. Owen and Helen would be above suspicion in

Germany — this was to save them — personally I felt that I would be deserted, tho I did not say so. But Owen said: "In the event that we go to Germany I have in mind three or four alternatives for you Avery — tell me which appeals to you. Either you could go to *Valley and live with your folks, go to N. York and live in Ben E. Riche's mission & help sister Rich, live with my mother in Salt Lake, or stay here and improve our little home. What do you think about it? Without hesitating I said: "O, I prefer going to Salt Lake and live with your mother" What about this place"? Its stone it will stand." Why S. Lake? Because I can have a good time in S. Lake. No more was said on the subject, needless to say I felt resentful.

Owen and Helen had a way of clearing away all shadows and restoring a genial sweet spirit. The days that followed were delightful for the most part. Helen treated me like a real sister — always did.

Then the day arrived "cinco de mia" — the Mexico holiday when I went with Owen to hear his speech at the L.D.S. celebration. At 1 P.M. he & Helen departed for the City and went out of my life forever.

1904 and Aftermath

[no letterhead, typed]

Bethel, Jan Ist. 1904.

Dear Mattie÷

As distance forbids my making you a New Year's call I will write a few lines instead.

We have at last got through (for this time) the important business at our home and the result is another fine black-headed girl which weighed ten pounds when she was born.[1] Helen had quite a hard time but is feeling fine now. We feel very greatfull to the Lord for His goodness and that all is as well as it is with us. Helen says to tell you she has left it for you to have "the boy" which I sincerely hope you will do as the girls are getting to be in the large majority. Our little girl came at twenty minutes to eleven on the evening of Dec. 27th. Mamma got your letter and appreciated it very much. She said she would not be as stingy as I am with my letters so she let me read yours which I enjoyed very much also. I feel most thankfull for the feeling of friendliness and sisterly love which you girls have for each other.

Father was down recently and said it might be difficult for him to do what he hoped he could on our house but that he would try to do something. I told him not to worry himself at all about our affairs that we could hoe our own row, which we will do with the help of the Lord though it may cramp us for a year or so. I still feel that the Lord will open up our way and if the worst comes we will borrow enough to complete our home and then furnish it as we can afford to do so. If we can only keep well and contented we can master the minor troubles which may arise.

Mama is feeling fine in spirits and if she did miss her time a month and then go over some I can forgive that now that all is well and safe. M—— [Helen] has found a good place for Mary if she wants to come down and go to school before she joins you. My eyes still bother me some yet they are much better. I am trying it with glasses now when I read or write.

Let me know how the house is progressing and anything about the business connected therewith. Sister Welling is her with M—— [Mary Clark]. Give my love to the dear girls I am so glad you are all together for I know it will more satisfactory to you and I feel happy that the girls have been kind enough to do as they have done.[2]

Are you going to continue your domestic art class after the holidays? Do you not want some money outside what I send for the house? I do so wish you could spend this evening here or we could spend it there. I have been at home so long I feel now I must get out and rustle for a few months when I hope to take another short vacation.

Well dear may this new year bring to you all that your heart can wish for. May the Lord bless you abundantly as I feel that he has ever done. For my part I do not know how to express my gratitude for the great blessings we all enjoy. I thank you for the beautifull present you <u>girls</u> gave me for Christmass. God bless you both I appreciate it so much more coming from both of you than I would have done had just one of you given it to me̶l̶. It is certainly a beauty and I will appreciate it very much indeed.[3] May this find you in your usual happy, good spirits. Give my love to the girls and wish them a happy and blessed New Year for me.

With love and best wishes for your welfare and prayers for you always I am,

Affectionately,
Ivan.

P.S. Helen sends you love and New Years greetings.

[Letter 65: Owen to Avery]

[*no letterhead, typed*]

Bethel, Jan. 5th. 1904.

Dear ~~Mattie~~: Avery [*handwritten*][4]

Just a line tonight to let you know that all is well with us and to send you a check for $135. which will make the second payment on the house. One hundred of this comes from your father, twenty of it is your own.

If you need some money now for personal use let me know and I will send it to you. My eyes are bothering me quite badly to night so I will not write much. I feel that the Lord is opening up our way and that we will get the money to complete our home alright. This will be so if our faith fails not I am satisfied.

Remember me kindly to the girls and to Prest. Ivins, his fafily the Bishop Bro. Wilson and all the "folks".

Hoping this will arrive in time for you to make our payment to Prest. Ivins on the IIth. when it is due and that the Lord may continue to bless and preserve you I am with love from Auntie [Helen] and myself,
Affectionately,
Ivan (My father Owen) [*handwritten*]

[Letter 66: Owen to Avery]

[*no letterhead, typed*]
Bethel, Me. Jan. 16th. 1904.
Dear Mattie: — Avery [*handwritten*]
Your welcome letter was received several days ago but as I have been having an extra time with my eyes I have not ventured to write to anyone until today. I have some new glasses now and they promise all kinds of good things for me. While I was out of the City for about a week Sister M—— came down and has started fo school but during the few days I have been home I have not yet seen her. She will come down tomorrow and spend the day and we will have a good visit. My eyes are so much better that I feel most encouraged and do not anticipate much more trouble with them.

You had better send the mail as heretofore and Jimmy [C.] will forward mine to me. It is my intention to go to Chicago, leaving here next Wednesday and may be away from some weeks.

I am so glad you like your Christmass present and hope it will "fit" you soon alright.

You Goose of a girl ofcourse I have always thought of your condition and pray earnestly for your safety in that condition and that all may be well with you.[5] It will be just fine for you to have —— with you and if I can possibly make it possible will come to see you about March 15th. Do you think that would be too late? I could come earlier possibly but must be back here before the first. Am so glad our means are coming along alright and hope the work is progressing satisfactorally on the house.

Mama and baby [Rhoda] are getting along fine and everybody around the place is alright. Had a long visit with your father and will tell you somethings I cannot write. It made me feel badly dear to know that you cried yourself to sleep and I hope you will not let this occur again but that you will be comforted and cheered with the "prospects" of the future. I trust you wil pardon these excuses for letters as this is the first attempt for some time.

How would it do for me to send the mail to Junius R—— [Romney]? Could you not get it from him easier than any other place?

I will write him a letter if you wish and request him to see that you get it alright and without any bother to you. Are you still doing somethings with the Domestic Art, or have you finished your school work entirely? Am very anxious to hear anything new about our home and would like you to keep me posted.

Do you know of a room or two we could rent until our home is in shape to move into? If M—— [Helen] and I both come down it seems to me we would feel better even if we could get a room or two and move by ourselves before you are sick [childbirth], but if you can be made comfortable why the rest of us can get along. Of course if the house is completed according to contract we ought to be able to beging to move in about March 15th. but it would not be safe for you to move in at that time as the plaster and everything would be damp. We will waite and see how things progress and then act according to the conditions as they come up.

May God bless you my dear and may you feel cheerfull and contented at all times. Give my love to the girls [Roxie and Rhoda Taylor]. Hoping this may find you in good health and spirits and that you may ever enjoy Heavens protection and choicest blessings,

> With love and blessings I am,
> Affectionately,
> Ivan. (Owen) [*handwritten*]

[Letter 67: Owen to Avery]

[*no letterhead, typed*]

> Bethel, Me. Jan 22 nd. 1904.

Dear Mattie: —

We are just now enjoying the finest snow-storm of years. The sleighing has been fine for a week or more though I have not been doing very much sleigh-riding. On the evening of the eighteenth (I suppose you will remember the day) I took Mary out to Neff's to a delightfull party. As I could not celebrate this day with you I thought the next would be your sister.[6]

The husband of the Ladies you live with [John W. Taylor] and I expect to leave here in a few days for a trip through western Mont. and when we finish there I will go to Illinois as I, suggested to you in my last letter.

Mary is located in school now and she comes down to see us occasionally. I forgot to tell you in my last that we have named out sweet little daughter "Rhoda" after our friend I met down there [Rhoda Welling Taylor].

I think it would be a good thing to impress upon Mary that you would like her to come down not later than the 15th. of March if you think that will be soon enough. Make it early enough so you will be safe.

We will pack in the trunk just whatever you want. If the folks send the things from the north so that they can go right down without re-packing them why then we can use this trunk for something else, if not we will pack them in your trunk. If I were you I would tell the folks at home not to try to send the deer head. It will be so hard to ship and I would not like to take it from there anyway. I have one here I will try to get down sometime.

It is indeed nice of your Ma to make those neccessary things for you. She is one of the best souls on earth anyhow. I asked Mary to try and have the mirror sold and we can but another across the line and take it in you might mention this to her when you write.

It gives me a great deal of pleasure to know you are feeling suffi-ciently well to go and teach a class but I don't want you to do it for the sake of the money. I would not have you make that a consideration for any thing but if you are more contented by being busy and feel that you can continue it without imbarrassing you why it will be alright with me, otherwise I hope you will discontinue. You will nodoubt soon be in a con-dition where you will not care to be seen by many people and I want you to study your own feelings and indulge yourself from now on.

I am very glad to hear that the house is progressing so nicely and with the force you report at work it will surely not take a great while to complete it. My suggestion was to have the dining room done in "Walnut" black and I think some "red" paper will look well with it. It is possible that an "oak" finish would look quite as well and if you prefer it why have it by all means. I think White will be nice for the parlour and front bed-room and either white or "oak" for the hall. H—— [Helen] says she would have some light, clean color for the pantry such as a light "drab". I think the bath-room would be nice done in an immitation of oak or possibly the same color of the pantry. I do not like to see too great a varitey in one house. A very dark green will look nice with the white for window sash or a very dark red would go with the white.

Please ask Brother Romney what it will cost to paint the roof with one coat of "red" (such as they used on the Bowman house) oil paint. I would like to have it done if we can afford it.

I think it would be well if you feel like it, to order the paper throught the store. The dividend on our investment in the store will have to go for awhile to pay the interest on the investment so we had better not count much on "store pay" but whatever we order we will either pay the money for there or pay the interest here and draw the dividend there.

About the grates I do not think Brother Romney counted on putting them in on the contract price of the house; if he did I would let him order the "radiant"grate such as Brother Taylor bought for his home. If they were not included just let them go until I come down and I will try and bring them in with me. Please talk to Brother Romney about this and write me. The contract says the Contractor shall furnish all hardware but I do not [*illegible*]. He will do right with you in this as in all other matters. See that in finishing up the dining room they do not forget the "chair-railing". Do you think it possible that you can get moved into one or two rooms before you are sick?

I would prefer to order the bath-tub etc. You might however get the prices from the store on such a tub as you think we ought to have, a wash-basin, and closet fixtures. This will give me an idea when looking for these things and will let us know which would be the cheaper to bring them in or order them through the store. If you will see Bishop Bentley he will help you in these matters and may be able to make some valuable suggestions. Have Brother Romney order the sink, put it in and do the plumbing all ready to attatch the tub and basin.

In all these things when you do not know what to do ask Bishop Bentley for you can tell him I say he will be a father to you and get anything done for you in a proper way and for the least possible outlay of money. I want you to be suited in paper, paint and all other things. Be sure you are satisfied with a thing before you order or buy it and then all will be right. I don't want my suggestions to influence you from anything you have made up your mind to as being what you want in connection with your home. Will you also find out or get the Bishop to find out for you what a "Miller Monitor" Range will cost ordered through the Store? This is one of the most essential things we have to get and if it comes under $75. gold I think you had better order one. The small one is what we have here and it is plenty large enough. I think there are two sizes. They may tell you some other range is just as good or better but we want a Miller Monitor. I think Prest. Ivins has one of these and he may be able to tell you what would be the best way to order one. Unless you will be ready to move in before I can see about the bed-steads etc when I come down. I would order the paper at once.

In furnishing the house let us the get the essentials first. What we do have let it be good and then get other things as fast as we can pay for them.

You will have to get the Bishop help you order the window blinds. This should be done soon. I think I like the brown ones better than any other color. Better have them leave a hole large enough to get down through the pantry unless the hole from the outside through the foundation is large enough for a man to get through. I mean to make a little "trap door". I think this will give you something to study about for some time to come. May God bless and preserve you from every accident and unpleasant thing keeping your thoughts happy with the spirit of the Lord ever to be your companion that you may continue contented and thankfull.

> With love and blessings in which Helen
> joins me,
> Affectionately,
> Ivan.

[*handwritten across the bottom with sketch off to the side*]
Roof red
Floor "
3 Front rooms white
Dining R. Walnut
Hall White
Pantry drab light
Bath room oak
Red Sash Dark

[Letter 68: Helen to Owen]

[*no letterhead, typed*]

> Bethel [Provo], Feb. 4th 1904.

My dear Husband.

I have had three letters come back to me this last week and I am about disgusted with writing to you so I will not write but a few lines for fear this will be returned also. One I sent to Great Falls one to Byron and one to Omaha have all returned and the one Ibsent to Great Falls was opened at the office "by mistake" of course.

After sending y u the telegram to Chicago I wrote and sent itto Omaha and then I thought perhaps you would not be coming that way so you will not get any explanation of why Mary is not going until you reach your destination. I have determined to send all the letters that have been returned to me to Bro. Ivins so I will not have to write all the news over again. The Brother from across the street has been over talking to me for two or three hours. He doesnot seem to be very much excited. Suppose you will see all the proceedings so I will not send them to you.[7] I was going to send you all the papers but think you will see them where ever you are. I will send some of your mail that you can answer from there.

I have decided to let Anna take June up to Eden with her for a couple of weeks. I asked both the Grandmas and they thot it was all right to let her go and I think it will do June good to have a change. You know she can telephone any minute and can get home in three hours time if necessary.

I feel the responsibility of things resting on me considerably but hope I may be equal to the occasion. I do feel so badly about Asahels condition. I do hope it will not be so bad as was thought at first. The folks do not have a suspicion of ti and Ibcan assure you they will not get anything from me. We are all getting along nicely and are well and I feel that this is a very great blessing. I hope you are we ll and that when you get to the end of your journey you will find rest from your labors for awhile and enjoy a little leisure (which you so seldom have at home. From present indications you will have a prolonged visit. We will have to read between lines I think for it is not safe to tell too much in letters.[8]

I want you to know that you always have my support and co-operation in all things and that I continue to love you the same as always.

I feel more keenly all the time the great responsibility of the children's rearing and am at a loss to know how to deal with them allways. I get discouraged in this every few days. Fearing that I do not do as well as I might. Am going to have M. [Mary Clark] come down and stay with me while Anna is away. Your folks are all well.

> With my best love I remain,
> Yours, Nell.

[Letter 69: Helen to Owen]

[*no letterhead, typed*]

> Salt Lake City, Feb.9th.1904.

My Own Darling Owen: —

Would that I might write a letter that would convey to you the full measure of my love for you. But it seems that words are inaduqate for this but were you here to-day I am sure I could make you know myexact feelings. When your letter came to-day^,^ it filled my soul with great happiness. It was so full of words of comfort and love and breathed the same spirit of hopefullness that is ever present with my darling. It is strange^,^ but never the less true^,^ that a letter holds the power of carrying from you to me that "something" that we have talked about, which causes us to thrill with happiness and makes us feel how much we love each other. We know not what it is, but we know its effect. I am so thankful that we are truly mated and that each finds in the other^,^ that "being" who can satisfy thet longing for pure love and affection, while some of our fellows go thro life with an unsatisfied longing for companionship. Surely God has been kind to us. I love you more fondly every day of my life and realize in you my ideal. When I bwas a school girl I remember Bro. Brimhall[9] lectured one day to the young ladies of the [Brigham Young] Academy and in speaking of the ideals we should have, said we must have several ideals. We might have one which we might call "perfect," but which would seldom be found in this world; then we should have "the ideal we should like," and thirdly "the ideal we must have" for instance one who was moral, who belonged to the Church etc,

When we were married, my dear, I thought and knew you possessed all the qualities of, "the ideal I must have" and some of the ones of "the one I would like" and to-day I feel that your possess all the factors that make up my "perfect ideal." Now I do not mean to say that you are perfect <u>now</u> because if that were the case you would'nt be with me, but I believe I will see the time when you will be perfect and I my greatest desire is that I may be worthy to be your companion then.

You are a blessed, darling husband and are indeed my strong firm "oak." Not because of your age but because I feel that you are filled with virtues that make you strong to lean upon.

Well ym darling, I could go on^,^ and on^,^ in this strain and never tire of telling of my love for you, but it cannot be, I must hasten and tell you some <u>news</u>^;^ for isn't that what you asked of me? You called for news seasoned with affection. While this letter is seasoned with love you need not be surprised if some of them smack of "Ginger," knowing my disposition as well as you do.

Last night Will and Alice gave a little party. There were present^;^ The Stake Presidency and their wives[10]^;^ all the Mc.Ewan's and Woodruffesses^,^ and my friend from the "Valley"^;^ [Mary Clark] by special request. We had a very nice time. Had a game and your wife "<u>Helen</u>" took the prize, a nice Hymn book. I told them I cheated and they said they all did, so I concluded that I must have taken it for being the biggest cheater.

To-night Mary and I are going to the Theatre to see "David Harum."[11] I wish you were here to go with me. I always wish that, especially when I go to a good <u>love</u> [*underlined later by hand*] play. I wished you were here a dozen times last night and when Joe [Daynes] came into the Kitchen and kissed Blanche, that was about the last "straw"^,^ and came nearly breaking my heart, It made me so homesick to see you.

The children are all well and talk about papa all the time and want to know when he is coming home. Rhoda caught cold over in that draughty house last night I am afraid. She is quite cross to-day.

Sister [Elizabeth] Mc.Cune is going to have that party that she put off until I could go^,^ and now you are not here to go. It will be Thursday and I wish you were here to go with me and I am sure Sister M. will feel disappointed that you will not be there. The two boards are to be there and no doubt we will have a nice time. Will write you about it.

Last Saturday there was a telegram came from Senator Kearns[12] which I will enclose with this letter. The answer I sent back in written on it. I did not know where to find you or would have had the message forwarded to you. I was reminded quite forcibly too that if we wanted you ever so much we would not know where to get you by wire.

I have so many things to tell you but cannot talk them in a letter. So when you come home I will talk an arm off. Edwin Bennion wished me to thank you for that introduction you gave him at John M's. He may live to regret it, if he does not win the suit.

What would you think if you were to find the pannel out of the stairs door when you come? That's what you may expect to find. And your boy was the cause of it. I dont think you can say much about it when you stop to recall your boyhood days.

Well really my dear, it is impossible for me to write any more this time. The children have all come in and I need not say more to you about that for you can judge from past experiences how it is.

Write often to your "darling" and she will do better. I love you with all my heart and you know it better than I can tell you. Think of me <u>often</u> [*underline added later by hand*] and pray for me <u>always</u> [*underline added later by hand*] as I do for you.

> With my heart's best love I am Yours
> Affectionately,
> Helen.

P.S. Owen sends love and kisses to papa and is here at my elbow while I am writing it. [*added later at the bottom of the page, written by hand*]

Love to all my friends, Bro. and sisters Sessions[13] and Welch[14] especially —

[Letter 70: Helen to Owen]

[*no letterhead, typed*]

> Salt Lake City, Utah, Feb. 12th.1904.

My Dearest Owen: —

Am wondering if you received the letter I sent to Great Falls. If you did not, then you have had but one letter from me and are not feeling very kindly toward me, judging you from my own feelings when your letters do not come often.

Last evening Sister Brixen[15] escorted me to Sister [Elizabeth] Mc.Cune's party.[16] I will not attempt to describe the grandeur of her magnificent home.[17] All the members of the two boards with their escorts were present except a few who, like yourself, were unavoidably absent. Of the absent ones none were missed more than you and nearly everybody enquired about you. Sister Mc. said she put the party off until I could go and thought you were at home until a day or two ago and then it was to late. I did not enjoy the evening nearly as much as if you, my dear, had been with me. It isn't a bit nice to go alone. The first Presidency[18] was there and of your quorum, Bros Cowley, Clawson,[19] Hyrum [Mack Smith] and Geo.A.[20] ^and^ [Joseph W.] McMurrin, Wells[21] and Kimball[22] of the Seventies.

The party went off as nicely as it could with the large number of guests present. I do not think there can be as much real enjoyment at an affair of that size^,^ as when the guests are all in one or two rooms and can be nearer to gether. In fact I think our party was a model, don't you? Wish we could have another.

Bro. Cowley called to see Hattie and Wilma to-day and he and Bro. Frank Y. have found a place for them to go. Sister Wheeler has offered them a room or two at her house and they will move as soon as convenient. Bro. Empey started the ball to rolling. He thought it was an injustice to Heber to have them there. Was afraid some trouble yould come to him and wrote Heber so. I think the fact of the matter is, Gusta is sick and tired of having so many people around her and Ib cannot blame her much. I told her I would have Mary C. come down and stay with me and she did not object but says Ivy[23] is going to stay two weeks longer and Mary might as well stay that length of time and then come to our house. Hattie and Wilma will be away by that time and I can tell you I will be glad for I have felt the responsibility fo their being there all the time. I think it has taught me a lesson and I will not be so fast quick to ask favors in the future. It seems we have to learn all things by experience.

I am afraid that instead of getting broader I am growing more narrow. The circle of friends in whom I have perfect confidence is getting smaller instesd of larger. You will have to come home and give me a little of your "sage brush" tea to make me more liberal toward mankind. You and my Mother are about the only ones in whom I have perfect confidence and if you ever deceive me I am afraid I would never afterward place confidence in a living soul. So BEWARE. You will say I am turning Pessimist. Well I do feel rather pessimistic to-day. You are my panacea for all my ills.

We are going to have the reunion at your mother's on the First and you must be sure and be here.

Anna is just going up town for the butter so I must stop and send my letter with her.

I love you more dearly every day, you blessed sweet soul. I want to be to you what you would have me be, and wish I might never disappoint you in anything and finally grow to be your ideal. I wish I could be with you right now, to tell you how much I love you, with the variations you know. Write me sweet letters as you always do^,^ full of love and encouragement, and write often, for I live on the hope of getting one until it comes and then on the pleasure of reading it afterwards. The children are all well. Owen says ^"^send papa love and kisses for me.^"^

With love unbounded and kisses without number I am your^,^

Helen.

[Letter 71: Helen to Owen]

[*no letterhead, typed*]

Salt Lake City, Feb. 19th 1904.

My Dear Owen: —

It is nearly time for the mail man to come but I must write ao few lines before he comes for it has been a week to-day since I wrote to you. It seems almost impossible for me to write you for whenever I bring The typewritter out some one comes in to talk to me or the children make such a noise that I cannot tell what I am writting. They are all in here now making the greatest racket you ever heard and I suppose you would'nt mind being here in the mixup for a few minutes at least, would you dear?

I have been staying home for more than a week like a good girl until last evening Prest. [Frank Y.] Taylor telephoned over for me to come over to supper. They had The Bros. and sisters Cannon, Lutie and Gearge, Ray and John, Lennie and Dan and Naomi and I. We had a fine supper and a real sociable time.

Suppose you have read in the papers of the division of the Salt Lake Stake into four. They are going to call the new Stakes the "Ensign," the "Emegration," the "Pioneer" and the "Salt Lake." I think they are so appropriate. They will organize the "Emigration" next week and the others will be organized later so perhaps you will be here at the time.[24] I hope you can.

Gusta has been very ill for two or three days. Has had a gathering in her ear and yesterday it broke and we thought she would be better but she had a very bad night and feels very weak this morning. I feel quite worried about her. She has had so many things the matter with her lately and she looks very bad indeed. I hope when she gets over this she will gbe better permanently.

Ray [Winters] has been up for a few days and is trying to get a job on the Street car. He had to have four men's names to recommend him. He got Bro. Empey, Judge Booth, George J. Cannon for three and I put your nam down per mine. Is that all right? I believe he will do well on the car as he has had some experience with machinery at the Sugar factory for two years and has run a flour Mill for two years. I hope he gets the job.

The letter from the[Logan] Knitting factory has not come yet so I have not attended to that business yet. They sent for me to sign a note at the bank for [Utah] Sugar[25] stock. You did not tell me anything about it but as Prest. Winder[26] brought it to the bank I thought it was all right for me to sign it and did so. To-night is the Pacific Islander's entertainment in the Stake House[27] and an entertainment in our ward also. Prest. Taylor asked me to go with them to the Stake House but if I go anywhere I think I should go to our ward for I have not been there for so long.

I have told you all the news I could think of in a big hurry thinking every minute I must stop and you will find it a very mixed up affair but must forgive me bare with me.

I thank you darling for your confidence in me and your great faith in my prayers. As soon as I got your letter I knelt down and asked the Lord to bless you and grant the things you so much desired if it might be his pleasure to do so and if it would be for the good of the people and I feel sure it will all be well in the end and what ever is will be for the best.

I will say good bye and God bless you my dearest sweet heart. I love you with all the power of my soul and am so thankful that you love me and my greatest wish is that it may continue so thro out all eternity.

The children all send love and kisses to papa and will be glad to see you again.

With my heart's best love I am as ever yours,
Helen.

[Letter 72: Helen to Owen]

I addressed this to Byron, Big Horn Co, Utah Ha, ha. [*handwritten in pencil in the top margin*]

[*no letterhead, typed*]
                              Salt Lake City, Feb. 20th. 1904.
My Dearest Owen: — [28]

When I wrote you yesterday I had no idea of writing again to-day but as I have something especially to tell you, I do so willingly but not cheerfully.

Bro. C. [Cowley] came to Will [McEwan] yesterday and told him to have me say to you that you had better stay away a little longer as there is a possibility (and I̶m̶ might say probability) of your being subpoenied as a witness to go to Washington to testify in the Kearns case, which case I believe is intended to prove that Church influence was used in his election.[29] Now that I have learned this bit of news I think I understand what the telegram was about and I am inclined to think that perhaps you have had communication with your friend in the East and are probably better informed on the subjec^t^, than I am. The day your telegram came, the most <u>important</u> man at the office^,^ you know who thinks that of himself, phoned the message to me. I asked him if he had showed the telegram to Prest. S. [Smith] and he replied, a little sharply and with a tinge of reproof for my question, that he had <u>not</u>, it was nothing to do with Prest. S. but was expressly for you. About a week afterward this same Bro. (G.) [George Gibbs, secretary to the First Presidency] phoned me and^,^ in his accustomed nurveous way^,^ asked me if I had received any further information on the subject and if I should hear anything in the future to let him know immediately, that was provided that, eh, eh, eh — a — Owen was not at home. I determined right there and then that if I did hear anything I would not let him know a word for I think I know about how much confidence you have in him. I think it was his individual curiosity that prompted his inquiry. He may have heard somethigg more though. I heard some few days after the telegram came that Kearns wanted Bro. R. to edit the Tribune and I then supposed that was what he wanted communication with you for. At the time I was prompted to take John M. into confidence as my advisor but then I concluded that it was not of much consequence and thought I would say nothing about it.

I met Bro. C. [Cowley] on the street several days ago and he said he was going to find a conference somewhere right away and then find another right after that and so on and will not be seen around here very much and thought you better do the same. Now I don't like this at all for I want to see you very <u>muchly</u>. Prest S. says if there is any liklyhood of any of the brethren being subpoenied to go East he wants them to keep out of sight.

Bro. (who uses the umbrella) had a letter from our Bro. who writes in parables or I might say (the swearing president) and he was very much concerned over his two boys, Will and Hans. They have changed boarding places now and all is peace and I think all parties concerned are satisfied, I can assure you I feel somewhat easier for I felt quite a responsibility on my shoulders as things were.

Gusta is feeling qite a bit better this morning I am pleased to say. The doctor says she will be all right in a few days.

I went to the entertainment in the Ward with Alice and Will. Your mother, Blanche and Joseph and Naomi went also and we had a fine time. The occasion was a Theological class reunion and they had a banquet at which about two hundred people were present. There were some very fine toasts given by Sister Leone Horne,[30] Sister Tingey,[31] Bros.

Bradford, Thompson and others and they were very good. Oh yes, Miss Florence[32] was there, does'nt that make you wish you were there? I am sure you would have enjoyed it there were lots of pretty girls there and (she) looked sweet as ever, but hold your breath while I tell you there was a young man with her.

I will wait now and see if there is a letter for me to-day and if there is I may write some more.

The Postman has just been here and there was no letter so I will just say in conclusion that I love you dearly fondly [*underline added later by hand*] and with all my heart and am getting awfully homesick to see you. Let me know when you think you will be able to come home. You had better learn when the coast is clear from headquarters had'nt you? I will keep you posted on anything I hear.

Owen asked me this morni ng if farmers were baptized. I told him yes if they wanted to be mormons they were. He said well I'll be a farmer then but I won't be a mormon. He is afraid of being baptized it seems. He still askes his thousand and one questions every day but is pretty good for him and I dont expect him to be very good when I think of his mother!s failings. Little Rhoda is wearing all the hair off her head am afraid she will not have any left by the time we take her to fast meetin. Helen Mar is getting cuter every day and June can say "Dodo keep still," and we think that is so cute. She has changed the baby from "Rodo" to "Dodo." Well there is no use of me trying to make you understand how cute they all are but you know as well as I that they are the brightest, sweetest children that ever were born. They all send love to papa and Owen says he wants to send you a bushel of kisses and Helen Mar says "and me too." God bless my darling. May he keep you safe and well and return you to us safely in the near future. With fondest love I am as ever,

Yours most affectionately,
Helen.

[Letter 73: Helen to Owen]

This letter was returned from Omaha. [*handwritten in top margin*]

[*no letterhead, typed*]
Salt Lake City, Feb.24th. 1904.
My Dearest Owen: —
Your letter was placed into my hands this morning by a "special delivery boy" and I wasso excited I could scarcely read it. I was relieved when I read the contents and learned nothing was wrong with you. I immediately

took it up to the office and placed it into the hands of the gentleman to whom it was addressed. He was the only person in at the time, every one else being out to lunch. A lucky moment I considered it and was ^made^ to feel so welcome that I immediately felt quite at home. We had a nice little talk and, after reading your letter, he gave me the answer which I wired to you. He told me a few things which, by the way, I already knew, and said he thought things would develop within the next two or three days so that we would know where we were at. And you will see by to-day's paper, a clipping from which I send with this, that things are developing.[33] Said above all others that might be called to go on a mission you would be the one he would not want to go. He thinks that the excessive heat of that particular climate would be very damaging to your health, owing to the attack you had about three years ago. I am ^gr^ateful for the intrest he takes in your well being for I have felt anxious about you myself.

So I cannot expect you home until April Conference, well I do not know as it makes much difference whether you go before or after. You would just be at home a few days if you came now^,^ and that would be an aggrivation. We are getting along nicely and are all well, for which I feel extremely thankful.

Mary says that neither she nor her mother will go to St. George [Juárez] this spring as they think they can not well afford it. They think as far as help is concerned that there will be plenty of efficient help the^re,^ and that all will be well if they do not go now.

M. [Clark] is rather undicided and scarcely knows what course to pursue and I think her school is doing her practically no good, in fact she says so herse^lf.^

She has a friend who does not want her to go until he gets better acquainted with her. He has gone off with the Sheep and expects to be gone three months so things will not develop very rapidly. He wants to take a fishing trip up north next summer and I suppose he will want Prest. T. to go with him as he knows the way. I may have her come atay with me while you are away, then we could get better acquainted. A sister from granger is coming to take her over there for a day or two this week.

It is very late. Anna and Alice's girl have gone to the theater, I went last night. Your mother, Sisters Mc.Cune, Ward, Bro and sister Empey little Bessie Mc.Cune and I made up a box party. We enjoyed the play immensely.[34] It was one of the funniest things I ever saw, something after the style of "Floradora"[35] and was as funny as the "Burgomaster." It takes something pretty funny to make me laugh nowadays, and I did laugh several times last night, so you may know it <u>was</u> <u>funny</u>.

Sister Elmina Taylor broke her collar bone last week and we are going to fast for her to-morrow, as well as for all other members of the board who are ill. Gusta is still sick but is feeling a little better to-day.

The family and neighbors are all well, and a number of them send love to you. Alice and Blanche both have told me they have found out something about you and are going to — punch your head, they say, when you come home.

Well I will not write more to-night. Know that you always have my truest love from my heart of hearts, and that my prayers are ascending unceasingly for your comfort and blessing.

I am happy to subscribe myself your affectionate wife,

Helen. [*written by hand*]

[*handwritten on the back of the letter*] >over' P.S. The reason I sent the telegram as it was it looked funny to say "Fordie is well" "Rhoda is well," so I thought if I changed it a little you would understand.

The gentleman said if you had time to go South it was all right with him but he is not particular about that part, just so you do not come at present. He will let you know when he desires to meet you. There is a nice letter here from Mr. Wooldridge with some News paper clippings.

P.S.Have just heard that Hyrum M.[Smith], Bro Lyman[36] and Andrew Johnson have been subpoenied.

H.

[Letter 74: Helen to Owen]

[*no letterhead, typed*]

Salt Lake City, Mar. 1st. 1904.

My Dear Owen: —

Received your telegram yesterday morning and as your letters had not yet arrived I could scarcely understand it or know what to do but shortly after the letters came and with them one from St. George asking me to get several things to put in the trunk. I immediately wentup to see Mary and found her sick in bed at my sisters. She said neither she nor her mamma were going to take the trip which has been talked about so much. They consider it unnessary as far as help is concerned and if it is to be a pleasure they think they cannot afford it at present.

Mary says she has written and written for the things and they have not even packed them up yet. Her Father said he could not see the use of sendin them before the house was finished and Mary thinks herself that there is no use in getting in a hurry, a thing she never does, by the way. She says "you know pa is always so slow, he neverr does anything until the last minut.e" I had a notion to tell her she was a true daughter of her father for really I never saw any one much more deliberate than she is.

You get out of patience with me often for being so slow but I imagine you would be exasperated with her if you had to wait for her to"get ready"[37]

We talked matters over and have done the best we could with the judgement we have. Mary says the shortest possible time in which we could get the things from valley would be four days. Then we would have to repack and send them to you and how could we check the trunk with no one going. Mary says there is nothing but that will do if it gets there in a month from now so we decided to write to her father and have him bring the things when he comes to conference and then you would be here and could send them by some of the conference folks. I think this will be all right myself.

One of Mary!s particular "friends" does not desire her to go away just at present and I think she does not know what she wants to do herself yet. And is waiting to hear from her folks.

The Hundred dollars from Davis county bank was deposite on feb. 23rd. and when I spoke to Bro. Gibbs he said I just put $500.00 in the bank a few hours ago in accordance with your husband's instructions. I telephoned Eddie Ashton[38] regarding the one share of knitting stock and he said he had not sold yet because he could not get more than Ninety for it. I told him to sell immediately for that price if he could get no more. About three hours afterward he phoned that he had sold and placed the money in the bank to your credit. Then Jimmie said he would place the money from the office in the bank to-day. Now dont you think I have russled it in a hurry.

The money from the Logan knitting factory just come saturday night and I paid it on the interest and there yet remains $38.00 more to be paid, there were two notes ~~more~~ you know. Shall I pay it and if so where shall I get the money? The news sends a bill of $22.50 and say they will take scrip. I will not write more this time for fear you may not get it. I did not send an answer to your telegram because I thought you had left Chicago before it would reach you. We are just going over to the birthday party. Children are all well and we are trying to get along the best we can. Anna is going to stay with Lena for two weeks and is teasing me to let her take June with her. I have half a notion to let her go. Anna says she would not let her out of her sight one minute while she is away and would take the best of care of her. I do not know how I could get along with out her. What do you think about it?

I have so much to do the next few hours I am nearly beside myself. With the truest love from my heart of hearts, I am as ever yours affectionately, and with constant prayers for your success and happiness, I am yours,

Helen

[Letter 75: Helen to Owen]

[*no letterhead, typed*]

St. George, Mar. 6th. 19 .

Dearest Owen: —

Your letter written on March 1st. came yesterday and I was very glad to hear from you. I do hope you got my letter sent to Omaha. You would not understand why Mary did not go South unless you did.

We had a great excitement here last night. Donald [Daynes] had a very bad sore throat yesterday and also a fever but Blanche did not think it anything serious until evening she sent for the Dr. and he said he could not tell whether or not it was anything contagious for a while. He grew worse and about midnight He came again and pronounced it diphtheri. You can imagine how frightened I was. I stayed awake all night and to-day I have not had my eye off from the children all day. I will have to watch them every minute for weeks I suppose, for they do not know any better than to go right over there. Joseph [Daynes] is staying at your mother's so he can go to work and Estella [Donald's sister] and Sharp [Donald's brother] have gone to Mc.Farlanes to stay. I do not belie the case is a very bad one although they can not tell for a few days. The Dr. says he can tell by to-morrow just about how it will go. I thought at first I would go to Provo or somewhere but then I thought I would not get frightened and run away as I might get some other disease by going for the whooping cough is raging all over the country, so I decided it would be best for me to stay right here and watch the children carefully and trust in the Lord to keep the children well. Just a week ago Joseph went over to administer to Bro. Bradford's little child and at the time they did not know that it had diphtheria but found it out next day. The Dr. says that is where Donald got it from for it just takes a week for the disease to deveol after one has been exposed. Donald was out playing with all the children the evening before he took sick and in fact he went with his papa and mama down to the stake house the night before. I do not want you to become alarmed though for I think the Lord can prevent us from having it if we will be wise and careful to keep the children away now.

Anna and June went to Eden yesterday morning to stay two weeks and Mary has come down to stay with me. She has just come from Farmington where she has been for a few days. She says the folks are all w well. We are all well and I do not want you to worry about us but just give us your faith and prayers. I will write often to let you know how we all are.

Give my love to M. [Avery] and tell her I got her letter all right and will answer some time in the near future. I love you dear and all ways pray earnestly for your health and blessing and want you to be happy and I believe you are. My baby [Rhoda] is the sweetest thing you ever saw (You are missing all her sweetness. I would not be surprised if you did not come home for Conference. I have not heard anything but if it takes as long to get through with every witness as it does with Prest. Smith they will not be through with the investigation until conference and then they could get some who are away attending conferences ~~and will~~ if they should come home. When Prest. comes home I will keep ypu posted all right. He will know what will be done then. I think something will be done, don't you?

Well good night my darling and may you have all your heart desires is the desire of your affectionate,

Nell.

p.s. I have had three letters come back that I have written you and just to prove it I will send them to you. Please answer every one of hem immediately after you receive them.

N

[Letter 76: Helen to Owen]

[*no letterhead, handwritten*]

Salt Lake City.
Mar 8th 1904.

Dear Owen:

Your precious letter written at Omaha was received yesterday and consequently this letter is written with a pen, "Hand painted" so to speak.

Don't blame you for objecting to machine written letters. They are all right for business but not for love. I don't like them at all.[39]

Donald is better this morning and is getting along nicely. Judging from the noise I heard eminating from his bed room yesterday he will be well soon. He was having a "tantrum." The nurse was at a loss to know what to do. He had been so sick from the first when she came that he was pe^r^fectly docile until yesterday and his actions were astonishing to her. Am sending you news paper clippings and "returned" letters that will furnish you (good?) literature for weeks to come. I will not write again for some time, not at least until I give you time to read all this.

When I wrote those letters I understood them <u>perfectly</u> but on rereading them to-day after they are cold I am inclined to think you will experience some difficulty in understanding the parables.

I appreciate dearest, the genuine warmpth of your affection and can assure you it is repracated.

Life would indeed be an empty dream without your dear love and companionship. Sometimes I get so hungry for you I can scarcely wait to see you but then I always think there is an other "longing heart," and I must make some sacrifices for her sake. Now I wish I had'nt said that. I do not wish to complain or have you feel I am not satisfied.

I have my precious children and I am wrapped up in them heart and soul. They give me joy and comfort every hour. And I have so much to be thankful for the Lord knows my heart and He knows how grateful I am for all my many blessings although it would <u>seem</u> sometimes to others that I am ungrateful. The one fact, that God knows my every thought, hope and desire, is one of my greatests sources of happiness. I keep nothing from Him, although the my true feelings are sometimes hidden from the eyes of my fellows and it would seem to them from my actions that my motives were not right, there is only <u>One</u> who can judge me, and He is merciful and I feel will be charitable with me. Give my love to M. [Avery], tell her she has my prayers continually and I do hope you can be with her at the time she will need you so much.[40] Who knows you may be able to stay there for a longer period than you think. I would be glad for <u>her</u> <u>sake</u> if you could stay for a couple of months at least. Experience has taught me many lessons and I know how <u>she</u> needs you, better than she knows now, for she knows no dread, and the <u>dread</u> is about as much ^great^ as the real experience.

May God bless you my dear faithful, <u>truest</u> <u>friend</u> on earth. May every wish of your heart by gratified and may you have your full need of happiness in this life and endless joy in the great eternal life to come. Is the desire and prayer of

Yours Affectionately,
Helen Winters Woodruff.

[Letter 77: Owen to Avery]

[*letterhead, handwritten*]

Department of the Interior,
United States Land Office,

Mar. 8th, 1904

Dear Mattie÷

I wrote you from Boise [El Paso, Texas] and left it to be delivered by Bro.—— whom we expected when I was there but whom I now learn has gone in quite another direction.

Am now on my way back to Boise but will have to waite a few days at Diaz for M—— [Helen] and the Children who are coming with me. We expect to arrive at Provo [Colonia Dublán, Mexico] next Thursday and would like it very much if the Bishop can get Edward Eyring[41] to meet us with his double rig. Leona[42] will also accompany us. We will have two or three trunks. We are coming with the President. All being well we should be in St. George [Colonia Juárez, Mexico] Thursday night, all being well. Keep that bed stead and get a pair of springs for it at once. Will explain all when I see you. I do hope all is well with you. God bless you dear and keep you from all evil.

With love
Ivan

[Letter 78: Owen to Avery]

[*letterhead, handwritten*]
Isaac W. Pierce
Lumber, Coal and Wood
Madera Aserrada, Carbon y Lena
Telephone 293

Ciudad Juarez Chic., Mex. Mar. 1904

My Dear Mattie ÷

This has been a "fierce" day and assure you we have all been very communicative with each other. We just have a moment here to drop you a line that you may know I remember you and pray the Lord to be good and [*illegible*] to you.

I love you dear and you are a patient, good, girl.

With love and blessings I am

Affectionately
Ivan.

[Letter 79: Helen to Owen]

[*Big Horn Basin Colonization Company letterhead, handwritten*]

March 12, 1904.

Dear Owen:

Just have time to write two or three lines before the "Postem" comes. Donald is almost well they say and it seems strange the Dr. says his disease is highly contagious but still has not put up a flag. Little Sharp took sick day before yesterday and Blanche could not stand it to have him away from her so they brought him and Estella both home. The Dr. is there now and says he is quite ill. I feel so thankful that we are all well and appreciate the great blessings of health more when I see others afflicted. There are two letters here that I cannot answer so will send them to you. Have written two letters since I received one from you. Got the bill from Chipman's yesterday and will send the check on Monday.

With love to you from all of us and ever praying for your blessings I am yours

Helen.

[Letter 80: Helen to Owen]

[no letterhead, handwritten]

Salt Lake City, Mar.16,1904

Dear Owen:

I am at present in conjoint, general board meeting[43] and thot before going home would "<u>drop</u>" you a few lines," although have not heard from you for nearly a week.

Suppose by this time you have received all my letters ~~by~~ that were returned and which I sent you again.

I wish we had a little of your sunshine and dust and you had some of our mud it is simply awful. Just as soon as the mud dries up a little here comes the snow and rain again. I am thoroughly sick of it.

You will perhaps be anxious to know how the children are knowing that Blanche's children have the diphtheria. Little Sharp has been very bad indeed but now they think both the children are out of danger but the nurse has come down with it now and they have her to wait on.

I have been very worried about this but could do nothing but hope and pray. I have kept good watch of them all the time.

Helen Mar was sick yesterday but had just eaten something that upset her stomach and vomited nine times during the day and after fasting all day and night is all right to-day.

Our meeting has just commenced with Bro. Golden Kimball presiding. If I get a good letter from you to morrow will perhaps write again.

Will give you a few minutes of this meeting. The first subject is June Conferences. Well they are too slow I will have to go on with my letter. You know how intensely interesting these meetings usually are.

Have just barely seen Prest. Smith and Prest. Lyman. But have not spoken to them.

Your ma has written to Bro. Dameron telling him he might have the Deseret farm, that is, hers and wants to know what you want to do with yours? You will get a letter from Bro. Seaman so will decide what you want to do and let him know.

Will ask Prest. Smith when you will be able to come home and suppose he will let you know tho as he knows where you are. Bro. Roberts[44] has just come in and taken the chair.

Give my love to M [Avery]. How is the house progressing?

I will close now with my heart's best love to you

I am Yours as ever,

Helen.

[Letter 81: Owen to Avery]

[no letterhead, handwritten]

Ciudad Juarez

May 7th 04

Dear Avery÷

We arrived here all well last evening, tho we had a very hot, dusty trip. We expect to go on this morning. Both Helen and I did not realize how much anxiety we would have about you all until we got started and then we became aware of the fact that two or three weeks would be a long time for a Mama to leave her little babies.[45]

We hope you will try and write very often and say just how all is going at home.

Please tell Bro. Romney I did not get a chance to see him and make a partial settlement with him but will do so when I return. I wish dear if you hear anything about the $500.00 which your father spoke to us about you would write to me here c/o Isaac W. Pierce so I can get it on my return for if we do not get this money as expected I will have to make arrangements to borrow it before I can settle with Bro. Romney. If it is so we can use it it should be deposited to my credit in the State Bank the same as the $200.00 which came from Uncles.

I wish I knew now what our program would be so that if we are to remain long I could get some things to help fix up with while in the City. There may be some word for me here on my return.

I hope you will be carefull and not try to do much work until you get your usual strength back. Be carefull of the babies and keep them from harm. I hope all will be well with little baby Ruth & her Mama and all the babies. God bless and preserve you from all harm.

With love and prayers for you I am,

Affectionately

Ivan

Our address will be: 5a Humboldt No. 50, Mexico D.F.

[Letter 82: Owen to Avery]

[*no letterhead, handwritten*]
Guernavaca, Mex.
May 18th 1904.
Dear Mattie:
We came down last Saturday and have been in almost a continual string of Conference meetings here ever since. It has been highly interesting to me visit with and labor among this strange people. The country too and it's vegitation is highly interesting to us. We have had a good Conference and are to hold another one next Sunday and Monday at Azunta, will then return to the City of Mexico and after a few days start for home. Helen & baby Rhoda are well. This climate seems to quite agree with them. The rains have started here as I hope they have at the Colonies.

We all remembered and observed the "Special Fast" last Sunday, asking the Lord to send rains to the Colonies.

The elders and all our party are well except Leona [Taylor] who has been quite ill but is better now. It is a great treat to come down here into the tropics where since the rain started it is cooler than it was farther North. I do hope all is will with you and the Children. Take good care of the darlings and give my love to them. If you answer this at Juarez I will get it.

May God bless and be with you to keep you all well and happy. Helen sends love

Affectionately
Ivan

[Letter 83: Owen to Avery]

[*no letterhead, typed*]
City of Mexico, May 20th. 1904.
Dear Mattie: —
We arrived here from Guernavaca last night and found your two letters, also the ones you forwarded to us. It was a feast for us to hear from you all at home but we are sorry you are not feeling well and I do hope you will take care of yourself and not overwork.

I cannot tell just when we will start home as we hold Conference at Czumba Sunday and I think it will be about Wednesday before we will get started back home. It is more than likely that I will go to the Salt River Valley and attend to the work which the Presidentcy have instructed me to attend to before returning to Juarez but of course the folks will come home with Prest. Ivins.

Like you I wish we knew just what our future programme will be so we would ħ know what to do about fixing up and it is more than likely I will know when I return to Ciudad Juarez as I look for a letter from the Presidentcy at that place.

I was very sorry that the rain spoiled the alabastine and it is too bad Bro. Romney can not fix the roof and chimney satisfactory.

If he has not yet had it painted I wish you would ask him to attend to it and have enough coats of good thick paint put on zafter all the holes are sodered up) to keep it from leaking.

Ask Brother Romney if the smoking of the chimney is not caused by the flue having been filled up with mud when the men were finishing the chimney and it is possible that so much has dropped into the stove that it will not draw until you clean the stove out underneath.

Write me at once to Ciudad Juarez and send whatever mail there is for me. It is quite interesting to labor among these natives for awhile but I fancy it would be most difficult for me to learn to relish their food.

I hope you will have sufficient rain to start the grass and make things fresh and beautifull.

Be carefull of yourself and the children and don t try to do much else. May God bless you and keep you well, with love,

Affectionately,
Ivan

P.S. I hope when I come home I will feel well and natural and not be so cross and disagreeable as I was before. My voice has been good all the time down here and I feel well and natural.

[Letter 84: Avery to Owen]

[*no letterhead, handwritten*]

Colonia Juarez
May 30, 1904.

Dear Ivan÷

As you requested I write and send your mail. Your letter came to late Saturday to send your mail that day.

The children are well and we talk to them about Papa and Mama.

Why should I keep it longer, I will have to tell you. Who else should know? I am suffering, I have been tried and why? It is all I can stand now, Elder Duffin has been in, he said he knew I was feeling bad and came to talk to me. I thank the Lord that he came.[46]

The last two or three days I have felt stronger and have more nurse for my darling babe.

Well, go and do your duty and visit the stake you mentioned and I pray God to bless you, preserve your health and give you success in that labor.

With Love,
Mattie.

[Letter 85: Avery to Owen]

[no letterhead, handwritten]

Colonia Juarez
June 1, 1904.

Dear Ivan ÷

We just got the dreadful news that you have the small-pox. I am quite ill but will endeavor to write. You will likely all have them wont you ~~are~~ is the whole company exposed? I am so sorry it happened, it will no doubt keep you there a month longer. If there is any possible way let us know how you are often, and we can write to you all the time. Little Rhoda is almost sure to have them after nursing her mother, what a horrible thing.

I have been sick and nervous. The day you say Helen took sick I was my worst and was feeling badly too. Elder Duffin came in and talked to me a long time and accounted for your not writing.

The children are perfectly well and tell Helen not to worry about them one bit. We haven't much to do but take care of ourselves and we ought to do that well I should think. And don't worry about me, I am up and around and am stronger now than when you left.

The stove draws better since we cleaned it out. I sent all your mail to Cuidad Juarez.

May the Lord hear and answer our prayers at this time and heal dear Helen and keep the rest of you from having it. I do hope dear that you don't take sick and little Rhoda.

May God bless you, O may He be mindful of you all in that affliction.

With love to you and Helen
Avery.

P.S. Is it the black small-pox?

[Avery's "Autobiography and Recollections": Excerpt D (pages 52–54)]

After 48 years
May 5 1952 [*in left margin*]

May 5th, 1904 Owen and Helen left for the City of Mexico with Pres. Ivins, his daughter Florence, Leona Taylor, daughter of John W. Taylor, Kate Spillsbury and a group of missionaries. They expected to tour the L.D.S. mission hold conferences and see the sights of this historical city. The missionaries were to enter their field of labor. A few days previous to their departure Pres. Ivins had advised Owen that he and Helen should be vaccinated for black smallpox along with all the others taking the trip. Owen replied: "We are in the hands of the Lord, he will take care of us," So Pres. Ivins did not further press the subject. All went well the first part of their journey and their letters to us were proof enough that they were all having a delightful time at Guaravaca and other beauty spots, until Helen became very ill starting with that dread disease. [Owen and Kate Spillsbury took are of Rhoda *in left margin*] Letters came to us telling of the anguish that filled the days until she passed away June 7th. Little Rhoda, a nursing baby of five months, was brought back to El Paso with a missionary caring for her and Owen met his mother here and gave the baby over to her to take back to Salt Lake.

Owen had been at Helen's side continuously during her illness and death. She was buried in the City of Mexico. Owen had decided to rest a while at the border before returning to Juarez — sent me a telegram from El Paso to that effect. On his second day there however, he took with a severe headache and feared he was starting with the disease. Next morning he ran a temperature and sent word to Pres. Ivins who traveled the 175 miles to be at Owen's service, was able to get him entered into a detention hospital in El Paso. Alonzo Taylor, a missionary, also had the disease and occupied the same room and he told me the details of their illness together, after Owen passed away June 20 and Alonzo got well and returned to Juarez. He brought me a few personal belongings of Owen that had been thoroly sterilized — letters etc. He said that really Owen was recovering from his illness, his temperature leaving and he felt so good he wanted to sit up. He reached for his trousers at the foot of his bed but the strain on his heart was too much — without a word more he was gone. The sorrow that filled my heart can't be described. It seemed I wept buckets of tears in the days that followed. Two wonderful people who left me well and happy never returned and their four children made orphans. My own child fatherless. I was now a widow.

After a few weeks Frank Y. Taylor came to Mexico to get the children and Anna the maid but <u>no</u> it would not do for me to cross the border. I remained in Mexico almost a year longer. Rented part of my home to a Dr. Farr and her husband and to Wilma and Hattie Robinson. The girls and I cooked and ate our meals together sharing expenses. Each of us had one child. Baby Ruth was my comfort and blessing, and when she was only five months old I took her with me to St.Louis to the world's Fair. Sister Luella Cowley was my traveling companion — and a loyal and true friend. The trip brought me some benefit — helped me to look outward instead of ^to^ my own plight, to some degree.

My sweet mother came to Mexico to comfort me and wanted to take me back with her but was advised it wouldn't do. Surrounded by friends in an all Mormon community I still had much to be thankful for.

Finally, May 1st, 1905 I received word that I might come home in safety. Mayme Bennion & I waved our last goodbye to the Southland — each with a daughter in our arms.

I turned my house and lot over to Pres. Ivins to rent and eventually sell which he did. A Mr. Duthie bought the place for much less than it cost us and it was years before I received the final payment — near the time of the revolution when the colonists were forced to leave their homes. Some of then later returned & got back their houses and I was told the Duthies did so. Before I left Mexico I visited Owen's grave in a beautiful cemetary in [Entered may 5 '52 *in left margin*] El Paso. It was against the law of Mexico to move Helen's remains till after twenty years. It was never done. I've made this long sad story short — just the high spots.

People throughout the church were shocked by the sudden and tradgic death of Owen and Helen. Letters and telegrams were sent to the family from missions, stakes of Zion everywhere. Memorial services were held and resolutions of respect — lofty tributes were spoken and read. Helen had served several years on the M.I.A. board, traveled with Owen and without him visiting the many Stakes of the church. Both were widely known and loved.

There were a few people who figured out for themselves just why this young couple had been taken in death while yet so useful happy and successful. Some such comments came to my attention such as: They died as near to the cause in line of duty, or they gave their lives for the principle meaning pologamy" or they were spared the humiliation of being ex. — they lost their lives for breaking the law of the church and state — the Manifesto.

Equally good people held these various interpretations spoken in my presence some of then to which I generally answered — "let God be the judge," I only know how humble and sincere they were in their conviction that they were doing the right thing in the sight of God. They followed the dictates of those in authority over them at the time and had their blessing. "From the desires of your heart, ye shall be judged"

Also I learned that Pres. Smith's first comment on receiving notice of Owen's and Helen's death was: "This never needed to have happened. Helen came to me for advice regarding a trip to Mexico I told her it was best she not go. A second time she came to me, I told her again to not go, but she didn't follow my counsil, she went."

[Alonzo L. Taylor's Journal] [47]

Alonzo L. Taylor

Thursday, May 26
The doctor came and examined Sister Woodruff and said she had small pox. Apostle Woodruff asked Elders Pomeroy, Henning, and myself to assist him in the caring for his wife, and Katy is to stay and take care of baby.

Friday 27
Elder Pomeroy and I sat up all night with Sister Woodruff. She is broken out all over her body with small pox. All of the folks left the mission house except Elders Pomeroy, Henning, and myself and Katy Spilsbury who stays in an adjoining room and tends Sister Woodruff's baby. We had to keep an oiled silk on our patients face to prevent pitting. It is impossible to get a nurse to come so we Elders do all the waiting on Sister Woodruff and the kitchen work also. Apostle Woodruff of course takes the lead in caring for his wife and we all are doing what we can for her recovery. It is quite a trying experience.

Saturday May 28
Last night we divided the night into 3 sections. I took the first and sat up till one o'clock. Elder Henning sat up till 3 and Elder Pomeroy the balance of the night. Sister Woodruff is getting better slowly but is broken out quite bad and is very weak. Katy left with the baby and is going to stay at a place over on Guerrero street as it was considered safer. Prest. Ivins, Elders Pomeroy and Harris have been hunting another place to live as they do not want to risk this place any more as mission headquarters. It is quite lonesome here now as we are left alone to care for Sister Woodruff . . . .

Sunday May 29
As Elder Pomeroy had to tend to so much work on the outside it was thought best for him to stay out of the sick room. Bro. Henning and I watched all night last night. He sat up til 10 o'clock and I took the balance

of the night. Sister Woodruff was quite bad last night is breaking out very badly. At 7:40 p.m. Prest. Ivins wife and 2 daughters Miss Taylor and Eliza Clayson left for home on the Central train. Bro Woodruff is going to try to get Lozado or Juana to come down and assist us then he wants me to do the running for them. The mission headquarters were changed to 23 _____.

Monday May 30
This morning Bro Pomeroy procured a trained nurse to wait on Sister Woodruff so Bro Woodruff told me to disinfect well so I could stay on the outside and run errands so I changed clothing all around and took a good bath, saturating all my clothes with carbolic acid. Sister Woodruff has a bad case of smallpox and is very sick.

Tuesday May 31
Bro Woodruff discharged the nurse as she did not understand her business and charged 15.00 a day. So he asked me to return to the sick room and assist but as I got ready to change my clothes we heard that Juana was coming so as I was needed for errands I stayed out.

Wednesday 1st
I put in a hard day to day buying drugs groceries etc. I went up town about 12 times some of the times on foot and some of the times in the car. Sister Woodruff is a little better but still very sick. Juana is a great help in this trouble.

Thursday 2nd
I again spent the day running errands up town was on the go all day long buying medicine and things for Sister Woodruff to eat she is gradually getting better but is very weak and very much discouraged in fact she asked for Bro Woodruff to pray for her to die the eruption is very painful.

Friday 3
As Bro Woodruff was so worn out and needed help as bad, I decided at his suggestion to return to the sick room and help wait on Sister Woodruff. The eruption had developed so much that I was about frightened when I saw her. Great white blisters filled with pus were standing out all over her body and wherever they had broken were sores it was a terrible sight. As Bro Woodruff was so worn out and Bro.Henning not well I watched the patient all night alone except that I called Juana a couple of times to assist me. There was scarcely a minute all night when I wasn't working with her.

Saturday 4
Sister Woodruffs condition remains practically the same only I think she is getting gradually weaker and will have a hard struggle to recover. I again set up all night so Bros Woodruff and Henning could rest.

Sunday 5
Our patient continues very weak and is suffering very much from a dryness of her tongue and throat. I sat up till 3 in the morning.

Monday 6
We are all about worn out caring for our patient, cooking trying to keep this old disease trap of a house in order. Sister Woodruff is apparently no better. Bro Woodruff went to hospital to arrange for her removal tomorrow.

Tuesday 7
Bro Woodruff & I sat up till 10 o'clock last night giving our patient milk and brandy for stimulants. She was delirious all the time. Bro. Henning and Juana took the second watch and at 3:45 a.m. Bro. Henning came rushing up the steps to where Bro. Woodruff and I were sleeping on the roof, and told us to come at once for sister Woodruff was dying and scarcely had we reached her bedside when she passed peacefully away after having suffered since May 23 with a most loathing and virulent form of smallpox. Her suffering has been something fearful and for her, death was surely a relief. Bro Woodruff felt terrible and Bro Henning and I did what we could to console him but of course our efforts were very feeble in so great an affection. I then went out to Santa Maria and notified Bro Pomeroy and Harris of her death and Bro Henning went to Hotel   and notified Bishop Johnson and family. I then went and engaged the Layendecker undertaking establishment to take charge of the body and attend to the burial. At 7:30 a.m. I took charge of the washing and laying out of the body and was assisted by 3 men from the undertakers. It was a terrible task as the body was covered with the small pox so bad that we could scarcely touch it without taking off the skin. Later Bros Woodruff and Henning dressed the body with the clothes that Sister Johnson and Harris had prepared. I then went to the undertakers and arranged for a coffin for 60.00 A grave in the American Cemetery Number 85 for $225.00, Two cars for transporting the corpse and attending brethren and sisters at a cost of $25.00 and pall bearers, etc. for $18.00. Making a total cost of $328.00 At 4 o'clock the body was taken from the House in Humboldt to the car on Guerrero street. The accompanying Brethren and sisters entered the other car and an hour later we were at cemetery. There we all surrounded the grave and sang

"O My Father." Bishop Johnson then dedicated the grave and we then sang "Rest for the Weary Soul" Bro Harris then offered a closing prayer and the grave was covered while a sorrowing band of brethren and sisters looked on in silence. Those present at the burial were Apostle Woodruff, Bishop Johnson and wife, Lucy and three daughters, Jenny, Lulu and _____. Bro Harris and family, Miss Katy Spilsbury, Sister Woodruff's baby, Rhoda, Elders T. E. Pomeroy, Paul Henning, P. A. Williams, James Mayhim, Antoine Ivins and myself. Apostle Woodruff and Elder Henning and I then took a room in Hotel Edison and spent a very quiet night in a nice cool clean room which we appreciated after so many nights of watching and worrying. It was a terrible blow to Bro Woodruff but he stood it bravely and manfully and reconciled himself to the ordeal.

[Kate Spilsbury's Recollections][48]

The next year, [1904] I taught the second grade in Col Juarez. We held a school in the basement of the church house. Liza Clayson, Lizzie Butler, Ernest Hatch and myself were the faculty there. In the spring of the year, there was an excursion to Mexico City for $50.00, round trip. Brother Anthony W. Ivins was going with his family — Anna and Florence, and Antonne was already there studying law. Leona Taylor (apostle Taylor's daughter), Apostle Abram O. Woodruff and wife, Helen Mar, Pres. and sis. Ivins, Liza Clayson and I were in the party to go. We arrived in Mexico City after two days traveling from Colonia Juarez. President Hyrum S. Harris was president of the Mexican Mission at that time, and he made us so welcome at the Mission home. At conference time, all the elders came in, and we enjoyed them so much. We also enjoyed visiting the different branches with the Elders and meeting with the saints.

One Sunday afternoon, after we had visited all day in the little branch of Amecameca, we were coming home on the train, and Sister Woodruff took violently ill with a high fever and headache. We arrived in Mexico City at noon from Amecameca and she was still very sick, and gradually getting worse. They called in the Doctor who diagnosed her sickness as Black Small Pox. This was just like a bomb shell exploding in our midst. Pres.Ivins moved his family out of the mission home immediately, and headquarters were transferred to Toluca. Brother and Sister Harris and all the children went over there also. If the city Health officials had known about Sister Woodruff's illness, they would surely have taken her to the pest house to die, so they dared not let it be known at all. Elder Alonzo L. Taylor had just been vaccinated for this dread disease, and Elder Heming had had it, so they volunteered their services to Apostle Woodruff to assist him in the illness of his wife. Her baby was just five months old and they were not able to find a wet nurse to take care of it for them. This left Liza Clayson and I there alone. After much consideration she decided to go home with the Ivins family so I volunteered my services to Apostle Woodruff to help care for the baby. Apostle Woodruff was most grateful and appreciated so much my offer to help, and he gave me a beautiful blessing and promised me in the name of the Lord that if I would stay and help him that I would not contract this dreaded disease. From that time on, I had absolutely no fear of it. He found me a room with a Mrs. Conley, a lady with whom Edmund Richardson had stayed during the time he was studying law in Mexico City. This lady was very kind and good to us and allowed me to do our washing and ironing there. We had a lot of difficulty in finding good that would agree with the baby. Brother Woodruff and Elder A. L. Taylor would take turns coming to see us every other day, and did whatever they could to help us out, certainly they did much in giving me encouragement and moral support.

Sister Woodruff was getting steadily worse. They didn't have a doctor and these two men were taking care of her the best they could. She finally lapsed into a coma,, and after two weeks illness, she died [7 June]. Plans were made immediately to return to the U.S. after burying her there. Bishop Derby Johnson and his wife and three daughters were visiting Mexico, and they held a lovely graveside service for her. That night, Brother Woodruff, A. L. Taylor, the baby and I got on the train to return to El Paso. He telegraphed his mother and Brother-in-law to meet him there, which they did. Brother Woodruff was sick with a high fever all the way to El PaSO. He was breaking out with small pox, too. After travelling 48 hours, we arrived in Ciudad Juarez and were taken immediately to the home of brother James Mortensen. The next A.M. arrangements were made to smuggle Brother Woodruff across the line and he was put in a pest house in El Paso. Brother Woodruff's mother took the baby, and they took A. L. and me and got us a room in a hotel in Juarez. A. L. was sick all day, he too was coming down with the dreaded disease. Still, I was not afraid of taking it, as I had been promised by an Apostle of the Lord that I would not.

The next morning A. L. was smuggled over to El Paso and put in the pest house there. Sister Woodruff took the baby and went back to Salt Lake, and I took the train and came home. Father met me at the train, and I was taken to the Ranch to stay alone until all danger was past. A. L. and Brother Woodruff was suffering intense pain and such a high fever. He passed away on the [20th] of June 1904.

[Emma Woodruff's Letters to Avery]

[*no letterhead*]

Salt Lake Temple Aug 19th 1904

My dear Daughter

Avery I have tryed week after week to get an hour to spend writing to you and others but the moment I get home from the Temple there is something crowding upon me all the time I am perfectly ashamed and feel that it is wicked for me to neglect you so but if you could see what I have to do I am sure you would forgive me. It was several weeks after I returned home before I could sit up long enough to write a letter and then what could I write that would be any comfort to you or any one I have been so sorely tried that I could not do or say anything to comfort anyone I am ashamed of the way that I have treated Brother Ivins after all that he has done for us and wish that you would assure him that he has my most sincere gratitude for what he has done for me and mine I do not feel that I shall ever be able to repay him for his kindness and unselfish devotion to my darling son. I think I can realize how Rachel of old felt when she was weeping for her Children and could not be comforted because they were not I feel as if I never could rise above this crushing blow that has been dealt me and if it was not for the hope that we have for the future I do not know how I could ever live But there I must stop this or you will wish that I had not written now Anna and the children got home all right the I was thankful to have them with me they are all very well and now my greatest desire is to have you home so that you can assist me to carry the load of responsibiliti that rests upon us for I feel that it is yours as well as mine Mrs. Grant thinks that the children should be divided up amongst Helens folks or that Mrs. Booth should take them But I could not consent to either arraingment I think the care of the Children rests entirely with you and me and so long as I have a home and am able in any way to care for them they shall never be seperated. My darlings last request to me was to have his children <u>all</u> raised togather and I shall be faithful to his wish. My house is their proper home and I shall never consent for them to be scatered around the Country. Now all I want is for the time to come when you can come home and take the responsibility off me so that I can attend to my other duties I am coming to the Temple occasionly so as to hold my place until you come home.

Owen had a shotgun and a rifle belonging to his Father. I do not know whare they are as they are not here if they are there I would like to have them brought home some time. I suppose you have some of your mutual friends with you give my love to them. Give my kind love to Katie Spillsbury and tell her if she ever comes to S.L. to come and make her home with me. Well I do not know of anything more of interest to write you but will try to write more often if you have to stay there which I do hope will not be for long. The girls all send love to yourself and bay Ruth. Give my love to _____ and tell her kind words of sympathy Asahel and Family are still in Chicago which makes it still more lonely than if they were home. I have one of Nellie's boys with me and Anna is still with me but as there has been no provision made for the Children as yet I do not know how long I will be able to keep some kind of help for the present. Well I hope you will write to to me occasionally and I will try to write whenever I can get time with much love to yourself and dear little Ruth I am as every your loving Mother Emma Woodruff

[*no letterhead*]

S.L. City March 14th 1907

My dear Daughter Avery I have tryed for months to write to you I receive your very welcome letter a long time ago but I always have so much to do that I cannot do anything that can be put of. I wish that you were here to help me about the children Mrs. Winters and Anna Rosenkilde are determined to take the Children from me and live in Owens house and I think if you were here to assert your rights that it would be a good thing for I dont want to give the Children up but I have talked to President Smith about it and I shall abide by his decision abut if they take the Children I shall not stay here I will rent my house and get me a small place in the City when are you coming north I hope you will at least come and made me a good long visit I will not be tormented with Anna whatever happens for the has been so insolent to me this winter that cannot put up with her any longer only until Mr Grant gets home when we will have this thing settled Well I hope I shall see you before a great while how is dear little Ruth I want to say lots of things to you which I cannot write.

With much love to yourself and Ruthie
I am as ever your
friend and Mother
Emma Woodruff

"I cannot understand why our bright joyous lovely Helen should be called home in the bloom of her life, but we feel that there is a greater work for her in another sphere" Susie Winters Bennion

The Woodruff Circle of Family and Friends

Allen, Dr. Samuel H. Physician in Salt Lake City. Born August 15, 1862, in Mt. Pleasant, Utah.

Ashton, Edward M. Insurance salesman and stockbroker in Salt Lake City.

Bailey, Josie E. Married Frank F. Allred August 20, 1902.

Beebe, Clara Martisha Woodruff. Sister of Owen. Born July 23, 1868. Married Ovando Collins Beebe August 3, 1887.

Beebe, Ovando "Van" Collins. Brother-in-law of Owen. Married Clara Martisha Woodruff, Owen's sister, August 3, 1887.

Bennion, Edwin T. Brother-in-law of Avery. Brother of Heber Bennion and polygamous husband of Mary Minerva Clark, Avery's sister. Born April 8, 1868, in Salt Lake City.

Bennion, Ethelyn "Ethel." Niece of Helen. Daughter of Heber Bennion and Susan Winters, Helen's sister. Born August 6, 1886.

Bennion, Heber. Brother-in-law of Helen. Married Susan Marian Winters, Helen's sister, September 11, 1885. Polygamist married also to Mary Bringhurst (1902) and Emma Jane Webster (no date). Brother of Edwin T. Bennion.

Bennion, Heber, Jr. Nephew of Helen. Son of Heber Bennion and Susan Winters, Helen's sister. Born January 30, 1888.

Bennion, Mary Elizabeth Lindsay. First wife of Edwin T. Bennion. Born September 29, 1870, in Salt Lake City. Married in 1892.

Bennion, Rulon Oscar. Nephew of Helen. Son of Heber Bennion and Susan Winters. Born November 14, 1900.

Bennion, Sterling Alfred. Nephew of Helen. Son of Heber Bennion and Susan Winters. Born January 27, 1899.

Bennion, Susan Marian Winters. Sister of Helen. Born June 25, 1859, in Payson, Utah. Married Heber Bennion September 11, 1885, in Pleasant Grove, Utah.

Booth, Delia Ina Winters. Sister of Helen. Born May 16, 1854, in Pleasant Grove, Utah. Married John Edge Booth in 1887.

Booth, John Edge. Brother-in-law of Helen. Born June 29, 1847, in England. Married Delia Ina Winters, Helen's sister, in 1887. Judge of the Fourth District Court.

Booth, Milton. Nephew of Helen. Born May 21, 1888, to John Booth and Delia Winters.

Brimhall, George H. Professor of pedagogy and later president at Brigham Young Academy. Born December 9, 1852, in Salt Lake City.

Brixen, Julia M. Born in Sweden and baptized into LDS Church at thirteen. Sent to work in Utah to raise money to emigrate her family. Married Andrew Brixen. Called to serve in the YLMIA in 1898.

Burgon, Willard C. Bishop of Union Ward, 1900–1910. Born November 4, 1854. Trained as a mason.

Burrows, Emeline Woodruff. Half-sister of Owen. Daughter of Wilford Woodruff and Sarah Delight Stocking. Born July 26, 1863, in Salt Lake City. Married David Creeland Burrows August 18, 1887.

Cannon, Caroline "Carlie" Young Croxall. Daughter of Brigham Young. Born February 1, 1851. Married George Q. Cannon in 1884 after divorcing Mark Croxall.

Cannon, George M. Cashier of the Zion's Savings Bank and Trust Company in Salt Lake City. Born December 25, 1861, in St. George, Utah. Served with Asahel Woodruff, Owen's brother, in the Stake Sunday School of the Granite Stake.

Cannon, George Quayle. Ordained an LDS apostle in 1860 and served as a counselor to LDS Church presidents Brigham Young, John Taylor, Wilford Woodruff, and Lorenzo Snow. Born January 11, 1827, in England.

Clark, Ann Eliza Porter. Mother of Avery. Born October 22, 1862, in Porterville, Utah. Married Hyrum Don Carlos Clark November 11, 1880.

Clark, Heber D. Brother of Avery. Born July 16, 1887.

Clark, Hyrum Taylor. Brother of Avery. Born October 3, 1885, in Idaho.

Clark, Hyrum Don Carlos. Father of Avery. Born February 13, 1856, in Farmington, Utah. Married Ann Eliza Porter November 11, 1880, in Salt Lake City. Married Mary Alice Robinson December 27, 1903, in polygamous marriage.

Clark, Mary Minerva. Sister of Avery. Born December 1, 1883. Married Edwin T. Bennion in 1903 polygamous marriage.

Clawson, Rudger A. Ordained an LDS apostle in 1898. Born March 1, 1857, in Salt Lake City. Served a four-year prison term for unlawful cohabitation under Edmunds Act.

Cowley, Lenora Taylor. Married Matthias Cowley as a plural wife September 16, 1905. Born March 28, 1885.

Cowley, Matthias F. Ordained an LDS apostle in 1897. Born August 24, 1858, in Salt Lake City. Left the LDS Church in 1905 over its anti-polygamy policy. Reinstated in 1936.

Crosby, Jesse W. Born June 22, 1848. Married to Sarah Pauline Clark.

Called in 1900 to help colonize the Bighorn Basin. Served as first counselor to Byron Sessions in Big Horn Stake Presidency.

Daynes, Winifred Blanche Woodruff. Sister of Owen. Born April 9, 1876,
in Salt Lake City. Married to Joseph J. Daynes Jr. December 18, 1895.

Daynes, Florilla Woodruff. Niece of Owen. Daughter of Joseph and
Blanche Woodruff. Born November 18, 1896.

Daynes, Joseph Donald. Nephew of Owen. Son of Joseph and Blanche
Daynes. Born October 1, 1898.

Daynes, Joseph John. Born April 2, 1851, in Norwich, England. Father of
Joseph Daynes Jr., brother-in-law to Owen. Salt Lake City Tabernacle
organist for thirty years.

Daynes, Joseph John, Jr. Brother-in-law of Owen. Married Winifred
Blanche Woodruff December 18, 1895, in Salt Lake City.

Dougall, Maria Young. Daughter of Brigham Young. Born December
10, 1849. Raised by Zina D. H. Young after mother's death. Married
William B. Dougall. Called in 1887 as counselor to Elmina Taylor on
the General Board of the YLMIA.

Empey, Emma Jane Evans. Wife of Nelson A. Empey. Born June 11, 1835.

Esplin, Henry Webster. Born October 20, 1854, in Nephi, Utah. Married
Phinena Cox. Bishop of Orderville, Utah, from 1884 to 1910.

Eyring, Edward Christian. Born May 27, 1868. Married Caroline Cottam
Romney in 1893 and her sister Emma Cottom Romney in 1903, sisters
of Junius Romney. Resident of Colonia Juárez.

Freeman, Ivy Leona. Niece of Helen. Born October 6, 1883, in Pleasant
Grove, Utah. Daughter of William and Mary Ann Freeman, sister of
Helen. Married John W. Adams March 15, 1905.

Freeman, Mary Ann Winters. Sister of Helen. Born January 3, 1862, in
Mt. Pleasant, Utah. Married William Hamblin Freeman November 25,
1880, in Salt Lake City.

Freeman, Ruby. Niece of Helen. Born November 7, 1890, in Pleasant
Grove, Utah. Daughter of William and Mary Ann Freeman. Married
Roscoe Derrick Sorensen March 27, 1913, in Salt Lake City.

Freeman, William Hamblin. Brother-in-law of Helen. Born February 4,
1858, in Harriman, Utah. Married Mary Ann Winters November 25,
1880, in Salt Lake City.

Gates, Emma Lucy. Born November 4, 1880, in St. George, Utah. Daughter of
Jacob and Susa Young Gates. Married Albert E. Bowen on June 30, 1916, in
Salt Lake City. Trained in opera at Berlin's Royal Conservatory of Music.

Gibbs, George. Personal secretary to the First Presidency of the LDS Church.
Son, also named George, companion of Owen's on a hunting trip.

Goddard, Emma. Born April 19, 1861, in England. Married Benjamin
Goddard in 1883. Called to the YLMIA General Board in 1896 and
served on the Journal Committee.

Graham, Julia Sessions. Daughter of Byron Sessions. Married Walter Graham. Resident of Bighorn Basin community.

Grant, Heber Jeddy. Helen's brother-in-law. Born November 22, 1856, in Salt Lake City. Married Lucy Stringham in 1877, Augusta Winters in 1884, and Emily Wells in 1884. Ordained an LDS apostle in 1882 and set apart as church president in 1918. When Grant served as president, Augusta was the only one of his wives still living.

Grant, Hulda Augusta "Gusta" Winters. Sister of Helen. Born July 7, 1856, in Payson, Utah. Married Heber J. Grant in 1884.

Grant, Rachel Ridgeway Ivins. Mother of Heber J. Grant. Born March 9, 1821, in New Jersey. Married Jedediah M. Grant November 29, 1855.

Hickman, Ella. Wife of Professor J. E. Hickman of Brigham Young Academy. Aunt of Ovando Beebe.

Horne, Clara Leone. Niece of Martha Horne Tingey. Born October 10, 1878, in Salt Lake City. Married Ambrey Nowell in 1904.

Hyde, Annie Taylor. Daughter of President John Taylor. Born October 20, 1849. Married a son of Orson Hyde. Considered the founder of the Daughters of the Utah Pioneers. Called to serve as first counselor to Bathsheba Smith on LDS Relief Society General Board in 1901.

Ivins, Anthony W. President of Juárez Stake in Mexico. Born in 1852. Married Elizabeth Ashby Snow, daughter of Erastus Snow, in 1878. Ordained an LDS apostle in 1907.

Kearns, Thomas. Non-LDS U.S. Senator. Born April 11, 1862. Member of Utah Constitutional Convention. Became millionaire in Park City, Utah, mining industry. Built Kearns Mansion, now Utah Governor's Mansion, on South Temple Street as his personal residence. Elected by the Republican legislature as U.S. Senator in 1901, with the rumored support of LDS president Lorenzo Snow.

Kelsch, Louis A. Associate of LDS apostle Mathias F. Cowley. Born April 28, 1857. Married Rosalia Esther Atwood.

Kelsch, Rosalia Esther Atwood. Wife of Louis A. Kelsch.

Kimball, Jonathan "J" Golden. Son of Heber C. Kimball. Born June 9, 1853, in Salt Lake City. Called as one of the Seven Presidents of the Seventy in 1892. Served on the YMMIA General Board.

Lambert, Martha. Nurse of Helen during childbirth.

Lund, Anthon Henrik. Counselor of Joseph F. Smith. Born May 15, 1844, in Denmark. Ordained an LDS apostle in 1899.

Lyman, Francis Marion. LDS apostle ordained in 1880. Born January 12, 1840, in Illinois, the eldest son of Amasa M. Lyman. Served on the YMMIA General Board.

Maeser, Karl G. President of Brigham Young Academy in Provo, Utah. Born January 16, 1828. Called by Brigham Young to organize academy in 1875.

McClellan, J. J. Tabernacle organist who replaced Joseph Daynes.

McCune, Elizabeth Claridge. Wife of Alfred W. McCune, wealthy businessman in Salt Lake City who built the McCune Mansion.

McEwan, Emma Woodruff. Niece of Owen. Born July 9, 1902, to William McEwan and Mary Alice Woodruff.

McEwan, Mary Alice Woodruff. Sister of Owen. Born January 2, 1879. Married William McEwan November 16, 1897.

McEwan, William. Brother-in-law of Owen. Born November 16, 1871. Married Mary Alice Woodruff November 16, 1897.

McMurrin, Joseph W. LDS apostle ordained in 1898. Born September 5, 1858. Served as one of the Seven Presidents of the Seventy in 1897 and on the YMMIA General Board. Helped Owen organize Bighorn Basin community.

Murdock, Joseph Royal. Utah State Senator elected in 1900. Born August 11, 1858, in Salt Lake City. Served as member of Utah State Constitutional Convention.

Paul, Joshua Hughes. President of LDS University in Salt Lake City. Born January 20, 1863. Taught for nine years at the University of Utah, was associate editor of the *Salt Lake Herald*, was president of the Agricultural College of Utah, and was editor of the *Deseret News* for a short time.

Pierce, Isaac Washington. High council member of Juárez Stake. Born August 22, 1839. Moved to Colonia Diaz, Chihuahua, Mexico, with his two polygamous families in 1890. Established a retail lumber business there in 1898.

Richards, DeForest. Governor of Wyoming elected in 1893. Born August 6, 1846, in Alabama. Married Elise Ingersoll in 1871. Moved west in 1885 and settled in Douglas, Wyoming, in 1886.

Roberts, Brigham Henry. Prolific writer of LDS Church history and biography. Born March 13, 1857. Ordained to the First Council of the Seventy in 1888.

Romney, Junius. Born March 12, 1878, in St. George, Utah. Resident of Colonia Juárez and later president of the Juárez Stake.

Rosenkilde, Anna. House girl employed by Helen.

Sessions, Byron. Big Horn Stake president called in 1901. Born November 7, 1851, in Bountiful, Utah. Married Idella Win Twombly in 1870. Called to help colonize Bighorn Basin in 1900.

Sessions, Idella Win Twombly. Wife of Byron Sessions. Born June 16, 1856. Married Byron Sessions in 1970.

Smith, Bathesheba W. Fourth general president of the LDS Relief Society. Born May 3, 1822, in West Virginia. Married to George Albert Smith. Charter member of the Relief Society when Emma Smith presided. Received her endowments from the Prophet Joseph Smith.

Smith, George Albert. Cousin to the Prophet Joseph Smith. Born June 26, 1817, to LDS Church Patriarch John Smith and Clarissa Lyman. Ordained an apostle in 1868 and served as first counselor to Brigham Young. Married to Bathesheba Smith.

Smith, Hyrum Mack. LDS apostle ordained in 1901 by his father, Joseph F. Smith. Born March 31, 1872, to Joseph F. Smith and Edna Lambson. Married to Ida Elizabeth Smith.

Smith, Ida Elizabeth Bowman. Wife of Apostle Hyrum Mack Smith.

Smith, Joseph F. LDS apostle ordained in 1866 and named counselor in First Presidency by Brigham Young. Born November 13, 1838, in Far West, Missouri, to Hyrum Smith and Mary Fielding. Served as counselor to church presidents John Taylor, Wilford Woodruff, and Lorenzo Snow. Ordained fifth president of the church in 1901.

Smoot, Reed. U.S. Senator elected in 1903 and apostle. Born in 1862 to Abraham Owen Smoot and Anne Kirstene Morrison.

Snow, Lorenzo. Fourth president of the LDS Church. Set apart in 1898. Born April 3, 1813, in Ohio. Ordained an apostle in 1849. Served as counselor to Brigham Young. Married Sarah Ann Prichard, his third wife, April 21, 1845.

Snow, Sarah Ann Prichard. Third wife of Lorenzo Snow. Born November 29, 1826.

Talmage, James E. Apostle ordained in 1911. Born September 21, 1862, in England. Married May Booth June 14, 1888.

Talmage, May Booth. Wife of LDS apostle James E. Talmage. Born 1868. Married June 14, 1888. Called to the YLMIA General Board in 1892.

Tanner, Joseph Marion. General Superintendent of LDS Church Schools and member of General Sunday School Board, serving with Owen. Born March 26, 1859, in Payson, Utah. Received degree from Harvard University. President of the Agricultural College in Logan until he resigned in 1900 over polygamy. Husband of six wives, one of whom, Annie Clark Tanner, was a relative of Avery.

Taylor, Elizabeth Campbell. Wife of Frank Young Taylor. Married in May 1844.

Taylor, Elmina Shepherd. General President of the YLMIA. Born September 12, 1830, in Middlefield, New York. Married George Hamilton Taylor in 1856.

Taylor, Frank Young. First President of the Granite Stake, set apart January 28, 1900. Born November 4, 1861. Son of President John Taylor and brother of Annie Taylor Hyde.

Taylor, John Whittaker. LDS apostle ordained in 1884. Born May 14, 1858, in Provo, Utah. Son of John Taylor. Resigned apostleship in 1905 and was excommunicated in 1911.

Taylor, Nellie Eva Todd. Polygamous wife of John W. Taylor, married September 23, 1888. Born January 13, 1869.

Taylor, Rhoda Welling. Resident of Colonia Juárez. Married August 29, 1901, to John W. Taylor as polygamous wife along with her sister Roxie.

Taylor, Roxie Welling. Resident of Colonia Juárez. Married August 29, 1901, to John W. Taylor as polygamous wife along with her sister Rhoda.

Tingey, Martha Horne. General YLMIA President, succeeding Elmina Taylor in 1905. Born October 15, 1857, in Salt Lake City. Called as second counselor to President Taylor in 1880.

Tippetts, Brigham L. First counselor in Big Horn Stake Presidency. Born August 1, 1880, in Brigham City, Utah. Member of original scouting party to the Bighorn Basin with Owen.

Welch, Charles A. Second counselor in Big Horn Stake Presidency. Appointed by Owen to keep the books of the Bighorn Basin project and run the commissary.

Wells, Heber M. First governor of Utah. Born August 11, 1859, to Daniel Wells and Martha E. Harris.

Wells, Rulon. One of the Seven Presidents of the Seventy ordained in 1893. Born July 7, 1854. Served on the General Board of the YMMIA.

Wilson, Guy Carlton. Principal of Juárez Academy, appointed in 1897. Born April 10, 1864, in Fairview, Utah. Supervisor of the LDS Church School System. Counselor to Anthony W. Ivins in Juárez Stake Presidency. Polygamist with three wives: Elizabeth Hartsburg, Agnes M. Stevens, and Anna Ivins.

Winder, John R. Counselor in LDS Presiding Bishopric, set apart in 1887. Born December 11, 1821, in England. Set apart as counselor to LDS President Joseph F. Smith in 1901.

Winters, Arthur Ray. Brother of Helen. Born May 16, 1871, in Pleasant Grove, Utah.

Winters, Mary Ann Stearns. Mother of Helen. Born April 6, 1833, in Missouri. Married Oscar Winters August 16, 1852.

Winters, Oscar. Father of Helen. Born February 7, 1825, in Ohio. Married Mary Ann Stearns August 16, 1852.

Woodruff, Arabell Jane Hatch. Sister-in-law of Owen. Born April 2, 1859. Married David Patten Woodruff, Owen's half-brother, February 19, 1877.

Woodruff, Asahel Hart. Brother of Owen. Born February 3, 1863, to Emma Smith and Wilford Woodruff in Salt Lake City. Married Naomi Abbott Butterworth December 14, 1887.

Woodruff, Asahel Hart Jr. Nephew of Owen. Born February 13, 1893, to Asahel Hart Woodruff and Naomi Abbot Butterworth.

Woodruff, Clara Martisha. Sister of Owen. Born July 23, 1868.

Woodruff, David Patten. Half-brother of Owen. Born April 4, 1854, to

Wilford Woodruff and Sarah Brown in Salt Lake City. Married Arrabell Jane Hatch February 19, 1877. Moved to Bighorn Basin in 1893 with first LDS colonists. Called to Big Horn Stake High Council in 1901.

Woodruff, Emma Rose. Niece of Owen. Born in 1896 to Asahel Woodruff and Naomi Butterworth.

Woodruff, Emma Smith. Mother of Owen. Born March 1, 1838, in Missouri. Married Wilford Woodruff March 13, 1853, as his third wife.

Woodruff, Helen Mar. Daughter of Helen and Owen. Born January 1, 1901, in Salt Lake City.

Woodruff, John Jay. Half-brother of Owen. Born August 14, 1873, to Wilford Woodruff and Sarah Delight Stocking. Married Annie L. E. Nielsen January 24, 1903.

Woodruff, June. Daughter of Helen and Owen. Born June 24, 1902, in Salt Lake City.

Woodruff, Naomi Butterworth. Sister-in-law of Owen. Born March 21, 1864, in England. Married Asahel Hart Woodruff in 1887.

Woodruff, Rhoda. Daughter of Helen and Owen. Born December 28, 1903, in Salt Lake City.

Woodruff, Ruth. Daughter of Avery and Owen. Born April 11, 1904, in Mexico.

Woodruff, Sarah Delight Stocking. Fifth wife of Wilford Woodruff. Born June 26, 1838.

Woodruff, Torrey Brigham Newton. Nephew of Owen. Born November 15, 1894, to Arabell Jane Hatch and David Patten Woodruff in Bighorn, Wyoming.

Woodruff, Wilford, Jr. Half-brother of Owen. Born March 22, 1840, in Iowa to Phoebe Whittemore Carter and Wilford Woodruff. Married Emily Jane Smith in 1867 and later two plural wives.

Woodruff, Wilford Owen. Son of Helen and Owen. Born October 31, 1899, in Salt Lake City.

Young, Brigham, Jr. Son of Brigham Young. Born December 18, 1836. Ordained LDS apostle on February 4, 1864.

Young, Seymour B. Physician and surgeon. Born October 3, 1837, to Jane Bicknell and Joseph Young in Kirtland, Ohio. Served as one of the Seven Presidents of the Seventy and later as an LDS apostle.

Young, Zina D. H. LDS General Relief Society President. Born January 31, 1831, in Watertown, New York.

Notes

Introduction

1. *Doctrine and Covenants* 132: 3 (Salt Lake City: The Church of Jesus Christ of Latter-day Saints, 1981), 281. This verse of LDS scripture from Section 132 on the new and everlasting covenant of marriage embodies the divine imperative Joseph Smith felt regarding the establishment of plural marriage among the Latter-day Saints
2. Gerry Avant and Douglas D. Palmer, "A Love Story, A Drama, A Miracle," *Deseret News,* July 24, 1993.
3. Avant and Palmer, "Love Story."
4. *Doctrine and Covenants* 132.
5. Richard L. Bushman with the assistance of Jed Woodworth, *Joseph Smith: Rough Stone Rolling* (New York: Knopf, 2005), 437.
6. Bushman, *Rough Stone Rolling,* 440.
7. Ibid., 526–27.
8. Avery's account of Owen's behavior during their courtship reflects this pattern.
9. Bushman, *Rough Stone Rolling,* 492–93.
10. R. Carmon Hardy, *Solemn Covenant: The Mormon Polygamous Passage* (Urbana: University of Illinois Press, 1992), 18.
11. Wilford Woodruff, "Manifesto," *Proceedings at the Semi-Annual General Conference of the Church of Jesus Christ of Latter-day Saints,* October 6, 1890, 2–3.
12. B. H. Roberts, *Comprehensive History of the Church* (Provo: Brigham Young University Press, 1965), 341.
13. *Doctrine and Covenants,* "Official Declaration 1." According to Robert J. Woodford in "The Story of the Doctrine and Covenants" (*Ensign,* December 1984), "Most usually, the Manifesto was on a separate page that was glued in; some printings, especially vest-pocket editions, didn't contain the Manifesto as a regular part of the text until the 1921 edition" (37). Hardy, in *Solemn Covenant,* notes there is some evidence that the voting to sustain the Manifesto was not unanimous and that some in attendance abstained from voting (135).
14. Roberts, *Comprehensive History of the Church,* 218.
15. Kenneth Godfrey, Audrey M. Godfrey, and Jill Mulvey Derr, *Women's Voices: An Untold History of the Latter-day Saints, 1830–1900.* (Salt Lake City: Deseret Book, 1982), 341.
16. Eliza Avery Clark (Woodruff) Lambert, "Autobiography and Recollections of Eliza Avery Clark (Woodruff) Lambert, 1882–1953."Abraham Owen Woodruff Collection, box 6, folder 21. L. Tom Perry Special Collections & Manuscripts, Harold B. Lee Library, Brigham Young University, Provo, Utah. 69–70.
17. Andrew Jenson, *Latter-day Saint Biographical Encyclopedia* (Salt Lake City: Deseret News, 1901), 1: 172–73.

18. Ibid., 1: 173.
19. Interestingly, this story is told in the Clark family, not the Woodruff family. It was told to Richard Lambert by his uncle, Heber Clark, Avery's brother.
20. *Deseret News,* June 30, 1897.
21. Scott G. Kenney, ed, *Wilford Woodruff's Journal: 1833–1898 Typescript,* vol. 9, 1 January 1, 1889, to September 2, 1898 (Midvale, Utah: Signature Books, 1983), 489.
22. May Boothe Talmage, "Helen Winters Woodruff," *The Young Woman's Journal: Organ of the Young Ladies' Mutual Improvement Associations* 15 (1904): 292.
23. Ibid., 293.
24. Hulda Augusta Grant, ed, "Mothers in Israel: Autobiography of Mary A. S. Winters," *The Relief Society Magazine* 3(1916): 577–78.
25. Ibid.
26. Susa Young Gates, ed., "Notes about Women," *The Young Woman's Journal: Organ of the Young Ladies' Mutual Improvement Associations of Zion* 10 (1899): 287–88.
27. Talmage, "Helen Winters Woodruff," 293.
28. Abraham Owen Woodruff, "Diary," June 30, 1899, Woodruff Collection, box 1.
29. Ibid., October 31, 1899.
30. Ibid., December 31, 1900.
31. Perhaps the most comprehensive treatment of post-Manifesto polygamy based on primary archival materials and related to the Woodruff's experience is found in an article by D. Michael Quinn, "LDS Church Authority and New Plural Marriages, 1890–1904," *Dialogue: A Journal of Mormon Thought* 18, no. 1 (1985): 9–105. As some of the documents Quinn consulted in his research for this article have subsequently been made inaccessible to scholars by the LDS Church, we cannot verify either his research or his conclusions. See also Hardy's *Solemn Covenant,* which relies heavily on archival materials as well as on Quinn's seminal article.
32. Hardy, *Solemn Covenant,* 190.
33. Kurt D. Graham, "The Mormon Migration to Wyoming's Big Horn Basin" (master's thesis, Brigham Young University, 1994), 20–21.
34. Ibid.
35. Ibid., 7.
36. Ibid., 24.
37. Ibid., 40.
38. According to the Register of the Woodruff Collection, Owen married Avery in January 1901, although Woodruff Family Group Sheets list their marriage date as November 1, 1900. Quinn also identifies January 1901 as the month of the marriage, with January 13 being the likely day (89). It is possible that Quinn read Owen's journal entry for that date and found, as Lu Ann indicated in an earlier draft of this introduction, that he had drawn a temple in connection with that entry to commemorate the marriage, though he made no other reference to it. Owen's journal entry for November 1, 1900, included in the Woodruff Collection, makes no reference to a marriage having taken place that day. Further, there is a reference in Letter 67 (Owen to Avery) suggesting that January 18 may be the marriage date: "On the evening of the eighteenth (I suppose you will remember the day) I took Mary out to Neff's to a delightfull party. As I could not celebrate this day with you I thought the next would be your sister."

39. Graham, "Mormon Migration," 82.
40. Ibid.
41. Woodruff, "Diary," May 27, 1900.
42. Woodruff, "Diary," August 28, 1900.
43. Woodruff, "Diary," August 30, 1900.
44. Lambert, "Autobiography and Recollections," 34.
45. Ibid., 37.
46. Ibid., 41–42.
47. Again, Quinn indicates January 13, 1901, to be the probable date (89), although Letter 67 suggests January 18 to be the date.
48. Hardy, *Solemn Covenant*, 389.
49. Ibid., 209.
50. Lambert, "Autobiography and Recollections," 12.
51. Lambert, "Autobiography and Recollections," 44.
52. Quinn, "LDS Church Authority," 89.
53. Hardy, *Solemn Covenant*, 389.
54. Ibid., 209.
55. Woodruff, "Diary," January 11, 1900.
56. Quinn, "LDS Church Authority," 89.
57. Fortunately, Avery did not destroy every letter from Owen, as many are extant in the Woodruff Collection.
58. Lambert, "Autobiography and Recollections," 44.
59. Ibid., 46.
60. Helen May Winters Woodruff, "Be Ye Not Unequally Yoked," *Young Woman's Journal* 13 (1903): 205.
61. Zina Diantha Jacobs Huntington Smith Young and Bathsheba W. Bigler Smith were distinguished women in the LDS community. Both had been polygamous wives of LDS leaders and had held high church positions. It is significant that Helen knew both of them well and that she had confided in them her polygamous secret. Helen's use of the title "Aunt" also demonstrates a familiarity with them, because children in polygamous households used this title to refer to other wives/mothers in the immediate family. At this time, LDS women were beginning to forfeit the privilege of pronouncing blessings, a practice that was once fairly common but now does not occur.
62. Helen mentions this point in a letter to Avery on January 1, 1904.
63. Hardy, *Solemn Covenant*, 175.
64. Ibid., 174.
65. Lambert, "Autobiography and Recollections," 48.
66. Ibid., 49.
67. Ibid., 44–45.
68. Milton R. Merrill, *Reed Smoot: Apostle in Politics* (Logan: Utah State University Press and Department of Political Science, 1990), 20.
69. Wayne Stout, *History of Utah*, Vol. 2, *1896–1929* (Salt Lake City: Wayne Stout, 1968), 148.
70. Merrill, *Reed Smoot: Apostle in Politics*, 30–31.
71. Woodruff Collection, box 4, folder 11.
72. Merrill, *Reed Smoot: Apostle in Politics*, 42.
73. Ibid.
74. Harvard S. Heath, "Reed Smoot: The First Modern Mormon" (PhD dissertation, Brigham Young University, 1990), 107.
75. Ibid., 108.

76. Ibid., 109.
77. Quinn, "LDS Church Authority," 89. Quinn's position on this issue cannot be verified by available documentation.
78. Carrie A. Miles, "Polygamy and the Economics of Salvation," *Sunstone* 111 (August 1998): 41.
79. Ibid., 36.
80. Ibid., 37.
81. Heath, "Reed Smoot: The First Modern Mormon," 109.
82. Hans P. Freece, "Mormon Chiefs Confess." Printed and distributed by Hans P. Freece, Attorney at Law, 35 Wall Street, New York City, NY.
83. Merrill, "Reed Smoot: Apostle in Politics," 48.
84. Ibid., 56.
85. Woodruff Collection, box 4, folder 11.
86. Lambert, "Autobiography and Recollections," 50. Avery notes that, according to Owen's journal, he voted to uphold President Smith contrary to his personal feelings. Because the 1904 portion of Owen's journal is unavailable to scholars, this vote cannot be verified.
87. Quinn, "LDS Church Authority," 100.
88. Ibid., 100.
89. Lambert, "Autobiography and Recollections," 50.
90. Ibid.
91. As discussed in Eric Bluth's BYU master's thesis, "Pus, Pox, Propaganda and Progress: The Compulsory Smallpox Vaccination Controversy in Utah, 1899–1901," the Utah legislature and two of Salt Lake City's newspapers fought a heated battle over compulsory vaccinations. The LDS Church never publicly opposed voluntary vaccinations, but because the *Deseret News* was viewed as the church's mouthpiece, its anti-vaccination stance was perceived as an official church statement. Church authorities differed in opinion regarding the issue. Opponents of compulsory vaccination believed exaggerated stories circulating from Europe regarding vaccinations' side effects and also feared loss of American liberties. Proponents of compulsory vaccinations, including the *Salt Lake Daily Herald*, championed science to control the dreaded disease. Ironically, the most outspoken anti-vaccination individual, Charles Penrose, editor of the *Deseret News*, replaced Owen in the Quorum of the Twelve Apostles upon his death from smallpox.
92. Lambert, "Autobiography and Recollections," 53–54.
93. Ruth May Fox, "Helen," *Young Woman's Journal* 15 (1904): 291.
94. Woodruff Collection, box 4, folder 7.
95. Avant and Palmer, "Love Story," 3–4.

1899

1. Florilla Woodruff Daynes, daughter and eldest child of Joseph J. Daynes and Blanche Woodruff, and niece of Helen and Owen. Florilla was born November 18, 1896, and died July 17, 1899. Family information such as this comes primarily from LDS family group sheets from the Church of Jesus Christ of Latter-day Saints Family History Library.
2. Winifred Blanche Woodruff Daynes was born April 9, 1876, and was married to Joseph J. Daynes Jr. on December 18, 1895. Blanche was Owen Woodruff's younger sister. Blanche was just twenty years old when Florilla died.

3. Emma Smith Woodruff was born March 1, 1838, in Adam-Ondi-Ahman, Missouri, and was married as the third wife to Wilford Woodruff on March 13, 1853. She gave birth to eight children.

4. Joseph John Daynes Jr. was born November 7, 1873, in Salt Lake City, Utah. He married Winifred Blanche Woodruff on December 18, 1895, in the Salt Lake Temple.

5. Asahel Hart Woodruff was born February 3, 1863, in Salt Lake City, Utah. He married Naomi Abbott Butterworth on December 14, 1887. Asahel was the third child born to Wilford Woodruff and Emma Smith and was the elder brother of Owen.

6. Ovando Collins Beebe was married to Clara Martisha Woodruff, Owen's sister, on August 3, 1887.

7. Jenson, *Latter-day Saint Biographical Encyclopedia*, 1: 746. John J. Daynes Sr. was born April 2, 1851, in Norwich, England. He was the father of Joseph John Daynes Jr., brother-in-law to Helen and Owen. Daynes was the tabernacle organist for thirty years.

8. *Deseret Evening News*, July 18, 1899. John J. Daynes, the tabernacle organist and Florilla's grandfather, played several numbers on the new organ as part of the dedication ceremony for the Sevier Stake tabernacle. Interestingly, Owen's journal indicates that in August of 1900 he "had an interview with Professor J. J. Daynes who feels bad towards me thinking I have been the means of his removal as church organist. This is not true."

9. Possibly Nellie Eva Todd Taylor, who was born January 13, 1869, and became a polygamous wife of John W. Taylor September 25, 1888. She had eight children and died February 11, 1945.

10. Susan Marian Winters Bennion, Helen's sister, was born June 25, 1859, and married Heber Bennion on September 11, 1885.

11. Mary Ann Stearns Winters, Helen's mother, was born April 6, 1833, in Missouri. She married Oscar Winters on August 16, 1852.

12. Probably Sterling Alfred Bennion, seven months old, born January 27, 1899.

13. Arthur Ray Winters, Helen's brother, was born May 16, 1871, in Pleasant Grove, Utah.

14. Hulda Augusta Winters Grant, Helen's sister, was born July 7, 1856, in Payson, Utah. She married Heber J. Grant in 1884 as his second wife.

15. *Deseret Evening News*, August 19, 1899. A "grand welcome" was given for the Utah volunteers returning from Manila, after being away for approximately fifteen months. They were returning from America's war with Spain over control of Cuba and the Philippines. The welcome included parades, speeches, and presentations of badges.

16. *Deseret Evening News*, August 14, 1899. The stake conference was held in the Heber City tabernacle. Elder Amasa Lyman spoke on the end of plural marriage, that it was "revealed by God but rejected because of the small percentage who were willing to accept it and observe it."

17. Delia Ina Winters Booth, Helen's sister, was born May 16, 1854, in Pleasant Grove, Utah. She married John Edge Booth in 1887.

18. Apparently, Avery began her "Autobiography and Recollections," on January 17, 1951, and finished it on May 5, 1952. In this excerpt, she recounts her first encounter with Owen during the summer of 1900 and details the events that are referred to only obliquely in the 1900 correspondence that follows this excerpt. Avery's recollections, unlike the correspondence, were written many years after the events, so they lack the immediacy of the letters and are

mediated by Avery's retrospective purpose. In addition, Avery undoubtedly told these stories many times over the years, so their narrative performance has a rehearsed, canonized quality about it. She seems very sure about her version of this part of her life.

19. Mary Minerva Clark, Avery's sister, was born December 1, 1883. She would marry Edwin T. Bennion in a 1903 polygamous marriage

20. *Valley means Star Valley, Wyoming. B.Y.C. is Brigham Young College in Logan, Utah.

21. Ann Eliza Porter Clark, Avery's mother, was born October 22, 1862, in Porterville, Utah, and married Hyrum Don Carlos Clark on November 11, 1880, in Salt Lake City. She had fourteen children.

22. Hyrum Don Carlos Clark, Avery's father, was born February 13, 1856, in Farmington, Utah, and married Ann Eliza Porter November 11, 1880, in Salt Lake City. He also married Mary Alice Robinson December 27, 1903, in a polygamous marriage. He died July 2, 1938.

23. Jensen, *Latter-day Saint Biographical Encyclopedia*, 1:216. Joseph W. McMurrin was ordained an apostle in 1898 and shared the Bighorn Basin development assignment with Owen. He was born September 5, 1858. He served as one of the Seven Presidents of Seventy in 1897 and served also on the Young Men's Mutual Improvement Association (YMMIA) General Board.

24. Hyrum Taylor Clark, Avery's brother, was born October 3, 1885, in Oakley, Idaho. Heber Don Carlos Clark, another brother, was born July 16, 1887, in Oakley, Idaho.

25. Round dancing is choreographed group ballroom dancing in which movements are called or cued by a "cuer," in a manner somewhat similar to square dancing.

1900

1. Avery and her sister Mary were attending Brigham Young College in Logan, Utah. They began their studies in 1899. Avery writes in her "Autobiography and Recollections," (17–18), "We were thrilled to be in college but in truth this was the beginning of our high school training. Mary and I were so thrilled with school that at the end of the second term that first year we wrote home begging out parents to let us stay on just six weeks longer for summer school. . . . Our enthusiasm for learning pleased them and I think influenced their decision when in the Fall we were again ready to return to B.Y."

2. Avery wrote of this experience in her autobiography (43), "In a week or so but without warning I answered a knock on our door. There stood Owen Woodruff as white as a sheet — he was frightened and so was I. . . . He treated me as if I were a queen tenderly touching my hand. There was no love making, just beautiful, lofty words of devotion to the principle we were contemplating living and for each other and Helen."

3. According to early Mormon doctrine, the first wife must give her consent to subsequent polygamous marriages, following the pattern of Abraham and Sarah when Sarah gave Hagar to wife. On July 12, 1843, the Prophet Joseph Smith received a revelation concerning the marriage covenant, including the plurality of wives. This revelation is recorded in Section 132 of the Doctrine and Covenants. Verses 64 and 65 explain the "law of Sarah": "And again, verily, verily, I say unto you, if any man have a wife, who holds the keys of this power, and he teaches unto her the law of my priesthood, as pertaining to

these things [plural marriage], then shall she believe and administer unto him, or she shall be destroyed, saith the Lord your God; for I will destroy her; for I will magnify my name upon all those who receive and abide in my law.

"Therefore, it shall be lawful in me, if she receive not this law, for him to receive all things whatsoever I, the Lord his God, will give unto him, because she did not believe and administer unto him according to my word; and she then becomes the transgressor; and he is exempt from the law of Sarah, who administered when I commanded Abraham to take Hagar to wife."

4. Historian Thomas Alexander, Brigham Young University, explains that temple fast meetings were held monthly up to the early years of the twentieth century. Participants included family members of general authorities, as well as prominent church members.

5. Lorenzo Snow was born April 3, 1814 in Ohio. He was ordained an apostle in 1849, served as a counselor to Brigham Young, and was set apart as president of the church in 1898. He died in 1901. *Deseret News Church Almanac*, 1991–1992 ed. (Salt Lake City: Deseret Press, 1992), 38

6. Ibid., 40–44. Counselors to President Snow were Joseph F. Smith and Rudger Clawson.

7. Ruby Freeman was born November 7, 1890, and was the daughter of William Freeman and Mary Ann Winters. She was Helen's niece.

8. Jenson, *Latter-day Saint Biographical Encyclopedia*, 1: 563. Frank Young Taylor, the son of President John Taylor and brother of Annie Taylor Hyde, was born November 4, 1861. He was called to serve as the first president of the Granite Stake on January 28, 1900. He was also one of the architects for the Manti Temple.

9. William McEwan, born November 16, 1871, and Mary Alice Woodruff, born January 2, 1879, were married November 16, 1897. They had eleven children. Mary Alice was Owen's younger sister.

10. Louis A. Kelsch, born November 28, 1857, was married to Rosalia Esther Atwood, born October 18, 1858. Kelsch was a friend and an associate of Apostle Matthias Cowley.

11. Wife of Nelson A. Empey. His first wife, Ella, died in 1890. Empey's second wife, Emma Jane Evans, was born June 11, 1835, and died October 24, 1919.

12. Helen's veiled remarks about her state of mind in this paragraph refer to Owen's impending marriage to Avery Clark as a plural wife. Her anxiety over losing her exclusive marriage relationship with Owen informs this and her subsequent letters.

13. Jenson, *Latter-day Saint Biographical Encyclopedia*, 1: 174. Owen was called as an apostle to head the colonization of the Bighorn Basin in Wyoming. He was given this assignment by the First Presidency.

14. Jenson, *Latter-day Saint Biographical Encyclopedia*, 1: 541–42. Jesse W. Crosby was born June 22, 1848. He was married to Sarah Pauline Clark. Crosby was called in 1900 to help colonize the Big Horn Basin and was called to serve as first counselor to Byron Sessions in the Big Horn Stake presidency.

15. Jenson, *Latter-day Saint Biographical Encyclopedia*, 1: 311. Anthony W. Ivins, born in 1852, was married to Elizabeth Ashby Snow, daughter of Erastus Snow, in 1878. He served as president of the Juárez Stake in Mexico and was called to be an apostle in 1907.

16. *Deseret News Church Almanac*, 41. George Quayle Cannon was born January 11, 1827, in England. He was ordained an apostle in 1860 and served as a counselor to Brigham Young, John Taylor, Wilford Woodruff, and Lorenzo Snow.

President Cannon left for the Sandwich Islands to attend their fiftieth anniversary of missionary work. He died in 1901, shortly after returning from this trip.

17. Caroline "Carlie" Young Croxall Cannon, a daughter of Brigham Young, was born February 1, 1851, and married George Q. Cannon in 1884. Caroline had been married previously to Mark Croxall and was the mother of eight children, only five surviving childhood. George Q. Cannon adopted these five children. She accompanied Cannon to the fiftieth anniversary celebration, along with three of her sons.

18. Sarah Ann Prichard, born November 29, 1826, was married to Lorenzo Snow on April 21, 1845, and was his third wife.

19. Miscellaneous references to the "Heber" who lives with Helen while he goes to school and helps around the house probably are to Heber Bennion Jr., nephew to Helen, born January 30, 1888.

20. Wilfred Owen Woodruff was born October 31, 1899, in Salt Lake City.

21. Maria Young Dougall, daughter of Brigham Young, was born December 10, 1849. Maria was eight years old when her mother died, so she was raised by Zina D. H. Young. She was called in 1887 to serve as a counselor to Elmina Taylor on the General Board of the YLMIA. Maria attended the suffrage convention in 1887 in Washington, D. C., and was married to William B. Dougall. Susa Young Gates, *History of the Young Ladies Mutual Improvement Association* (Salt Lake City: Deseret News, 1911), 98.

22. Ibid., 21, 26. Zina D. H. Young was born January 31, 1831, in Watertown, New York. Zina and Bathesheba Smith traveled thousands of miles organizing branches of the Retrenchment Association. Zina was president of the LDS Relief Society from 1888 to 1901. Bathesheba W. Smith was born May 3, 1822, in West Virginia and was the fourth president of the Relief Society. She received her endowments from the Prophet Joseph Smith and was a charter member of the first Relief Society when Emma Smith presided. Bathsheba was married to George Albert Smith.

23. Rachel Ridgeway Ivins Grant was the mother of Heber J. Grant. Born March 9, 1821, in New Jersey, she married Jedediah M. Grant November 29, 1855.

24. *Deseret News Church Almanac*, 49. Matthias F. Cowley was born August 24, 1858, in Salt Lake City, Utah. He was called as an apostle in 1897. Cowley was instrumental in converting Helen to the idea of plural marriage, and he later left the church over polygamy in 1905. He was reinstated in 1936 and died in 1940.

25. *Deseret Evening News*, October 28, 1900. Ella Hickman, thirty-four years old, was the wife of professor J. E. Hickman of the Brigham Young Academy. She died of dropsy (edema) and other ailments, leaving seven children.

26. Obviously, Helen and Owen kept his impending polygamous marriage to Avery a secret even from close family members at this time.

27. *Deseret Evening News*, November 10, 1900. The Wilford Woodruff monument in the Salt Lake City Cemetery was donated by funds from the YMMIA and from the Woodruff family, at a total cost of $1,500. It is made of solid granite and was erected by Elias Morris & Sons. On the north side is inscribed, "Fourth President of the Church of Jesus Christ of Latter-day Saints, 1889–1898." On the west side is inscribed the names of his wives. The dedicatory prayer was offered by Joseph F. Smith, with George Q. Cannon, Heber J. Grant, and Anthon H. Lund present.

28. Jenson, *Latter-day Saint Biographical Encyclopedia*, 2: 477–78. Joseph and Blanche Daynes were serving a mission in Great Britain from 1899 to 1901.

29. Ida Elizabeth Bowman was the wife of Apostle Hyrum Mack Smith. This line probably refers to their baby, Joseph Fielding Smith, who was born January 30, 1899.

30. Gates, *History of the Young Ladies*, 193–94. May Booth Talmage was born in 1868 and was married to James E. Talmage. She was called to serve on the YLMIA in 1892.

31. Jenson, *Latter-day Saint Biographical Encyclopedia*, 1: 702. Annie T. Hyde, daughter of President John Taylor, was born October 20, 1849. She was married to the son of Orson Hyde. She was considered the founder of the Daughters of Utah Pioneers. Annie was called to serve as first counselor to Bathsheba Smith on the General Board of the Relief Society in 1901.

32. These shadow allusions may refer to an analogy communicated earlier to Helen by Owen, perhaps to explain polygamous relationships.

33. This sentence undermines the sentiments Helen expresses in the foregoing paragraphs in response to Owen's "beautiful" letter, illustrating the dramatic shifts in the emotional swings she is experiencing.

34. *Deseret News Church Almanac*, 50. Hyrum Mack Smith, son of Joseph F. Smith and Edna Lambson, was born March 31, 1872. He was called to serve as an apostle in 1901 and was ordained by his father.

35. *Deseret News Church Almanac*, 38. Joseph F. Smith, son of Hyrum Smith and Mary Fielding, was born November 13, 1838, in Far West, Missouri. He was ordained an apostle and named counselor to the First Presidency in 1866 (age twenty-seven) by Brigham Young. He also served as a counselor to John Taylor, Wilford Woodruff, and Lorenzo Snow. He was ordained as president of the church in 1901 and died in 1918.

36. Jenson, *Latter-day Saint Biographical Encyclopedia*, 1: 200. Seymour B. Young, son of Joseph Young and Jane Bicknell, was born in Kirtland, Ohio, on October 3, 1837. He was a physician and surgeon and also served as a president of the Seventies and later as an apostle.

37. *Deseret Evening News*, November 6, 1900. In the presidential election with Bryan and Stevenson on the Democratic ticket and McKinley and Roosevelt on the Republican, the Republicans made a clean sweep, taking control of both houses.

38. Emeline Woodruff Burrows, daughter and second child of Wilford Woodruff and Sarah Delight Stocking, was born July 26, 1863, in Salt Lake City. She was married to David Creeland Burrows on August 18, 1887. Their last child was born in 1897, so perhaps this line refers to an illness.

39. Sarah Delight Stocking Woodruff was born June 26, 1838, and was the fifth wife of President Wilford Woodruff . She was the mother of eight children and died May 28, 1906.

40. John Jay Woodruff, son of Wilford Woodruff and Sarah Delight Stocking, was born August 14, 1873. He was married to Annie L. E. Nielsen on January 24, 1903.

41. Joshua Hughes Paul was born January 20, 1863, in Salt Lake City. He was president of the LDS University in Salt Lake City. Professor Paul taught for nine years at the University of Utah, was associate editor of the *Salt Lake Herald*, president of the Brigham Young College at Logan, president of the Agricultural College of Utah, and, for a short time, editor of the *Deseret News*.

42. Colonia Juárez, Chihauhua, Mexico, consisted of those residing on the Río Piadres Verdes in the state of Chihuahua, ten miles southwest of the Mexican town of Casas Grandes, sixteen miles southwest of Dublán, 150 miles west of

El Paso, Texas, and 120 miles west-northwest of Galego, the nearest accessible railway station on the Mexican Northwestern Railway. Colonia Juárez was the headquarters of the Juárez Stake of Zion.

The townsite was dedicated January 1, 1887, and named Juárez after the Mexican patriot and general. A ward was organized June 5, 1887, with George Sevey as bishop. Bishop Sevey was succeeded in 1898 by Joseph C. Bentley, who presided until the exodus to Arizona in 1912. The Juárez Stake included Colonia Chuichupa, Colonia Dublán, Colonia Garcia, Colonia Juárez, and Colonia Pacheco. It also included the settlements of Colonia Oaxaca and Colonia Morelos, which no longer exist.

43. Obviously, Owen gave Avery instructions to destroy his letters as evidence of their relationship, although it is clear by this collection that she did not destroy all of them.

44. The LDS University in Salt Lake City later became a high school.

45. *Deseret News Church Almanac*, 49. John Whittaker Taylor, son of John Taylor, was born May 14, 1858, in Provo, Utah. He was ordained an apostle in 1884, but resigned over polygamy in 1905 and was excommunicated in 1911.

46. Ibid., 41. Anthon Henrik Lund was born in Denmark on May 15, 1844. He was ordained an apostle in 1899 and served as a counselor to Joseph F. Smith.

47. Heber Bennion was born November 28, 1858, in Salt Lake City. He married Susan Marian Winters, Helen's sister, on September 11, 1885. He married two other wives, one in 1902 (Mary Bringhurst) and one with no date available (Emma Jane Webster). Heber Bennion was the brother of Edwin T. Bennion.

48. *Deseret Evening News*, November 17, 1900. A band of about fifty Yaqui Indians escaped from their reservation in southern Arizona and tried to drive away some livestock from a Mormon settlement. The Mormons gave chase. According to the article four Mormons and twelve Indians were killed.

49. Walter Graham and his bride-to-be, Julia Sessions, daughter of Byron Sessions, born 1883, were residents of the Bighorn Basin community.

50. Undoubtedly, Helen is referring to the time before Heber returned home.

51. Probably Rulon Oscar Bennion, born November 14, 1900. There is some confusion on the date of birth in the family history data.

52. Gates, *History of the Young Ladies*, 90–94. Elmina Shepherd Taylor was born September 12, 1830, in Middlefield, New York. She taught school until marrying George Hamilton Taylor in 1856. Elmina was called to serve as the president of the YLMIA. in June of 1880, which calling she held until her death in 1904.

53. Ibid., 113. The *Young Women's Journal* had previously been edited by Susa Young Gates, but upon her resignation, President Elmina Taylor, after earnest prayer and consideration, decided to appoint a committee that would have direct supervision over the journal's business and literary interests. May Booth Talmage was chosen as editor, with Augusta W. Grant and Emma Goddard as assistants. When President Taylor invited Sister Talmage to take over this position, he said, "It is my earnest desire that you should undertake this work; go home and say to your husband that you have been called to do it, and that if you will accept the call the Lord will bless you in your effort." Sister Talmage agreed on the condition that her name not be announced as editor, rather that it say "edited and published by the General Board."

54. Ibid., 209–11. Emma Goddard was born April 19, 1861, in England and emigrated to Utah with her parents. She was called to serve on the YLMIA General Board in 1896 and served on the Journal Committee. She was married to Benjamin Goddard in 1883.

55. Jenson, *Latter-day Saint Biographical Encyclopedia*, 1: 361. Joseph Royal Murdock was born August 11, 1858, in Salt Lake City, Utah. His vocations were farming, stock raising, and merchandising. He served as a member of the state constitutional convention and was elected state senator in 1900.

56. Apparently, Owen was not as regular a correspondent as Helen would have liked, as this letter demonstrates. Her displeasure may have been accentuated by her latent jealousy, although Avery is not alluded to here.

57. A reminder of the toll Owen's traveling had on his relationship with his family. Helen's support of Owen in his duties rarely wavered, as this gentle observation indicates.

58. *Deseret Evening News*, November 23, 1900. The opera opened with *The Singing Girl*, with Miss Nielson, Viola Pratt Gilette, Eugene Cowles, and Joseph Cawthorn.

59. Ibid., November 24, 1900. J. J. McClellan, tabernacle organist who replaced Daynes, gave an organ recital in the Salt Lake City Tabernacle to honor Viola Pratt Gillette and the opera company. There were approximately two thousand people in attendance. Miss Gillette was a former member of the tabernacle choir. Her voice was not entirely recovered from an illness that had settled in her vocal chords.

60. Ibid., November 22, 1900. The headlines declared, "Killed in Fight with Mormons. Apache Kid Meets His Death. A. O. Woodruff Present at His Burial." The article gave the following details: "Mr. Woodruff was one of the party that pursued the retreating Indians and assisted at the burial of the Kid. Mr. Woodruff said they will put in an application for the reward offered for him in the United States." The article also clarified with a dispatch from A. Ivins that no Mormons were killed in the raid.

    Owen recorded this event in his journal: "It happened to my lot to come onto the first two Indians lying together dead. I passed over them without saying anything and next found a full quiver with 60 well made arrows in it and a fine bow also. Next in my search I found a dead squaw. After the ground for some distance around had been searched to be sure there were no live Apaches in the bush we took off the belts, pistols, moqisons and the Chiefs Cap, then found a good, deep crevice in the rocks, spread out a blanket and laid it in the bottom, then placed the Chief (who was no doubt the famous "Apache Kid") in first, then the little girl down by his legs and the squaw on top. We covered them with another good blanket and then laid about three feet of rock on top of them. These Indians were all well clad in native attire, the old chief wore a belt filled with 45–70 shells, the squaw carried a knife, pistol and many trinkets. The little one had a knife in the belt. They were the most savage looking group I have ever seen. We followed the trail of those who escaped but did not find them nor their tracks. We returned to the Harris Ranch, had a dance and spent the night."

61. The problems of keeping up a regular correspondence while Owen was traveling must have been enormous, as Helen had to guess where to send her letters based on the schedule Owen provided her. As this letter indicates, Helen's letters often missed Owen.

62. The secret Helen refers to here may refer to Owen's impending marriage to Avery.

63. It would appear that "tea party" was an idiom for childbirth. At this time Helen was pregnant with Helen Mar, who would be born January 1, 1901.

64. Asahel Hart Woodruff Jr. was born February 13, 1893, and was a nephew to Owen and Helen. He would have been about eight years old.

65. Helen's reaffirmation of her love for Owen here, with the caveat of "something changed" in her, obviously as a result of his impending marriage to Avery, and her reference to "duty" and "true happiness in the Eternal World," underline the notion that their entering into polygamy was fundamentally a religious decision.

66. David Patten Woodruff was born April 4, 1854, to Wilford Woodruff and Sarah Brown. He became one of the first Mormon settlers in Wyoming in 1892. Woodruff died January 24, 1937.

67. Arabell Jane Hatch Woodruff was born April 2, 1859. She was married to David Patten Woodruff February 19, 1877, and was the mother of twelve children. She died January 13, 1923.

68. Willard C. Burgon, born November 4, 1854, served as the bishop in the Union Ward from 1900 to 1910. He was trained as a mason. Frank Esshom, *Pioneers and Prominent Men of Utah* (Salt Lake City: Utah Pioneers Book Publishing, 1912), 672.

69. Martha Lambert was Helen's nurse, as mentioned in Owen's October 31, 1899, journal entry recording Wilford Owen's birth.

70. Avery was selecting names for the codes they would use in letters so people wouldn't suspect that she and Owen were entering into a polygamous union.

71. Avery's recollections here are mediated, of course, by the time between these events and her recording of them. The passage of time can have a way of ameliorating past events, but it can also have the opposite effect. Here and in the passages to follow, it is clear that in 1952 and 1953 Avery insists on the elevated nature of her polygamous relationship with Owen and Helen.

72. In a way, Mary did find herself in Avery's shoes when she married Edwin T. Bennion in a 1903 polygamous marriage.

73. George Gibbs's father, also named George Gibbs, was serving as secretary to the First Presidency.

1901

1. In 1901, an anti-vaccination debate raged in Utah. Educational leaders were convinced that a vaccination act would be the best measure to prevent the spread of smallpox in the public schools. This conviction led the State Board of Health to issue a proclamation to all schools in the state requiring that all pupils be vaccinated as a condition to their admission into all public schools. This proclamation went into effect 1 January 1901. Utahans protested, viewing the proclamation as a violation of human rights and liberties. Citizens placed heavy pressure on lawmakers to enact legislation which would supersede the public health regulation. The legislature passed the new act, but Governor Wells vetoed it, saying, "The bill would be a step backwards, with disastrous consequences." Stout, *History of Utah*, vol. 2, 120. Ironically, Owen's later refusal to be vaccinated against smallpox would result in his and Helen's deaths from the disease.

2. Probably Helen Mar Woodruff, born January 1, 1901.

3. Karl G. Maeser was born January 16, 1828. He was called by Brigham Young in 1875 to organize the Brigham Young Academy in Provo. Maeser died February 15, 1901, in Salt Lake City.

4. Avery was born March 9, 1882.

5.   George Q. Cannon died April 2, 1901.

6.   Jenson, *Latter-day Saint Biographical Encyclopedia*, 1: 722–23. Heber M. Wells, the son of Daniel Wells, was born August 11, 1859, and was the first governor of Utah, serving two terms.

7.   Since 1896, a racket had developed in Utah involving the alleged violators of Chapter 7 — "That if any male person, hereafter cohabits with more than one woman, he shall be guilty of a misdemeanor, and on conviction thereof shall be punished by a fine of not more than $300.00, or by imprisonment for not more than six months" — and the paid informer who sought out these violators and reported them to the prosecuting officials. This business had become very lucrative to a Mr. Charles M. Owen. Abel John Evans of Lehi, the president of the Senate, in an attempt to stop Owen in his campaign to harass the polygamists, wrote and submitted the Evans Bill to the State Senate. Stout, *History of Utah*, vol. 2, 121–24. The Evans Bill was proposed as a way to offer a measure of amnesty to a few surviving polygamists. The proponents of the bill felt that Utahns had proved themselves as loyal Americans who could be trusted. Opponents of the bill, and many politicians and citizens outside of Utah, perceived it as a way for the Mormons to reestablish polygamy. The governor vetoed the bill, which had previously been sustained by the Senate with a vote of 9 to 9. *Deseret Evening News*, March 16, 1901. In defense of his veto, Governor Wells was quoted in the *Senate Journal*: "In my opinion nothing can be clearer than that this bill, if passed, would be welcomed and employed as a most effective weapon against the very classes whose condition it is intended to ameliorate . . . I find also the solemn feeling that this bill holds out only a false hope of protection, and that in offering a phantom of relief to a few, it, in reality, invites a deluge of discard and disaster upon all." Stout, *History of Utah*, 124.

8.   Stout, *History of Utah*, vol. 2, 124. Charles M. Owen also later became a prominent figure in the anti-Smoot campaign, traveling to Washington, D.C., to testify against the church. He even posed for the press cameras with Mormon temple garments.

9.   Since Apostle Matthias Cowley was a polygamist, there is insufficient data to know which Sister Cowley this entry refers to.

10. Ethelyn Bennion, the daughter of Heber Bennion and Susan Winters, was born August 6, 1886. She was fifteen years old at this time and was Helen's niece.

11. Idella Winn Twombly Sessions, born June 16, 1856, was married to Byron Sessions in 1870. She was the mother of twelve children.

12. Jenson, *Latter-day Saint Biographical Encyclopedia*, 1: 563. Elizabeth Campbell was married to Frank Young Taylor in May 1884 and was the mother of eight children.

13. *Deseret News Church Almanac*, 39. Heber Jeddy Grant was born November 22, 1856, in Salt Lake City. He married Lucy Stringham in 1877, Hulda Augusta Winters in 1884, and Emily Wells in 1884. Grant was called to serve as an apostle in 1882 and was set apart as the president of the LDS Church in 1918.

14. Andrew Jenson, *Encyclopedic History of the Church of Jesus Christ of Latter-day Saints* (Salt Lake City: Deseret News, 1941), 373–74. The Japan Mission was opened in 1901 by Apostle Heber J. Grant, assisted by elders Louis A. Kelsch, Horace S. Ensign, and Alma O. Taylor. They arrived in Yokohama, Japan, by the steamship *Empress of India*, from Vancouver, British Columbia, on August 12, 1901. Grant dedicated the land of Japan for missionary work on

September 1, 1901, and he baptized the first convert, Hijime Nakazawa — a former Shinto Priest — on March 8, 1902. Gusta Grant and Apostle Grant's daughter Mary joined them later that month. Grant and his family left Tokyo on September 8, 1903, succeeded by Horace S. Ensign as president of the mission.

15. Helen was pregnant.
16. The Dayneses completed a two-year mission to Great Britain.
17. Jenson, *Latter-day Saint Biographical Encyclopedia*, 3: 380–81. Emma Lucy Gates was described as Utah's greatest singer. Gates studied at the Royal Conservatory of Music in Berlin, Germany, and made her debut at the Royal Opera House in Berlin. Gates also played the piano and violin. She married Albert E. Bowen in 1916 and lived in Logan.

1902

1. The groundbreaking for the Big Horn colony's first canal, the Sidon Canal, took place on May 27, 1900.
2. Jenson, *Encyclopedic History*, 163. The town of Cowley, Wyoming, is seven miles northwest of Lovell, eight miles northeast of Byron, and about ninety-five miles south of Billings, Montana. Cowley was founded by Latter-day Saint settlers in 1900 when the Shoshone Branch of the LDS Church was organized with William C. Partridge as presiding elder. Soon after the organization of the Big Horn Stake in 1901, the Shoshone Branch was reorganized into the Cowley Ward, in honor of Apostle Matthias F. Cowley, with Partridge as the bishop. On this same occasion, the townsite of Cowley was dedicated.
3. Jenson, *Latter-day Saint Biographical Encyclopedia*, 3: 74. Henry Webster Esplin was born October 20, 1854. He was married to Philena Cox and they were the parents of twelve children. Esplin was the bishop of Orderville from 1884 until 1910.
4. While the details to this specific incident are unavailable, it appears from Avery's later writings that Emma Woodruff was an assertive and formidable woman. Living in such close proximity to Owen's mother and sisters may have led to the usual family problems for Helen.
5. The site for the new Cowley meetinghouse had been dedicated and the cornerstone laid on November 19, 1901.
6. Charles A. Welch was a polygamist, having three wives: Mary Louis Hinckley, Abbie Burton, and Emma Rosetta White Bull. Once established in the Big Born Basin, Welch had his other wives join him. D. Kurt Graham, "The Mormon Migration to Wyoming's Big Horn Basin" (master's thesis, Brigham Young University, 1994), 82.
7. Ibid., 65. Charles A. Welch served as second counselor to Byron Sessions in the Big Horn Stake Presidency. Owen appointed Welch to keep the books of the Big Horn Basin project and run the commissary.
8. Torrey Brigham Newton Woodruff, the son of David Patten Woodruff and Arabell Jane Hatch, was born November 15, 1894, at Sunshine, Wyoming, in the Bighorn Basin. He married Ruby Stone Asbury in 1922 and died January 17, 1947.
9. David Patten Woodruff had recently been called by Owen to serve on the stake high council.
10. Helen was pregnant with their third child, June Woodruff.
11. Possibly Wilford Woodruff Jr., Owen's half-brother.

12. Wedding announcement in Abraham Owen Woodruff Collection. Josie E. Bailey married Frank F. Allred on August 20, 1902.

13. Emma Woodruff McEwan, daughter of Alice and Will McEwan, was born July 9, 1902, in Sunshine, Wyoming, in the Bighorn Basin.

14. It appears that Avery Clark was moving to Colonia Juárez, perhaps because of pregnancy.

15. Jenson, *Latter-day Saint Biographical Encyclopedia*, 1: 709–10 and Lambert, "Autobiography and Recollections," 13. Joseph Marion Tanner was born March 26, 1859, in Payson, Utah. He received a university degree from Harvard, chiefly in the study of law. Tanner served as president of the Agricultural College in Logan until 1900 when he resigned over issues of polygamy. He also served as general superintendent of church schools and was a member of the LDS General Sunday School Board, serving with Owen. Tanner had four wives, one of which, Annie Clark Tanner, was a relative of Avery, staying with the Clark family for a period of time while living on the underground.

16. Lovell, Wyoming, is situated on the Shoshone River. It was an important station on the Chicago, Burlington, and Quincy Railroad. The city came into existence in 1900, and, at the same time, a ward was organized with Haskell S. Jolley as the bishop. Lovell is about twenty miles south of the Montana border.

17. Brigham Young Jr., son of President Brigham Young, was born December 18, 1836. He was ordained an apostle February 4. 1864.

18. T. Earl Pardoe, *The Sons of Brigham Young* (Provo, Utah: Brigham Young University Alumni Association, 1983), 223–24. Guy C. Wilson was born April 10, 1864, in Fairview, Utah. He was a polygamist, having three wives: Elizabeth Hartsburg, Agnes Melisda Stevens, and Anna Ivins. Wilson was chosen as the principal of Juárez Academy in 1897. He was also named the supervisor of the LDS Church School System, where he served from 1897 until 1912, traveling thousands of miles to set up new schools for the church. Wilson was also a counselor to Anthony W. Ivins in the Juárez Stake Presidency.

19. Young died eight months after this talk, on April 11, 1903.

20. It would appear from Owen's remarks that Avery has had a miscarriage while living in Colonia Juárez.

21. Owen (AOW) is referring to his brother Asahel Hart Woodruff (AHW).

22. After Avery's miscarriage in September, she moved back to Logan from Colonia Juárez to continue her schooling.

23. Apostle Reed Smoot's campaign for senator was in full swing, with a vote to be held in January 1903. The issue of polygamy was one of the attacks against Smoot during this time.

24. Owen was planning to have Avery and their future children live in Colonia Juárez after she finished up her schooling.

25. Apparently, Owen sees birth control as a positive side effect of their separation because it would be difficult for Avery to stay in school if she were to become pregnant again.

1903

1. Reference to the border customs house at El Paso, Mexico.

2. Edwin T. Bennion was born April 8, 1868, in Salt Lake City. He was Heber Bennion's brother and Susan Winters Bennion's brother-in-law.

3. Mary Elizabeth Lindsay Bennion was born September 29, 1870, in Salt Lake City. She married Edwin T. Bennion in 1892 and gave birth to twelve children.

4. Mary Minerva Clark, sister to Avery, became Edwin Bennion's polygamous wife in 1903, when she was not quite twenty years old. This letter appears to concern the establishing of that polygamous relationship.

5. Possibly Sister Edwin "Teddy" Bennion.

6. Naomi Butterworth Woodruff was born March 21, 1864, in England. She married Asahel Hart Woodruff in 1887 and was the mother of six children.

7. Emma Rose Woodruff was the daughter of Asahel Woodruff and Naomi Butterworth. There is no birth date listed, but she was born in 1896 at the earliest. She was approximately seven years old at this time and was Owen's niece.

8. Letterhead in Abraham Owen Woodruff Collection. The Logan Knitting Factory was located in Salt Lake City and manufactured "Union Suits, L.D.S. Garments, and Hosiery." Joseph Morrell was the president, with Melvin J. Ballard as vice president. The board of directors also included Owen Woodruff and Matthias Cowley.

9. George M. Cannon, cashier of the Zion's Savings Bank and Trust Company in Salt Lake City. Abraham Owen Woodruff Collection. He was born December 25, 1861, in St. George and was serving with Asahel Woodruff in the stake Sunday school of the Granite Stake. Jenson, *Latter-day Saint Biographical Encyclopedia*, 1: 566.

10. Anna Rosenkilde, a house girl employed by Helen Winters Woodruff.

11. Joseph Donald Daynes, son of Joseph Daynes and Blanche Woodruff, was born October 1, 1898. He was Owen's nephew and cousin to Wilford Owen.

12. Jenson, *Encyclopedic History*, 382. Juárez Stake Academy grew from a one-room log cabin in 1897 to a modern school building in 1904. Approximately three hundred students could take courses from twelve teachers. The school closed in 1930.

13. Owen and Avery had made plans for Avery to relocate to Colonia Juárez, Mexico.

14. This may be another reference to complaining polygamous wives living in Colonia Juárez.

15. Avery had relocated to Colonia Juárez, Mexico.

16. Helen was about seven months pregnant.

17. Possibly, Avery and Mary's mother, Ann Eliza Clark, was pregnant at this time. Family group sheets show three children born after 1899 but the dates are unavailable.

18. Jenson, *Encyclopedic History*, 373–74. The Grants were returning after Heber J. Grant had opened up the Japan Mission for the church.

19. Esshom, *Pioneers and Prominent Men*, 372. Dr. Samuel H. Allen, a physician in Salt Lake City, was born in Mt. Pleasant, Utah, on August 15, 1862.

20. *Deseret Evening News*, November 1, 1903. The play *Ben Hur* was presented at the Salt Lake Theater for seven nights. It was a major production presented by a traveling company that had recently performed in Denver. The Salt Lake Theater usually presented smaller productions because of the time and costs involved.

21. Jenson, *Latter-day Saint Biographical Encyclopedia*, 1: 494. John Edge Booth, born June 29, 1847, in England, married Delia Ina Winters in 1887. Booth was judge of the Fourth District Court. Milton Booth, eldest child of John

Booth and Delia Winters, was born May 21, 1888, and was about fifteen years old at the time. Delia was Booth's third wife, the other two wives being deceased; she cared for her own four children and four children from Booth's previous marriages.

22. Helen is expecting another child in December 1903. Rhoda was born December 28, 1903.
23. The house in Colonia Juárez for Avery.
24. Rhoda Welling Taylor lived in Colonia Juárez and was married August 29, 1901, to John W. Taylor as a plural wife.
25. Avery has been teaching school at the Colonia Juárez Academy. She is pregnant and will deliver Ruth April 11, 1904.
26. These sisters were plural wives of Apostle John W. Taylor.
27. Because this section of Owen's journal is not included in BYU's Special Collections, Avery's comments on this issue cannot be verified.

1904

1. Rhoda Woodruff was born December 28, 1903.
2. Avery had moved from the Ivins home to share a home with Roxie and Rhoda Taylor, John W. Taylor's polygamous wives.
3. Helen wrote Avery in early December 1903 to suggest a Christmas gift of a stallion for Owen from the both of them. Apparently, they followed through with this gift.
4. Apparently, Owen decided to cross out the code name and substitute Avery's real name.
5. A reference to Avery's pregnancy.
6. The eighteenth of January is obviously an important anniversary for Owen and Avery, probably of their marriage, despite Quinn's claim for the thirteenth.
7. Heath, *Reed Smoot: The First Modern Mormon*, 120. The Reed Smoot hearings conducted by the Committee on Privileges and Elections in the U.S. Senate in Washington, D.C., had been scheduled to begin in February 1904 but were postponed until March to allow the prosecution more time to prepare.
8. Merrill, *Reed Smoot: Apostle in Politics*, 47. The Committee on Privileges and Elections was preparing a list of potential witnesses, including many apostles, to testify regarding the church's involvement in polygamy and politics. The committee chairman, J. C. Burrows, made it clear that his investigation was "to be as wide as the ocean and that the protestors could present a general pattern of church activity without being required to make any definite and personal tie with Smoot."
9. Jenson, *Latter-day Saint Biographical Encyclopedia*, 1: 714–15. George H. Brimhall was born December 9, 1852, in Salt Lake City. He was educated as a teacher and became a professor of pedagogy at Brigham Young Academy.
10. Jenson, *Encyclopedic History*, 296. The Granite Stake Presidency included Frank Y. Taylor (president) and Edwin "Teddy" Bennion (first counselor) at this time.
11. *Deseret Evening News*, February 9, 1904. This dramatization of Westcott's novel about "rural life" was presented at the Salt Lake Theater on February 8, 1904. The audience was a bit disappointed in the production because the actor who usually played the lead was not on this tour. The replacement was not nearly as good.

12. Roberts, *Comprehensive History*, 345. Thomas Kearns was born April 11, 1862, and was a member of the Utah constitutional convention. He became a millionaire in the mining industry in Park City and built what is now the Utah governor's mansion on South Temple Street. Kearns was elected by the Republican legislature as a United States senator in 1901. It was charged, however, that Mr. Kearns, a non-Mormon, was elected senator because of the influence of President Lorenzo Snow.

13. Jenson, *Latter-day Saint Biographical Encyclopedia*, 1: 300. Byron Sessions was born November 7, 1851, in Bountiful, Utah. He was the son of Perregrine Sessions and the grandson of Patty Bartlett Sessions. He was called to help colonize the Bighorn Basin in 1900 and in 1901 was called to serve as the Big Horn Stake President.

14. Charles A. Welch served as second counselor to Byron Sessions in the Big Horn Stake presidency.

15. Gates, *History of the Young Ladies*, 217. Julia M. Brixen was born in Sweden and baptized a member of the church at age thirteen. She was sent to work in Utah to raise money to emigrate her family. She met and married Andrew Brixen and was called to serve in the YLMIA in 1898.

16. Ibid., 213. Elizabeth Claridge was born in England in 1842. She later married Alfred W. McCune, a wealthy businessman, in 1872. She was called to the YLMIA Board in 1898.

17. Ibid., 421. An earlier party given at the McCune home was described in the *Young Woman's Journal*, giving a sense of the magnificence of their parties: "The spacious rooms were profusely decorated with flowers and palms. The rich treasures of the McCune home, the statuary, rugs, pictures and bric-a-brac, were an education to many whose souls hunger after beauty and who rarely see it amplified in artistic creation.

   "In the far corner of the long parlor suite, a delightful Japanese retreat was formed, and here was an inexhaustible well of iced lemonade served out by two lovely girls clad in gorgeous Japanese raiment.

   "Out on the west lawn, a large floor was laid, waxed and smooth. Seats surrounded this floor, a fine band discoursed quadrilles and reels all the evening; seats were everywhere, on porches, under trees, beside the shrubbery, while over all there sparked and flashed innumerable electric lights, making the scene like an illuminated fairy-land. Bunting and flags draped the pillars and swung from corner to corner. Over the door glittered an electric star, which paled and dulled the light of the moon, shedding warmth and welcome to all."

18. The First Presidency of the Church of Jesus Christ of Latter-day Saints consisted of President Joseph F. Smith, John Rex Winder (first counselor), and Anthon H. Lund (second counselor).

19. Jenson, *Latter-day Saint Biographical Encyclopedia*, 1: 174. Rudger A. Clawson was born in Salt Lake City, Utah, on March 1, 1857. He was called to be an apostle in 1898. Clawson was one of the first victims under the Edmunds Act and thus served a four-year prison term for unlawful cohabitation. He also married Pearl Udall well after the second Manifesto was issued in 1904.

20. Ibid., 1: 37. George Albert Smith was born June 26, 1817, to Patriarch John Smith and Clarissa Lyman, a cousin to Prophet Joseph Smith. He served as first counselor to President Brigham Young and was called to serve as an apostle in 1868. Husband of Bathesheba Smith.

21. Ibid., 1: 212. Rulon Wells was born July 7, 1854. He was called to serve as one of the Seven Presidents of the Seventy in 1893 and also served on the General Board of the Young Men.

22. Ibid., 1: 210. J(onathan) Golden Kimball, son of Heber C. Kimball, was born in Salt Lake City on June 9, 1853. He was called to serve as one of the first Seven Presidents of the Seventy in 1892. He also served on the General Board of the Young Men.

23. Ivy Freeman was born October 6, 1883, to William Freeman and Mary Ann Winters. She married John Winifred Adams March 15, 1905, and died November 14, 1922.

24. *Deseret News Church Almanac*, 179. The Granite Stake was divided to form three additional stakes: the Liberty Stake (February 26, 1904), the Pioneer Stake (March 24, 1904), and the Ensign Stake (April 1, 1904), making a total of four stakes.

25. The Utah Sugar Company was located in Lehi, Utah. The board of directors included Thomas Cutler, Heber J. Grant, Joseph F. Smith, David Eccles, W. B. Preston, James Jack, George M. Cannon, Barlow Ferguson, George H. Taylor, and J. R. Winder.

26. Jenson, *Latter-day Saint Biographical Encyclopedia*, 1: 244–45. John R. Winder was born December 11, 1821, in England. He was called to serve as a counselor in the Presiding Bishopric in 1887 and was called as first counselor to President Joseph F. Smith in 1901.

27. *Deseret Evening News*, February 20, 1904. A reunion of the missionaries who had served in the Sandwich Islands was held in the Granite Stake tabernacle on February 19, 1904. Joseph F. Smith and Frank Y. Taylor were in attendance. There was a dance following the entertainment.

28. This letter was probably deliberately written so that no one outside of Helen and Owen's inner circle of friends would be able to decode it easily.

29. According to a letter written on February 27, 1904, from Reed Smoot to Owen, the subpoena that Owen received was to act as a witness in the Smoot case.

30. Clara Leone Horne was born October 10, 1878, in Salt Lake City. She was Martha Horne Tingey's niece. Leone married Ambrey Nowell in 1904.

31. Gates, "Notes About Women," 287–89. Martha H. Tingey was born October 15, 1857, in Salt Lake City. She was called to serve as Elmina Taylor's second counselor in the YLMIA in 1880. With the death of Elmina Taylor in 1905, Martha was called to assume the presidency.

32. Possibly Florence Ivins, daughter of Anthony and Elizabeth.

33. *Deseret Evening News*, February 24, 1904. The article reported that the subpoenas were starting to be served by Marshal Heywood in the Senator Smoot case. Those subpoened would have to testify in Washington, D. C. Apostle John Henry Smith was the first one served and it was suspected that President Joseph F. Smith would likely be served some time during that same day.

34. The play *A Chinese Honeymoon* had a very successful engagement at the Salt Lake Theater. It was a musical comedy in two acts, written by George Dance with music composed by Howard Talbot. *Deseret Evening News*, February 24, 1904, and *A Chinese Honeymoon* sheet music, 1901.

35. Gerald Bordman, *The Oxford Companion to American Theatre* (New York: Oxford University Press, 1984), 263. *Floradora* is an 1899 English musical comedy based on the book by Owen Hall, with the lyrics written by E. Byrd Jones and Paul Rubens and the music composed by Leslie Stuart. The story is about a

young heiress, her rights to a famous perfume, and an attempt to cheat her out of those rights. Its opening run in New York was one of the longest of its era in the American theater.

36. Francis Marion Lyman was born January 12, 1840, in Illinois, the eldest son of Amasa M. Lyman. He was called to be an LDS apostle in 1880 and also served on the General Board of the Young Men. Jenson, *Latter-day Saint Biographical Encyclopedia*, 1: 136. Apostle Lyman's testimony in the Smoot case did not go well. Reed Smoot suggested that Lyman did not grasp the meaning of the questions asked him. Heath, *Reed Smoot: The First Modern Mormon*, 81. Apostle Lyman admitted his guilt in the matter of cohabitation and also admitted his intention to continue the practice of polygamy, knowing that this practice was against the laws of the land and the law of God as revealed in the Manifesto. Merrill, *Reed Smoot: Apostle in Politics*, 48.

37. Mary Clark, now a plural wife of Edwin T. Bennion, was making plans to move to Colonia Juárez to be with her sister Avery and away from anti-polygamy conflicts. Apparently, Mary would be taking some of Avery's belongings to Mexico.

38. *Salt Lake City Telephone Directory*, 1902. Edward M. Ashton was an insurance salesman and stockbroker in Salt Lake City.

39. Nineteen of Owen's thirty-two letters to Avery are typed, perhaps to help him maintain his anonymity. None of his five letters to Helen are typed.

40. Avery was due to deliver her daughter, Ruth, who was born April 11, 1904. Unfortunately, Owen was not present at the birth.

41. Edward Christian Eyring, a resident of Colonia Juárez, was born May 27, 1868. He married Caroline Cottam Romney in 1893 and her sister Emma Cottom Romney in 1903, and was the father of eighteen children. Caroline and Emma were sisters of Junius Romney. Eyring died December 18, 1957.

42. Lenora Taylor was born March 28, 1885, and married Matthias Cowley as a plural wife Spetember 16, 1905. Lenora died January 8, 1971.

43. Gates, *History of the Young Ladies*, 221. In 1896, the General Superintendency of the LDS Young Men's Association suggested that the Young Ladies' Association join them in a conference once a year. Prior to that time, the two associations had always met separately. This pattern on the general level was set for the stakes to follow.

44. Jenson, *Latter-day Saint Biographical Encyclopedia*, 1: 205–06. Brigham Henry Roberts was born March 13, 1857, in England. He was ordained to the First Council of the Seventy in 1888. He was a prolific writer of history and biography.

45. Owen and Helen have left their children, with the exception of Rhoda, with Avery while they tour Mexico on church business.

46. Avery had many postpartum complications and was very unwell at the time.

47. MS 9604, Archives, The Church of Jesus Christ of Latter-day Saints, Salt Lake City, Utah.

48. Account of Kate Pearl Spilsbury in Brown, *The Life and Posterity of Alma Platte Spilsbury*, 159–61.

Bibliography

Alexander, Thomas G. *Things in Heaven and Earth: The Life and Times of Wilford Woodruff, a Mormon Prophet.* Salt Lake City: Signature Books, 1991.

Avant, Gerry, and Douglas P. Palmer. "A Love Story, A Drama, A Miracle." *Deseret News* July 24, 1993, 3–4.

Bluth, Eric. "Pus, Pox, Propaganda and Progress: The Compulsory Smallpox Vaccination Controversy in Utah, 1899–1901." MA thesis, Brigham Young University, 1993.

Bordman, Gerald. *The Oxford Companion to American Theatre.* New York: Oxford University Press, 1984.

Brown, Viva Skousen Spilsbury. *The Life and Posterity of Alma Platte Spilsbury.* Provo, UT: V. S. Brown, 1983.

Deseret Evening News, July 18, 1899, August 14, 1899, August 19, 1899, October 28, 1900, November 6, 1900, November 10, 1900, November 17, 1900, November 22–24, 1900, November 1, 1903, February 9, 1904, February 20, 1904, February 24, 1904.

Deseret News Church Almanac, 1991–92. Salt Lake City: Deseret Press, 1992.

Doctrine and Covenants. Salt Lake City: The Church of Jesus Christ of Latter-day Saints, 1981.

Esshom, Frank. *Pioneers and Prominent Men of Utah.* Salt Lake City: Utah Pioneers Book Publishing, 1912.

Freece, Hans P. "Mormon Chiefs Confess." Printed and distributed by Freece, Attorney at Law, 35 Wall Street, New York, New York.

Fox, Ruth May. "Helen." *Young Woman's Journal* 15 (June 1904): 291.

Gates, Susa Young. *History of the Young Ladies Mutual Improvement Association.* Salt Lake City: *Deseret News,* 1911.

———. "Notes About Women." *The Young Woman's Journal* 10 (1899): 287–89.

Godfrey, Kenneth, Audrey M. Godfrey, and Jill Mulvey Derr. *Women's Voices: An Untold History of the Latter-day Saints, 1830–1900.* Salt Lake City: Deseret Book , 1982.

Graham, D. Kurt. "The Mormon Migration to Wyoming's Big Horn Basin in 1900." MA thesis, Brigham Young University, 1994.

Grant, Hulda Augusta, ed. "Mothers in Israel: Autobiography of Mary A. S. Winters." *The Relief Society Magazine* 3 (1916): 577–78.

Hardy, Carmon. *Solemn Covenant: The Mormon Polygamous Passage.* Urbana: University of Illinois Press, 1992.

Heath, Harvard S. "Reed Smoot: The First Modern Mormon." PhD diss., Brigham Young University, 1990.

Jenson, Andrew. *Encyclopedic History of the Church of Jesus Christ of Latter-day Saints.* Salt Lake City: Deseret News, 1941.

———. *Latter-day Saint Biographical Encyclopedia.* Salt Lake City: Deseret News, 1901.

Kenney, Scott G., ed. *Wilford Woodruff's Journal: 1833–1898 Typescript.* Vol. 9. Midvale, UT: Signature Books, 1983.

Lambert, Eliza Avery Clark Woodruff. "Autobiography and Recollections, 1882–1953." Abraham Owen Woodruff Collection, Box 6, Folder 21. L. Tom Perry Special Collections & Manuscripts, Harold B. Lee Library, Brigham Young University, Provo, UT.

Merrill, Milton R. *Reed Smoot: Apostle in Politics.* Logan: Utah State University Press and Department of Political Science, 1990.

Miles, Carrie A. "Polygamy and the Economics of Salvation." *Sunstone* 111 (August 1998): 34–45.

Pardoe, T. Earl. *The Sons of Brigham Young.* Provo, UT: Brigham Young University Alumni Association, 1983.

Quinn, D. Michael. "LDS Church Authority and New Plural Marriages, 1890–1904." *Dialogue: A Journal of Mormon Thought* 18 (Spring 1985): 9–105.

Roberts, Brigham H. *Comprehensive History of the Church.* Provo, UT: Brigham Young University Press, 1965.

Stout, Wayne. *History of Utah.* Vol. 2 *1896–1929.* Salt Lake City: Wayne Stout, 1968.

Talmage, May Boothe. "Helen Winters Woodruff." *The Young Woman's Journal* 15 (1904): 293–94.

Taylor, Alonzo. Journal. MS 9604. Archives, The Church of Jesus Christ of Latter-day Saints, Salt Lake City, Utah.

Woodruff, Abraham Owen. Abraham Owen Woodruff Collection. L. Tom Perry Special Collections & Manuscripts, Harold B. Lee Library. Brigham Young University, Provo, UT.

Woodruff, Helen Winters. "Be Ye Not Unequally Yoked." *The Young Woman's Journal* 14 (1903): 203–5.

Woodruff, Wilford. "Manifesto." In *The Proceedings at the Semi-Annual General Conference of the Church of Jesus Christ of Latter-day Saints,* October 6, 1890, 2–3. Salt Lake City: The Church of Jesus Christ of Latter-day Saints, 1890.

Index